Calvin
and
World Mission

Thomas Schirrmacher
(Ed.)

Calvin and World Mission

Essays

edition afem
mission classics 6

Thomas Schirrmacher
(Ed.)

This book ist part of the series edition afem – mission academics,
ed. by Klaus W. Müller, Bernd Brandl,
Thomas Schirrmacher and Thomas Mayer.
http://www.missiologie.org

Bibliographic information published by the Deutsche Nationalbibliothek
The Deutsche Nationalbibliothek lists this publication in the Deutsche National-
bibliografie; detailed bibliographic data are available in the Internet at
http://dnb.d-nb.de.

ISBN 978-3-941750-20-3 (VTR)
VTR Publications
Gogolstr. 33, 90475 Nürnberg, Germany, http://www.vtr-online.de

ISBN 978-3-938116-84-5 (VKW)
VKW (Culture and Science Publ.)
Friedrichstr. 38, 53111 Bonn, Germany, http://www.vkwonline.de

ISSN 0944-1085 (edition afem – mission classics)

© 2009

Cover Illustration: VTR
Editorial: Ron Kubsch and Titus Vogt
Layout: Titus Vogt

Printed in the UK by Lightning Source

Contents

Schirrmacher: Introduction 9
    Articles from 1882 to 2002 9
    Not a Defense of Calvinism 9
    Predestination and Responsibility 11
    The Reformed Origin of Modern Protestant Mission 12

McFetridge: Calvinism as an Evangelizing Force (1882) 15

Schlatter: Calvin und die Mission (1909) 29

Kochs: Calvin und die Mission (1909) 41

Pfisterer: Der Missionsgedanke bei Kalvin (1934) 47
    I. 47
    II. 50
    III. 57

Edwards: Calvin and Missions (1936) 61

Zwemer: Calvinism and the Missionary Enterprise (1950) 67
    I. Calvin and Missions 67
    II. Calvinism and Islam 73

Van der Berg:
Calvin's Missionary Message: Some Remarks about
the relation between Calvinism and Missions (1950) 79

Chaney:
The Missionary Dynamic in the Theology of John Calvin
(1964) 93
    Introduction 93
    I. Calvin's Missionary Principles 95
        The Calling of the Gentiles 95

    The Progress of the Kingdom 97
    The Gathering of the Church 98
    Personal Christian Responsibility 100
  II. Calvin's Missionary Influence 102
    Calvin's Doctrine of Election 102
    Calvin's Eschatology 105
    Calvin's Concept of the Glory of God 108
    Christian Compassion 108
  III. Conclusions 109

Clowney:
The Missionary Flame of Reformed Theology (1976) 111
The Glory of God – The Goal of Missions 112
The Grace of God the Source of Missions 114
The Kingdom of God the Power of Missions 118

Pogson: Calvin's Missionary Thought and Practice (1990) 123

Nicholls: The Theology of William Carey (1993) 129
Biblical Foundations 130
Christology for Mission 131
The Gathered Church 132
Faith and Culture 136
Integral Mission 138

Hulse: John Calvin and his Missionary Enterprise (1998) 141
An Outline of Calvin's Life 141
Missionaries sent into France 143
Conclusion 145

Van Neste:
John Calvin on Evangelism and Missions (1998) 147
Introduction 147
Historical Context 147
Calvin's Writings 149
Calvin's Activity 151
Conclusion 153
    Selected Bibliography 153

Contents

James, III: Calvin the Evangelist (2001) 157

Beeke: John Calvin –
Teacher and Practitioner of Evangelism (2001) 163
Calvin: Teacher of Evangelism 164
Calvin: Practitioner of Evangelism 168
Evangelism in the Congregation 169
Evangelism in Geneva 171
Evangelistic Efforts in France 173
Evangelism in Brazil 174
Calvin's Missionary Spirit and Election 177
A Word of Encouragement 179

Simmons:
John Calvin and Missions: A Historical Study (2002) 183
Introduction 183
Calvin's Theology of Missions 184
A Positive Statement 184
Charges against Calvin's Theology of Missions 186
The Great Commission 187
Predestination 188
Calvin's Missionary Endeavors 189
France 189
The Rest of Europe 191
Geneva: Refugee Center and Missionary Center 191
The Netherlands 192
England 193
Scotland 194
Poland 195
Hungary 196
Overseas Missions in Brazil 197
Conclusion 200
Bibliography 201
    Works Cited 201
    Extended Bibliography 202

Introduction

THOMAS SCHIRRMACHER

Articles from 1882 to 2002

At the end of the 'Calvin-Year', in which Christians all over the world celebrate Calvin's 500th birthday, finally we emphasize Calvin's role for establishing a Protestant mission theology which later led to a worldwide expansion of Protestant Christianity.

All articles from 1882 to 2002 have been left in their original version, with one exception: Joel R. Beek revised his article for this volume. The result is, that some information on Calvin can be found in several articles. But our aim was, to present major articles on the topic through 125 years of history and from different viewpoints, not to give one polished latest opinion on the topic.

Some of the articles discuss Calvin and his writings and thinking on mission alone. Some add the question, what kind of mission has been organized from Geneva during Calvins time, because Calvin did not only speak about evangelism and mission, but also helped establish it in reality, even though on a rather small scale compared to later centuries. Some articles go further, and follow the students and followers of Calvin and their relation to mission through history. Thus we sometimes have included the wider topic of 'Calvinism and Mission', whereby we leave it to the authors to define 'Calvinism' in a broader or narrower way.

The final article by Scott J. Simmons is a good summary of 125 years of history. It presents the latest findings as of 2002, shows a good common sense of the researchers, and his bibliography at the end is a good bibliography for the whole book.

Not a Defense of Calvinism

This book has not been edited to defend 'Calvinism' and its dogmatic system. This has – even from Calvinism's own firm position – to be done on exegetical grounds, not on historical ones. Even if one could prove that Calvinism was more prone to mission than say – Lutheranism or Methodism, this would be no argument to its truth. Then one might just as well become Catholic, because the Jesuits surely were as busy as the Calvinists.

Even though this book is not a defense of Calvinism, some of the authors wrote their articles as a defense of Calvinism, or at least as very convinced Calvinists. Others write more from a neutral point of view as historical researchers. The editor of this volume and the 'Association of German Speaking Evangelical Missiologists', which edits the series, are grateful to what the Reformed branch of the Reformation has given to evangelical mission thought and practice, but are open to all branches of Evangelicalism who want to preach the gospel of Jesus Christ as testified in God's revealed Word. We believe, that dogma needs to be based on well informed exegesis, taking into account the history of exegesis and dogma, and not on historical arguments or samples of good or bad followers of a certain theology.

I already published a selection of articles on the theological forerunner of Calvin, the reformer Martin Bucer and his relation to Mission in the 'edition afem', as Bucer probably was the only real missiologist among the Reformers.[1] I also published the first dissertation written within our 'Martin Bucer Seminary' for a theological doctorate, on 'Luther and Mission'[2], written by the late Paul Wetter. In both cases, as the historical research was mainly done by German speaking authors, the original contributions are mostly not available in English, yet. We hope to translate the volume on Bucer into English in the future. The biographical volume on Bucer has been translated into English already and will be published soon. I also wrote a book on the theology of one of Calvin's heirs, William Carey, which has been translated into English already.[3] I am preparing a volume with English essays on Carey, too. Carey, even though in soteriology and other areas of systematic theology a Calvinist, was a Baptist. Thus my interest in 'Calvin and Mission' does not come from a narrow, confessional perspectives, but is interested in a broad discussion of the relationship of the 'evangelical' gospel as rediscovered in the Reformation to the history of world mission.

---

[1] Thomas Schirrmacher (ed.). Martin Bucer als Vorreiter der evangelischen Mission. Nürnberg: VTR & VKW: Bonn, 2006; see also the yearbook of our Martin Bucer Seminary: Thomas Schirrmacher (ed.). Anwalt der Liebe – Martin Bucer als Theologe und Seelsorger. VKW: Bonn, 2001; and my "Foreword Two: Bullinger and Bucer". S. xiii-xx in: George M. Ella. Henry Bullinger (1504-1575): Shepherd of the Churches. GO Publications: Durham (GB), 2007.

[2] Paul Wetter. Der Missionsgedanke bei Martin Luther. VKW: Bonn, 1996.

[3] Thomas Schirrmacher. Be Keen to Get Going: William Careys Theology. RVB: Hamburg, 2001^1; 2008^2.

Predestination and Responsibility

Having said this, as a Reformed missiologist and editor of the German edition of the first edition of Calvins 'Institutes of Christian Religion'[4], I nevertheless would like to add two thoughts.

1. Calvin's doctrine of predestination never denied human responsibility towards divine commandments, including the Great Commission.[5] Calvin was, after all, besides Martin Bucer the first and probably only Reformer to enjoin world mission. In 1556, he sent two missionaries to Brazil,[6] although the mission was destined to fail.

Calvin was blamed simultaneously to be too passive because of his doctrine of predestination, and to be too active and legalistic, because of his high view of God's commandment and man's responsibility and ability to fulfill it. But Calvin found both sides in the Bible, and so both sides were true and important for him at the same time.

We should learn from Calvin, that Biblical teaching always has to be understood as complementarity. All revealed truth is true at the same time.[7]

Augustine, Aurelius (354-430), bishop of Hippo (North Africa), called the theologian of grace, is the most important theologian of the Roman Catholic Church and spiritual father of all major Reformers, especially Luther, Zwingli and Calvin. In most of his writings Augustine discusses problems of mission,[8] as he was heavily involved in reaching heathen African tribal people and heathen Roman citizens. Gonsalvus Walter has com-

---

[4] Johannes Calvin. Christliche Glaubenslehre: Erstausgabe der 'Institutio' von 1536. with an introduction by Thomas Schirrmacher. VKW: Bonn, 2008.

[5] See Paul Jacobs, Prädestination und Verantwortlichkeit bei Calvin (Kassel, Germany: J. G. Oncken, 1937). For a modern Calvinist call for missions, see James I. Packer, Prädestination und Verantwortung, Neue Studienreihe 5 (Wuppertal, Germany: Brockhaus, 1964) [English title: Evangelism and the Sovereignty of God].

[6] Henry R. Van Til, The Calvinistic Concept of Culture (Grand Rapids, Mich.: Baker Book House, 1959) p. 93; Louis Igou Hodges, Reformed Theology Today (Columbus, GA: Brentwood Christian Press, 1995) pp. 101-104.

[7] For details see my "The Complementary Nature of Biblical Teaching", MBS Texte 29 (Theologische Akzente). Bonn: Martin Bucer Seminar, 2004, see under www.bucer.eu/international.html.

[8] Gerhard Metzger, Kirche und Mission in den Briefen Augustins, Allgemeine Missions-Studien 20 (Gütersloh, Germany: C. Bertelsmann, 1936); and F. van der Meer, Augustinus der Seelsorger (Cologne: J. P. Bachem, 1958).

bined those quotations to a full-orbed theology of mission.[9] Augustine reconciled the belief in double predestination with an urgent call, that it is the will of God to preach the Gospel everywhere. In his famous Letter No. 199,[10] Augustine denies that the Great Commission was already achieved by the apostles because, exegetically, the commission goes "till the end of the world" and practically, he knows of "innumerable barbarian tribes in Africa to whom the gospel has not yet been preached."[11] God had not promised Abraham the Romans alone but all nations. Before the return of Jesus Christ the majority of nations and people will become Christians.[12]

The Reformed Origin of Modern Protestant Mission

2. Theologians and historians generally ignore the origins of modern evangelical world mission in the middle of the sixteenth century. Calvinist, mostly Puritan pastors, who had immigrated to America from England, preached the Gospel to the Indians.[13]

In 1915, Maurus Galm demonstrated that modern Protestant mission began in the Netherlands, where Calvinist theologians were inspired by the missionary efforts of the Catholic Church.[14] Gisbert Voetius[15] (1589-1676)

---

[9] P. Gonsalvus Walter O. M. Cap., Die Heidenmission nach der Lehre des heiligen Augustinus, Missionswissenschaftliche Abhandlungen und Texte 3 (Münster, Germany: Aschendorrf, 1921).

[10] Maurice Wiles and Mark Santer ed., Documents in Early Christian Thought (Cambridge: Cambridge University Press, 1975) pp. 259-264); Norman E. Thomas ed., Classic Texts in Mission and World Christianity, op. cit., p. 18.

[11] Ibid. (both editions), Letter 199, Part 46.

[12] Ibid. (both editions), Letter 199, Part 47-49.

[13] R. Pierce Beaver ed., Pioneers in Missions: … A Source Book on the Rise of the American Missions to the Heathen (Grand Rapids: Wm. B. Eerdmans, 1966) pp. 11-15; see also my "Eschatology". S. 106-110 in: John Corie (Hg.). Dictionary of Mission Theology". InterVarsity Press: Nottingham (GB), 2007.

[14] Maurus Galm, Das Erwachen des Missionsgedankens im Protestantismus der Niederlande (München: Franz Xaver Seitz and St. Ottilien: Missionsverlag St. Ottilien, 1915). See the restrictions in A. Goslinga, "Die Anfänge der Mission in Holland", Allgemeine Missions-Zeitschrift 49 (1922) pp. 56,63,79-85.

[15] Jürgen Moltmann, "Voetius, Gisbert", Religion in Geschichte und Gegenwart Vol 3, ed. Kurt Galling (Tübingen, Germany: J. C. B. Mohr, 1986); Wilhelm Goeters, Die Vorbereitung des Pietismus in der reformierten Kirche der Niederlande bis zur labadistischen Krise 1670 (Leipzig: 1911) pp. 80-134; Ernst Bizer, "Die reformierte Orthodoxie und der Cartesianismus", Zeitschrift für Theologie und Kirche 55 (1958) pp. 306-372, on Voetius' book 'Disputationen über den Atheismus' (1639) (Bibliographical information p. 308, note 2).

discovered the connection between Reformed orthodoxy and the missionary orientation of Reformed Pietism[16] and wrote a thorough missionary theology.[17]

Gisbert Voetius, 1634-1676 professor of theology and Oriental languages in Utrecht, Netherlands, was an active member of the Synod of Dordt (1617/19) and a chief proponent of Calvinistic orthodoxy and the most influential Dutch theologian of the 17th century. At the same time, he was one of the spokesmen of the emerging mission oriented Reformed Pietism in the Netherlands and had personal contacts to English Puritans. His book 'Disputations on Atheism' (1639) and other books against philosophies of his time show him to be an evangelist to the well educated. Voetius is also the founder of the comparative study of religions for missionary purposes. Nearly all his books and tracts contain long sections on mission, which do not appeal and call to mission work but discuss all major problems of mission scientifically as a fourth part of Systematic Theology 'Theologica elenctica' beside Exegetical, Dogmatic and Practical Theology. Thus Voetius designed the first comprehensive mission theology written by a Protestant. He was well-read in Catholic mission literature. Following a distinction made in Reformed ethics, Voetius combines double predestination as God's absolute will with the conviction that God's moral will is world mission under Biblical promises.

The strict Calvinist, Dutch theologian Adrian Saravia (1531-1613), pastor in Antwerp and Brussels, as well as professor in Leyden (1582-1587), finally Dean in Westminster, according to Norman E. Thomas, was the only Reformer who abandoned the view that the Great Commission had already been fulfilled by the apostles, an opinion already thoroughly refuted by Calvin.[18] He had, however, forerunners of importance, such as the

---

[16] Jürgen Moltmann, "Voetius, Gisbert", op. cit., Col. 1432.

[17] On Voetius' missiology, see: Jan. A. B. Jongeneel, "Voetius' zendingstheologie, de eerste comprehensieve protestantse zendingstheologie", De onbekende Voetius, ed. J. van Oort et. al (Kampen, Netherlands: J. H. Kok, 1989) pp. 117-147; H. A. van Andel, De zendingsleer van Gisbertus Voetius, De onbekende Voetius (Kampen, Netherlands: J. H. Kok, 1912). On Voetius' theology in general, see: J. van Oort, ed., De onbekende Voetius, (Kampen, Netherlands: J. H. Kok, 1989); Ernst Bizer, "Die reformierte Orthodoxie und der Cartesaianismus", Zeitschrift für Theologie und Kirche 55 (1958) pp. 306-372. Wilhelm Goeters, Die Vorbereitung des Pietismus in der reformierten Kirche der Niederlande bis zur labadistischen Krise 1670, op. cit., pp.80-134.

[18] Norman E. Thomas ed., Classic Texts in Mission and World Christianity, op. cit., pp. 41-43.

Church Father, Aurelius Augustine, who was also the precursor of the Calvinist soteriological view of double Predestination.

Chaney has emphasized that modern Protestant world mission began with two Calvinist groups: the chaplains of the Dutch East India Company and with the Puritans, who tried to reach the Indians of North America.[19]

The reason for the almost exclusively Reformed nature of Protestant world mission from the sixteenth to the eighteenth centuries was the rise of the Netherlands (The East Indian Trading Company was founded in 1602) and England as sea powers;[20] two Protestant countries, whose churches had Reformed Confessions.[21]

---

[19] Charles L. Chaney, The Birth of Missions in America, op. cit., p. ix.

[20] Gustav Warneck, Abriß einer Geschichte der protestantischen Missionen von der Reformation bis auf die Gegenwart, op. cit., p. 39.

[21] Philip E. Hughes, "Thirty-nine Articles", Encyclopedia of the Reformed Faith, ed. Donald K. McKim, op. cit., p. 369. Hughes demonstrates that not only the Puritans, but also the Anglican Church was Reformed. The Thirty-nine Articles are Reformed in their view of the Scriptures, of salvation and of the sacraments. The standard commentary on the Thirty-nine Articles is W. H. Griffith Thomas, The Principles of Theology: An Introduction to the Thirty-Nine Articles (1930, repr. London: Vine Books, 1978) pp. xxxiii, xlix.

Calvinism as an Evangelizing Force (1882)

NATHANIEL S. MCFETRIDGE

Rev. Nathaniel Smyth McFetridge (sometimes MacFetridge) was born in Ireland, August 4, 1842; early home was at Catasauqua; received the second Fowler Prize Chaucer; graduated at Western Theological Seminary, 1867; pastor at Oil City, 1868-74; was the first pastor of the Wakefield Presbyterian church at Germantown, where he has been since 1874; preached the Annual Sermon before the Brainerd Society in 1878. He died in 1886.

This essay originally was published in Nathaniel S. McFetridge. Calvinism in History: A Political, Moral & Evangelizing Force'. Presbyterian board of publication; Philadelphia, 1882. The book has been reprinted 1989 and 2004.

    In this chapter our inquiry will be as to the evangelizing force of Calvinism. Has Calvinism, as compared with other systems of religious doctrine, shown itself to have been a power in the evangelization of the world? This is the most important question connected with any system of belief. All other questions are, in every Christian's opinion, subordinate to this. To save sinners and convert the world to a practical godliness must be the chief, the first and last, aim of every system of religion. If it does not respond to this, it must be set aside, however popular it may be.

    The question, then, before us now is, to whether the system of doctrines called Calvinism is the most acceptable and popular with the world, but whether it is eminently adapted to the conversion of sinners and the edification of believers.

    In determining this I shall proceed, as in the preceding chapters, according to the law, "The tree is known by its fruit."

    We may, however, premise, on the ground of the doctrines included in this system, that it is certainly most favorable to the spread of Christianity. Its doctrines are all taken directly from the Scriptures. The word of God is its only infallible rule of faith and practice. Even its doctrine of predestination, or election, which most men dislike, but which all Christians practically believe and teach, is granted by some of its bitterest opponents to be a transcript of the teachings of the New Testament.

    The historian Froude says: "If Arminianism most commends itself to our feelings, Calvinism is nearer to the facts, however harsh and forbidding those facts may seem."²² And Archbishop Whately says the objections against it "are objections against the facts of the case." So Spinoza and John Stuart Mill and Buckle, and all the materialistic and metaphysical philosophers, "can find," says an eminent authority, "no better account of the situation of man than in the illustrations of St. Paul; 'Hath not the potter power over the clay, to make one vessel to honor and another to dishonor?'" There never has been, and it is doubtful if there ever can be, an Arminian philosophy. The facts of life are against it; and no man would attempt to found a philosophy on feeling against fact.

Arminian theologians thought they had discovered the starting-point for a systematic philosophy and theology in the doctrine of "free-will;" but even that was swept away from them by the logic of Jonathan Edwards, and it has continued to be swept farther and farther away by Buckle and Mill and all the great philosophers. Hence it comes that to this day, there is not a logical and systematic body of Arminian divinity. It has as in the Methodist Church, a brief and informal creed in some twenty-five articles, but it has neither a Confession of Faith nor a complete and logical system of doctrine.²³ To make such a system it must overthrow the philosophy of the world and the facts of human experience; and it is not likely to do that very soon.

Now, the thought is, must not a theology which agrees with the facts of the case, which recognizes the actual condition of man and his relations to God, be more favorable to man's salvation than one which ignores the facts?

This is confirmed by the nature of the particular doctrines involved. We freely agree with Froude and Macaulay that Arminianism, in one aspect of it, is "more agreeable to the feelings" and "more popular" with the natural heart, as that which exalts man in his own sight is always more agreeable to him than that which abases him. Arminianism, in denying the imputation of Christ's righteousness to the believer, in setting him on his own works of righteousness, and in promising him such perfection in this life as that there is no more sin left in him – or, in the words of John Wesley, a "free, full and present salvation from all the guilt, all the power and all the in-being of sin"²⁴ – lays the foundation for the notions of works of supererogation, and that the believer, while in a state of grace, cannot commit sin. It thus powerfully ministers to human pride and self-glorification. Calvinism,

---

[22] Calvinism, p. 6.
[23] Humphrey's Our Theology, p. 68, etc.
[24] Gladstone's Life of Whitefield, p. 199.

on the other hand, by imputing Christ's righteousness to the believer, and making the sinner utterly and absolutely dependent on Christ for his salvation, cuts away all occasion for boasting and lays him low at the foot of the cross. Hence it cannot be so agreeable to the feelings of our carnal heart. But may it not be more salutary, nevertheless? It is not always the most agreeable medicine which is the most healing. The experience of the apostle John is one of frequent occurrence, that the little book which is sweet as honey in the mouth is bitter in the belly. Christ crucified was a stumbling-block to one class of people and foolishness to another, and yet he was, and is, the power of God and the wisdom of God unto salvation to all who believe.

The centre doctrine of Calvinism, as an evangelistic power, is that which Luther called "the article of a standing or a falling Church" – "justification by faith alone, in the righteousness of Christ alone." And is not that the doctrine of the gospel? Where does the Holy Spirit ascribe the merit of any part of salvation to the sinner?

But aside from that question, which it is not my purpose here to argue, would not reason dictate that that doctrine is most conducive to salvation which makes most of sin and most of grace?

Rowland Hill once said that "the devil makes little of sin, that he may retain the sinner." It is evident at once that the man who considers himself in greatest danger will make the greatest efforts to escape. If I feel that I am only slightly indisposed, I shall not experience much anxiety, but if I am conscious that my disease is dangerous, I will lose no time in having it attended to. So if I feel, according to the Arminianism, that my salvation is a matter which I can settle myself at any moment, even in the last gasp of dissolution, I shall be prone to take my time and ease in deciding it; but if, according to Calvinism, I feel that I am dependent upon God for it, whose pleasure, and not my own, I am to consult, I will naturally give more earnest heed to it.

Thus reason brings forward her vindication of Calvinism against the allegation that it is not favorable to the pursuit of salvation.

But perhaps some one may reply, "Has not the Methodist Church been more successful in her efforts to evangelize the world than any Calvinistic Church?" In answer I would say that I will give way to no one in my high estimate of that Church's piety and zeal and progress. I thank God, with all my heart, for what she has done, and I pray that she may never flag in her energy and success in winning souls to Jesus Christ. I admire her profoundly, and her noble army of men and women enlisted in the Master's service. May she ever go on, conquering and to conquer, until we all meet as one on the great day of the triumph of the Lamb!

But bear in mind that the aggressive Church has no well-defined system of doctrine, and that her Arminianism is of a very mild type, coming nowhere near that of High-Churchism or Roman Catholicism. Wherein lie the elements of her power and progress? I do not believe, and I am confident it cannot be shown, that they lie in her Arminianism or in the doctrines common to all the Christian churches, such as sin, Justification, regeneration and holiness, and in her admirable system of inerrancy, by which she keeps all her stations manned and sends forward fresh men to every new field. Let her preach Arminianism strictly and logically, and she will soon lose her aggressiveness, or become another institution than an evangelical Church of Christ.

Furthermore, Arminianism in the Methodist Church is but a century old. It has never passed through the years or the confusions through which Calvinism has passed. Will it continue in the ages to come to be the diffusive power which it has been for these years past? Of this I am persuaded, looking at the history and workings of religious opinions in the past: that the Church will be constrained in time to put forth a systematic and logical Confession of Faith,[25] out of which she will either drop all peculiarly Arminian doctrines, and so secure her permanency, or in which she will proclaim them, and by that means will inject the poison of death, as an evangelizing body, into her system. A thorough Arminianism and a practical evangelism have never yet remained long in loving harmony. Look at the history of doctrines as illustrated in the history of the Church of Rome, and you will see this clearly attested. Arminianism, in its principles, had been in operation in that Church for centuries when the Reformation broke forth, and what evangelistic work had it done? It had indeed converted almost the entire world, but to what had it converted it? It had formed and established the largest and most powerful Church which the world has ever seen, but what had it done for the salvation of human bodies and souls? It had made Romanists, but it had not made Christians equally as numerous. Was it not the very principles of the Calvinistic theology which flashed light upon the thick darkness, and threw fire into the corrupt mass, and lifted up the banner of the cross, so long trodden under a debased hierarchy, and revived the ancient faith of the Church, and established the great Protestant and evangelical denominations of Christians? Who but Calvinists – or, as formerly called, Augustinians – were the forerunners of the

---

[25] I do not forget, and do not disparage, Richard Watson's Theological Institutes.

Reformers? Such was Wycliffe, "the morning star of the Reformation;" such was John of Goch and John of Wesalia and John of Wessel, "the light of the world;" and Savonarola of Florence, who thundered with such terrible vehemence against the sins of the clergy and people, who refused a cardinal's hat for his silence, saying, "he wished no red hat, but one reddened with his own blood, the hat given to the saints" – who even demanded the removal of the pope, and, scorning all presents and promises and honors on condition of "holding his tongue," gave his life for the holy cause – another victim of priestly profligacy and bloodthirstiness. Every great luminary which in the Church immediately preceded the greater lights of the Reformation was in principle a Calvinist. Such also were the great national Reformers, as Luther of Germany, Zwingle of Switzerland, Calvin of France, Cranmer of England, Knox of Scotland. "Although each movement was self-originated, and different from the others in many permanent characteristics,"[26] it was thoroughly Calvinistic. These men were driven to this theological belief, not by their peculiar intellectual endowments, but from their study of the word of God and the moral necessities of the Church and the world. They felt that half measures were useless – that it was worse than folly to seek to unite a system of saving works with a system of saving faith. So "Calvinism in its sharp and logical structure, in its moral earnestness, in its demand for the reformation of ecclesiastical abuses, found a response in the consciences of good men."[27] It was it which swept, like a prairie-fire, over the Continent, devouring the fabric of works of righteousness. He who is most familiar with the history of those times will most readily agree with the startling statement of Dr. Cunningham (successor to Dr. Chalmers), that, "next to Paul, John Calvin has done most for the world."

So thoroughly was the Reformed world Calvinistic three hundred years ago that it was almost entirely Presbyterian.[28] The French Protestant Church was as rigidly Presbyterian as the Scotch Church. "There are many acts of her synod," says the late Dr. Charles Hodge, "which would make modern ears tingle, and which prove that American Presbyterianism, in its strictest forms, is a sucking dove compared to that of the immediate descendants of the Reformers."[29]

---

[26] Dr. Hodge.
[27] Dr. Fisher, Hist. Ref.
[28] Dr. Breed's Presbyterianism Three Hundred Years Ago.
[29] Const. Hist.

There was, of course, as there always has been, greater diversity in the matters of church government than in the doctrines of faith; yet even in these there was an almost unanimous agreement that the presbyterial was the form of government most in accord with the teachings of Scripture. Dr. John Reynolds, who was in his day regarded as perhaps the most learned man in the Church of England, said, in answer to Brancroft, chaplain to the archbishop, who had broached what was then called "the novelty" that the bishops are a distinct order superior to the ordinary clergymen, "All who have for five hundred years last past endeavored the reformation of the Church have taught that all pastors, whether they be called bishops or priests, are invested with equal authority and power; as, first, the Waldenses, next Marsilius Patavianus. then Wycliffe and his scholars, afterward Huss and the Hussites, and, last of all, Luther, Calvin, Brentius, Bullinger and Musculus. Among ourselves we have bishops, the queen's professors of divinity in our universities and other learned men consenting therein, as Bradford, Lambert, Jewel, Pilkington, etc. But why do I speak of particular persons? It is the common judgment of the Reformed churches of Helvetia, Savoy, France, Scotland, Germany, Hungary, Poland, the Low Countries and our own."[30]

If we now turn to the fruits of Calvinism in the form of devoted Christians and in the number of churches established, we shall see that it has been the most powerful evangelistic system of religious belief in the world. Consider with what amazing rapidity it spread over Europe, converting thousands upon thousands to a living Christianity. In about twenty-five years from the time when Calvin began his work there were two thousand places of Calvinistic worship, with almost half a million of worshippers, in France alone. When Ambrose Willie, a man who had studied theology at the feet of Calvin in Geneva, preached at Ernonville Bridge, near Tournay, in 1556, twenty thousand people assembled to hear him. Peter Gabriel had also for an audience in the same year, near Haarlem, "tens of thousands;" and we can judge of the theological character of this sermon from his text, which was, "For by grace are ye saved through faith; and that not of your self; it is the gift of God: not of works, lest any man should boast; for we are his workmanship, created in Christ Jesus unto good works, which God hath before ordained that we should walk in them."[31]

These are but two of the many examples of the intense awakening produced by the earnest preaching of the Calvinistic doctrines. So great were

---

[30] Breed's Presbyterianism Three Hundred Years Ago, p. 24, 25.
[31] Eph. 2:8-10.

the effects that in three years after this tie a General Synod was held in Paris, at which a Confession of Faith was adopted. Two years after the meeting of the Synod – that is in 1561 – the Calvinists numbered one-fourth of the entire French population.[32] And in less than half a century this so-called harsh system of belief had penetrated every part of the land, and had gained to its standards almost one-half of the population and almost every great mind in the nation. So numerous and powerful had its adherents become that for a time it appeared as if the entire nation would be swept over to their views. Smiles, in his Huguenots in France,[33] says: "It is curious to speculate on the influence which the religion of Calvin, himself a Frenchman, might have exercised on the history of France, as well as on the individual character of the Frenchman, had the balance of forces carried the nation bodily over to Protestantism, as was very nearly the case, toward the end of the sixteenth century." Certain it is that the nation would have had a different history from that which she has had. But it is interesting to mark how rapidly Calvin's opinions had spread in his native land, and to note the evangelistic effect of that system of doctrine which bears his name. Its marvelous evangelizing power lies no doubt in its scriptural thought and phraseology, and its intense spirituality and lofty enthusiasm and logical strength. Luther, though Calvinistic in his doctrinal beliefs, weakened his system by his concessions to princes and ceremonies. He "hesitated," says the historian Bancroft,[34] "to deny the real presence, and was indifferent to the observance of external ceremonies. Calvin, with sterner dialectics, sanctioned by the influence of the purest life and by his power as the ablest writer of his age, attacked the Roman doctrine respecting communion, and esteemed as a commemoration a rite which the Catholics revered as a sacrifice. Luther acknowledged princes as his protectors, and in the ceremonies of worship favored magnificence as an aid to devotion; Calvin was the guide of Swiss republics, and avoided, in their churches, all appeals to the senses as a crime against religion ... Luther permitted the cross and taper, pictures and images, as things of indifference. Calvin demanded a spiritual worship in its utmost purity." Hence it was that Calvinism, by bringing the truth directly to bear upon the mind and heart, made its greater and more permanent conquests, and subjected itself to the fiercer opposition and persecution of Romanism.

---

[32] Fisher, Hist. Ref.
[33] P. 100.
[34] Hist. U.S., I. pp. 277, 278.

"The Lutheran Reformation," says Dyer in his History of Modern Europe,[35] "traveled but little out of Germany and the neighboring Scandinavian kingdoms; while Calvinism obtained a European character, and was adopted in all the countries that adopted a reformation from without, as France, as the Netherlands, Scotland, even England; for the early English Reformation under Edward VI. was Calvinistic, and Calvin was incontestably the father of our Puritans and dissenters. Thus, under his rule, Geneva may be said to have become the capital of European Reform."

A similar testimony is that of Francis de Sales, who in one of his letters to the duke of Savoy urged the suppression of Geneva as the capital of what the Romish Church calls heresy. "All the heretics," said he, "respect Geneva as the asylum of their religion . There is not a city in Europe which offers more facilities for the encouragement of heresy, for it is the gate of France, of Italy and Germany, so that one finds there people of all nations – Italians, French, Germans, Poles, Spaniards, English, and of countries still more remote. Besides, every one knows the great number of ministers bred there. Last year it furnished twenty to France. Even England obtains ministers from Geneva. What shall I say of its magnificent printing establishments, by means of which the city floods the world with its wicked books, and even goes the length of distributing them at the public expense? ... All the enterprises undertaken against the Holy See and the Catholic princes have their beginnings at Geneva. No city in Europe receives more apostates of all grades, secular and regular. From thence I conclude that Geneva being destroyed would naturally lead to the dissipation of heresy."[36]

God had ordered it that Geneva, so accessible to all the nations of Western Europe, should be the home of Calvin, from which he could most efficiently carry on his work of enlightenment and civilization. And so important to the cause of Protestantism had that city become that upon it, in the opinion of Francis de Sales, the whole cause depended.

Almost marvelous indeed was the rapid spread of the doctrines of Calvinism. Dyer says[37]: "Calvinism, still more inimical to Rome than the doctrines of Luther, had, from Geneva, its centre and stronghold, spread itself in all directions in Western Europe. In the neighboring provinces of Germany it had in a great degree supplanted Lutheranism, and had even penetrated into Hungary and Poland; it was predominant in Scotland, and had

---

[35] Vol. 11. p. 7.
[36] Vie de Ste. Francois de Sates, par son neveu, p. 120.
[37] Hist. Mod. Europe, vol. 2. pp. 136, 392.

leavened the doctrines of the English Church ... The pope could reckon only upon Spain and Italy as sound and secure, with a few islands and the Venetian provinces in Dalmatia and Greece ... Its converts belonged chiefly (in France) to the higher ranks, including many of the clergy, monks, nuns, and even bishops; and the Catholic churches seemed almost deserted, except by the lower classes."

From this brief survey we are enabled to perceive something of the wonderful evangelizing force of this system of belief. It was the only system able to cope with the great powers of the Romish Church, and over-throw them; and for two centuries it was accepted in all Protestant countries as the final account of the relations between man and his Maker.[38] In fact, there is no other system which has displayed so powerful an evangelizing force as Calvinism. This becomes still more manifest in the history of the great revivals with which the Christian Church has been blessed.

Many are accustomed to think that revivals belong particularly to the Methodist Church, whereas, in fact, that Church has never yet inaugurated a great national or far-spreading revival. Her revivals are marked with localism; they are connected with particular churches, and do not make a deep, abiding and general impression on society. The first great Christian revival occurred under the preaching of Peter in Jerusalem, who employed such language in his discourse or discourses as this: "Him, being delivered by the determinate counsel and foreknowledge of God, ye have taken, and by wicked hands have crucified and slain." That is Calvinism rigid enough. Passing over the greatest revival of modern times, the Reformation, which, as all know, was under the preaching of Calvinism, we come to our own land. The era of revivals in this country is usually reckoned from the year 1792, but in 1740 there was a marked revival under the preaching of the Rev. Jonathan Dickinson, a Presbyterian clergyman. It was about this time also that George Whitefield, called in his day "the great Methodist," a clergyman of the Church of England and an uncompromising Calvinist, was startling the ungodly in Philadelphia. It is recorded that he threw "a horrid gloom" over this fashionable and worldly old town, "and put a stop to the dancing schools, assemblies and every pleasant thing." Strange, indeed, that dissipation and vanity are "pleasant things," while holiness and salvation from hell are disagreeable things! But this great man, in company with Gilbert Tennent, a Presbyterian clergyman, of whom Whitefield said, "He is a son of thunder," and "hypocrites must either soon be converted or en-

---

[38] Froude, Calvinism, p. 4.

raged at his preaching," was arousing multitudes by his fiery, impassioned, consecrated eloquence.

We speak of the Methodist Church beginning in a revival. And so it did. But the first and chief actor in that revival was not Wesley, but Whitefield. Though a younger man than Wesley, it was he who first went forth preaching in the fields and gathering multitudes of followers, and raising money and building chapels. It was Whitefield who invoked the two Wesleys to his aid. And he had to employ much argument and persuasion to overcome their prejudices against the movement. Whitefield began the great work at Bristol and Kingswood, and had found thousands flocking to his side, ready to be organized into churches, when he appealed to Wesley for assistance. Wesley, with all his zeal, had been quite a High-Churchman in many of his views. He believed in immersing even the infants, and demanded that dissenters should be rebaptized before being taken into the Church. He could not think of preaching in any place but in a church. "He should have thought," as he said, "the saving of souls almost a sin if it had not been done in a church."[39] Hence when Whitefield called on John Wesley to engage with him in the popular movement, he shrank back. Finally, he yielded to Whitefield's persuasions, but, he allowed himself to be governed in the decision by what many would regard as a superstition. He and Charles first opened their Bibles at random to see if their eyes should fall on a text which might decide them. But the texts were all foreign to the subject. Then he had recourse to sortilege and cast lots to decide the matter. The lot drawn was the one marked for him to consent, and so he consented. Thus he was led to undertake the work with which his name has been so intimately and honorably associated ever since.

So largely was the Methodist movement owing to Whitefield that he was called "the Calvinistic establisher of Methodism," and to the end of his life he remained the representative of it in the eyes of the learned world. Walpole, in his Letters, speaks only once of Wesley in connection with the rise of Methodism, while he frequently speaks of Whitefield in connection with it. Mant, in his course of lectures against Methodism, speaks of it as an entirely Calvinistic affair.[40] Neither the mechanism nor the force which gave rise to it originated with Wesley.[41] Field-preaching, which gave the whole movement its aggressive character, and fitted and enabled it to cope with the powerful agencies which were armed against it, was begun by

---

[39] Lecky, Hist. England, Eighteenth Century, vol. 2. p. 612.
[40] Bampton Lectures, for 1812.
[41] Wedgewood's Life of John Wesley, p. 157.

Whitefield, whilst "Wesley was dragged into it reluctantly." In the polite language of the day "Calvinism" and "Methodism" were synonymous terms, and the Methodists were called "another sect of Presbyterians."[42] The sainted Toplady said of the time, "Arminianism is the great religious evil of this age and country. It has more or less infected every Protestant denomination amongst us, and bids fair for leaving us, in a short time, not so much as the very profession of godliness ... We have generally forsaken the principles of the Reformation, and 'Ichabod,' the glory is departed, has been written on most of our pulpits and church-doors ever since."

It was Calvinism, and not Arminianism, which originated (so far as any system of doctrines originated) the great religious movement in which the Methodist Church was born.

While, therefore, Wesley is to be honored for his work in behalf of that Church, we should not fail to remember the great Calvinist, George Whitefield, who gave that Church her first beginnings and her most distinctive character. Had he lived longer, and not shrunk from the thought of being the founder of a Church, far different would have been the results of his labors. As it was, he gathered congregations for others to form into churches, and built chapels for others to preach in.

In all that awakening in this country it was such Calvinists as Whitefield, Tennent, Edwards, Brainerd, and, at a later day, Nettleton and Griffin, who were the chief actors. "The Great Revival of 1800," as it is called, began toward the close of the last century and continued for a generation into this. During that time it was one series of awakenings. It spread far and wide, refreshing and multiplying the churches. It was the beginning of all those great religious movements for which our century is so noted. The doctrines which were employed to bring it about were those, as a recent writer remarks, "which are commonly distinguished as Calvinistic."[43] "The work," says the another, "was begun and carried on in this country under the preaching and influence of the doctrines contained in the Confession of Faith of the Presbeterian Church."[44] "It is wonderful how the holy influence of Jonathan Edwards, David Brainerd and others of that day is to be traced at the root of the revival and missionary efforts of all sects and lands."[45]

---

[42] Bampton Lectures, for 1812. 22 Speer's Great Revival of 1800, p. 52.
[43] Speer's Great Revival. p. 52.
[44] Dr. Smil. Ralston's Letters.
[45] Speer's Great Revival. p. 112.

The revival which began in New England, and which was the greatest that had, until that time, been witnessed in the American colonies, resulted, under the blessing of God, from a series of doctrinal sermons preached by Jonathan Edwards.

But I cannot continue to specify instances. Let it be borne in mind that the men who have awakened the consciences and swayed the masses, and brought the multitudes to the feet of Jesus, not in a temporary excitement, but in a perpetual covenant, have been such Calvinists as Ambrose Wilde, and John Knox, and Thomas Chalmers, and George Whitefield, and Jonathan Edwards, and Griffin, Nettleton, Moody, and, last but not least, Spurgeon.

Calvinism may be unpopular in some quarters. But what of that? It cannot be more unpopular than the doctrines of sin and grace as revealed in the New Testament. But much of its unpopularity is due to the fact of its not being understood. Let it be examined without passion, let it be studied in its relations and logical consistency, and it will be seen to be at least a correct transcript of the teachings of the Scriptures, of the laws of Nature and of the facts of human life. If the faith and piety of the Church be weak today, it is, I am convinced, in a great measure because of the lack of a full, clear, definite knowledge and promulgation of these doctrines. The Church has been having a reign of candyism; she has been feeding on pap sweetened with treacle, until she has become disordered and weakly. Give her a more clearly-defined and a more firmly grasped faith, and she will lift herself up in her glorious might before the world. All history and experience prove the correctness of Carlyle's saying, that "At all turns a man who will do faithfully needs to believe firmly." It is this, I believe, that the Church needs today more than any other thing – not "rain-doctors," not religious "diviners," wandering to and fro, rejoicing in having no dogmatic opinions and no theological preferences; no, it is not these religious ear-ticklers that are needed – although they may be wanted somewhere – but, as history teaches us, clear and accurate views of the great fundamental doctrines of sin and grace. First make the tree good, and the fruit will be good. A good tree cannot bring forth evil fruit. It is not for us to trifle with these matters. Our time here is but for a moment, and our eternity depends on the course we take. Should we not, then, seek to know the truth, and strive, at any cost, to buy it, and sell it not?

By all the terrors of an endless death, as by all the glories of an endless life, we are called and pressed and urged to know the truth and follow it unto the end. And this joy we have, in and over all as the presence of a divine radiance, "that He which hath begun a good work in you will perform it until the day of Jesus Christ." So grant thou Holy Spirit of God, to begin the work in every one of us; and to thee, with the Father and the Son, shall be all the praise and the glory for ever Amen.

Calvin und die Mission (1909)

WILHELM SCHLATTER

Wilhelm Schlatter (1865-1943) arbeitete mehrere Jahre im Evangelisationswerk von Fritz Fliedner in Madrid und in der deutschen Seemannsmission von Pastor Harms in Sunderland (England) mit. Für dreieinhalb Jahre unterrichtete er an der Evangelischen Predigerschule in Basel und baute so den Kontakt mit der Basler Mission auf. 1910 begann Schlatter mit der Forschung über die Geschichte der Basler Mission neben seiner Arbeit als Pfarrer der Evangelischen Gesellschaft in Merishausen und St. Gallen (Schweiz). Ab 1916 veröffentlicht er eine dreibändige „Geschichte der Basler Mission 1815-1915". Im Laufe der Jahre entstanden viele weitere Bücher, neben solchen mit biblisch-theologischen und kirchengeschichtlichen auch eine ganze Reihe mit pastoraltheologischen Themen. Schlatter selbst hatte neben seiner abschließenden beruflichen Tätigkeit als Pfarrer im Dienst der Evangelischen Gesellschaft in Bern den vierten Band über die Fortsetzung der Missionstätigkeit der Basler Mission während der Zwischenkriegszeit ins Auge gefasst und dazu auch ein Manuskript verfasst, konnte dies aber nicht mehr umsetzen, da er im Anschluss an ein Herzleiden verstarb.

Erschienen in: Evangelisches Missions-Magazin (Verlag der Baseler Missionsbuchhandlung) NF 53 (1909), Heft 8 (August), S. 333-343.

Nicolaus Durand de Villegaignon, von Provinz in der Bretagne stammend, Maltheserritter, hatte als Galeerenoffizier mehrere Expeditionen mitgemacht und war im Jahre 1554 Vizeadmiral der Bretagne. Infolge eines Zerwürfnisses und da er sich in Frankreich nicht nach Gebühr anerkannt sah, legte er 1555 Coligny und durch seine Fürsprache dem Könige einen Kolonisationsplan vor. Jener erwärmte sich sehr für die Sache, und dieser gewährte die zur Ausführung erforderliche Unterstützung. Zwei schöne Schiffe konnten ausgestattet werden, und Villegaignon wusste sie zu füllen mit zwei verschiedenen Menschenklassen: Reformierte bewog er zur Mitreise durch die in Aussicht gestellte völlige Glaubensfreiheit (er versprach, die neue Kolonie nach der Genfer Kirchenordnung einzurichten), und mit Erlaubnis des Königs suchte er sich in den Gefängnissen von Paris arbeitsfähige Leute aus, welche er als Tagelöhner durch versprochenen schönen Lohn lockte.

Am 15. Juli 1555 schiffte er sich in Havre ein und langte im November in der Gegend von Rio de Janeiro an. Wir besitzen den Text eines Briefes an Calvin, in welchem Villegaignon seine Erlebnisse in Brasilien bis zum 31. Dezember 1557 (Datum des Briefes, vgl. Corp. Ref. Ca. Br. Nr. 2672) erzählt. Der Anfang war überaus schwer. Das Land war gänzlich unbebaut, Märkte gab es nicht, die Ernährung machte Schwierigkeiten. Die Portugiesen, die das betreffende Gebiet beanspruchten, ohne dass sie es hätten besetzen und behaupten können, nahmen eine unfreundliche Haltung ein, ebenso die wilden, rohen Eingeborenen, deren Umgang auch für die mitgebrachten Sträflinge eine große sittliche Gefahr bedeutete. Die Enttäuschungen bewirkten eine solche Entmutigung, dass manche, welche aus Rücksichten der Freundschaft mitgezogen waren, bald die Rückreise antraten. Er selbst aber – so schreibt er mit schönen Worten an Calvin – wollte sich nicht abschrecken lassen, auf den Bau des Reiches Christi dieselbe Sorgfalt zu verwenden, die er früher den weltlichen Dingen gewidmet hatte; da es sich um Christi Sache handelte, habe er Vorwürfe und Verleumdungen ertragen und auf Christus gebaut.

Um die Kolonie gegen die Feindseligkeiten und Einflüsse der Eingeborenen abzuschließen, verlegte er sie auf eine 2000 Schritte vom Festland entfernte Insel, die er nach dem hohen Protektor des Unternehmens Coligny nannte. Sie wurde in harter Arbeit befestigt. Weil die insulare Abgeschlossenheit den unzüchtigen Verkehr mit den Weibern der Eingeborenen abschnitt, zettelten 26 jener Tagelöhner eine Verschwörung an gegen Villegaignons Leben. Sie wurde ihm in letzter Stunde verraten. Durch entschlossenes Auftreten wurde er ihrer Herr. Der Hauptradelsführer wurde aufgeknüpft, die übrigen erlangten Verzeihung, da er sich seiner Leute nicht allzusehr entblößen konnte. Er erzählt: er habe nicht unterlassen, seine Umgebung nach Vermögen unter den Einfluss der christlichen Religion zu stellen, indem er Morgen- und Abendandachten anordnete; dadurch sei erreicht worden, dass der Rest des Jahres ruhiger verlief. Villegaignon hatte bald nach der Landung eingesehen, dass eine Vermehrung der reformierten Kolonisten der Unternehmung förderlich werden müsste, und deshalb mit den nach Europa zurückfahrenden Schiffen Briefe an Coligny und Calvin geschickt, in welchem er um Zusendung frommer Leute und um Prediger bat, zur innern Befestigung der Kolonie und zur Ausbreitung des Reiches Christi.

Coligny unterstützte seine Bitte, und in Genf gewährte man sie gern. Zwei Geistliche wurden von der Genfer Kirche abgeordnet: *Peter Richer*, genannte de l'Isle, früher Karmelitermönch, Doktor der Theologie, und *Wilhelm Chartier*, von Vitré, vornehmen Ursprungs. Sie verließen Genf

„mit derselben Freudigkeit des Geistes, welche sie früher bewiesen hatten", am 8 September 1556. Ein edler Edelmann, der sich in de Nähe Genfs niedergelassen hatte, ein Herr Philippes de Corguilleray, genannt du Pont („Pontanus"), reiste als ihr Protektor mit ihnen; auch Jean de Lery (später Pfarrer in Bern) schloss sich ihnen an; es waren im ganzen 13 tüchtige Männer, welche, um Christi Reich in die neue Welt zu bringen, Genf verließen. Sie besuchten Coligny und die Brüder in Paris und fanden „bei solchen, welche nach dem göttlichen Wort Verlangen hatten", finanzielle Unterstützung für die Anschaffung von Büchern und Kleidern und für die Reiseauslagen. Ein Sorbonnist Cointa gesellte sich zu ihnen, und eine beträchtliche Anzahl „derer von der Religion" (Glaubensbrüder) schloss sich an. In Honfleur sammelte sich die ganze Reisegesellschaft unter der Führung eines Neffen von Villegaignon, Bois le Conte. Am 19. November 1556 stach die kleine Kolonistenflotte in See; es waren drei Schiffe mit 80, 26 und 90 Passagieren, welche sich freuten, Gott in Freiheit zu dienen und für das Reich Christi zu wirken; eine beträchtliche Anzahl von Kindern, die man für besonders geeignet hielt, die Sprache der Eingeborenen zu lernen, soll eingeschifft worden sein, unter Aufsicht und Pflege einiger Jungfrauen und einer älteren Frau.

Die Überfahrt gelang unter Stürmen ohne Unfall. Am 10 März 1557 geschah die Landung in Brasilien. Über die drei ersten Wochen nach der Ankunft liegt uns ein anschaulicher Doppelbericht vor: ein Brief von Richer an einen unbekannten Adressaten (Corp. Ref. Ca. Br. Nr. 2609) und ein gemeinsames Schreiben der beiden Prediger Richer und Chartier an Calvin (Nr. 2615); jener vom 31. März, dieser vom 1. April 1557 datiert. Der Brief an Calvin beginnt mit der Bezeugung inniger Gemeinschaft: „Unsere Gemeinschaft, in welcher wir, durch die Bande des Heiligen Geistes verbunden, an dem einen Leibe Christi zusammenwachsen, vereint uns so innig, dass der ungeheure Raum, welcher uns leiblich scheidet, es nicht verhindern kann, dass wir im Geiste bei dir sind, in der Gewissheit, dass auch du uns im Herzen habest." Damit diese ihre Gemeinschaft wachse, wollen sie Calvin zum Genossen ihrer Sorgen und Freuden machen. Sie sind hocherfreut über die Aufnahme und Förderung, welche sie bei Villegaignon gefunden haben. Sie nennen ihn ihren „Vater" und „Bruder", welchen Gott selbst für sie bereit gehalten habe, „Vater – denn er nimmt uns wie Söhne auf; Bruder – denn mit uns ruft er den einen Vater an und glaubt an Jesus Christus, den einzigen Mittler, durch welchen allein er vor Gott sich gerecht weiß, und durch die innere Bewegung des Heiligen Geistes erfährt er in sich selbst, dass er ein echtes Glied Christi sei." Er habe Freude am göttlichen Wort und stehe seiner Familie in einer Weise vor, dass man an die Hausgemeinde bei Aquila und Priscilla erinnert werde. „Dies lässt uns hoffen, dass in Bälde große Gemeinden von hier ausgehen, welche das Lob Gottes verkündigen und das Reich Christi mehren." Sie bitten um Calvins Fürbitte, „damit Gott dieses Gebäude Christi, welches an diesem Erdenende begonnen ist, vollende"; er möge zu solchem Dienst der Fürbitte auch die Gottesfürchtigen anspornen.

Im Brief Richers an den Unbekannten finden sich genauere Mitteilungen über die getanen Schritte zur Förderung des Glaubenslebens. Am Tage nach der Ankunft der Prediger begehrte schon Villegaignon von ihnen, dass sie mit der Ausübung ihres Amtes beginnen sollten. Acht Tage später wurde auf sein Verlangen das Abendmahl gefeiert; er beteiligte sich mit seinen Leuten daran in augenscheinlicher Andacht und legte zur Erbauung der Gemeinde ein gutes Bekenntnis seines Glaubens ab. „Was hätte unserem Vorhaben besser entsprochen?"

Wenn so das Verhalten des Hauptes der Kolonie die Pfarrer das Beste hoffen ließ, so war freilich der Einblick in den Zustand der Eingeborenen, welcher in der kurzen Frist möglich war, um so weniger ermutigend. Richer redet davon ausführlich. Das Klima sei herrlich, die Gesundheit ausgezeichnet – „nur eines ist, das uns nicht wenig schmerzt und ängstigt. Das ist die Barbarei der Eingeborenen, welche nicht schlimmer sein könnte. Ich behaupte nicht, dass sie Menschenfresser seien, obwohl ihnen auch dies zuzutrauen wäre. Aber mich betrübt ihre geistige Stumpfheit, die inmitten ihrer Verfinsterung greifbar ist. Von Vatertugenden wissen sie nichts, Gutes unterscheiden sie nicht von Bösem; die Laster, welche unter den übrigen Völkern schon die Natur brandmarkt, verwechseln sie mit Tugenden, überhaupt wissen sie rein nichts davon, dass Laster schädlich sind. Kurz, in dieser Beziehung sind sie den unvernünftigen Tieren völlig gleich. Aber was das Schlimmste ist: dass ein Gott sei, ist ihnen in solchem Maße verborgen, dass sie weder auf sein Gesetz achten, noch seine Macht und Güte bewundern. Deshalb ist uns die Hoffnung, sie für Christus zu gewinnen, genommen. Das ist das Schwerste von allem, was uns auch am meisten beschwert. Da höre ich jemanden einwenden: „Gut, so sind sie eine unbeschriebene Tafel, welche leicht mit ihren Farben wird bemalt werden können, weil ihrem Glanz nichts anderes im Wege steht." Doch der weiß nicht, wie sehr die Verschiedenheit der Sprache hindert. Bedenke, dass es uns an Dolmetschern, welche dem Herrn treu wären, gebricht! Wir beabsichtigten, die Dienste solcher in Anspruch zu nehmen. Aber wir fanden, dass sie selbst ganz und gar Satans Glieder sind und nichts so sehr hassen, wie das heilige Evangelium Christi. So müssen wir in dieser Sache an uns halten und Geduld üben, bis die jungen Leute, welcher Herr von

Villegaignon zur Unterweisung in der Landessprache den Eingeborenen übergeben hat, genügende Fortschritte gemacht haben. Gott gebe, dass sie nicht an ihren Seelen gefährdet werden! Weil nun der Höchste selbst uns diese Amt anvertraut hat, hoffen wir, dieses Edomiterland werde einmal ein Besitztum Christi werden. Inzwischen zählen wir auf neue Ankömmlinge, damit durch den Umgang mit ihnen allen dieses barbarische Volk umgewandelt werde und unsere Kirche wachse ... Der Höchste wird für alles sorgen. Wir bitten angelegentlich, dass alle Kirchen für uns beten. Aus dem antarktischen Gallien. Dein P. Richerius."

Leider trat Villegaignons Unaufrichtigkeit bald an den Tag. Er hatte die Reformierten als folgsame Kolonisten an sich gezogen; nun, da er sie um sich hatte, zeigte er bald, dass er nicht ihres Sinnes war. Der mitgekommene Sorbonnist Cointa bereitete Schwierigkeiten. Er verlangte allerlei katholisches Ritual bei Abendmahl und Taufe. Villegaignon nahm eine zweideutige Stellung an und bewirkte, um den jüngeren Chartier los zu werden, dessen Entsendung nach Genf, damit er Calvins Gutachten über die Differenzpunkte einholte. Nach seiner Abreise und der Abfahrt der Schiffe ließ er seine Maske gänzlich fallen. Er soll erfahren haben, dass man am Hofe über seine Ketzerfreundlichkeit sich unwillig geäußert hatte; auch heißt es, der Kardinal von Lothringen habe ihn brieflich aufgefordert, die Ketzerei zu unterdrücken. Nun begannen die Leiden der Reformierten. Ihr Gottesdienst wurde ihnen verboten und musste, wie im Heimatlande, heimlich abgehalten werden; da er ihren Gehorsam gegen die Obrigkeit kannte, drückte er sie auf jede mögliche Weise.

Durch solches Verhalten Villegaignons wurde die ursprüngliche Absicht, eine christliche Kolonie auszubauen, als Grundlage für nachfolgende Arbeit an den heidnischen Landesbewohnern, vereitelt. Eine beträchtliche Anzahl Reformierter wurde, als sie Miene machten, ein bretonisches Handelsschiff zur Heimkehr zu benützen, aus Coligny nach dem Festlande vertrieben. Sie sahen hierin ein Zeichen zur Tätigkeit unter den Heiden und unterredeten sich eifrig mit ihnen, fanden auch offene Ohren und in ihren materiellen Bedürfnissen freundliche Unterstützung; de Lery gibt in seiner Reisebeschreibung ein kleines Wörterbuch über die Sprache der Topinambu, welches zeigt, dass sie sich mit Energie und Erfolg ihrer Erforschung widmeten. Überhandnehmender Mangel aber an allem Nötigen und die fortdauernden Hemmnisse, welche Villegaignon von seiner Insel her ihnen bereitete, brachten ihren Plan der Heimkehr zur Ausführung.

Die Seereise war fürchterlich. Das Schiff ließ, von Würmern ganz durchfressen, Wasser ein; der Untergang drohte. Fünf Mann zogen es vor, sich einem schwachen Boote und der Gnade des Villegaignon anzuvertrauen, und ruderten nach der brasilianischen Küste zurück. Dieser aber, anstatt den Geretteten barmherzig zu sein, machte ihnen den Prozess um des Glaubens willen. Einer soll sich zu den Wilden geflüchtet haben; vier aber legten ein treues, freudiges Bekenntnis ab, weshalb Villegaignon drei durch den Henker vom Felsen ins Meer werfen ließ; den vierten verschonte er, weil er die Kolonie nicht ihres einzigen Schneiders berauben wollte. Die Namen der drei Glaubenszeugen lauten: Pierre du Bordel, Matthieu Vermeil und Pierre Bourdon. Sie sind es wert, unvergessen zu bleiben als die ersten Glaubenszeugen der evangelischen Heidenmission.

Diejenigen, welche auf dem Schiffe geblieben waren, erreichten Frankreich, abgemagert bis auf Haut und Knochen. Villegaignon verfolgte sie heimtückisch, indem er ihnen unter Verschluss die abgeschlossenen Akten ihres Ketzerprozesses an den ersten französischen Magistrat mitgab. Dieser aber legte die Schriften beiseite und versagte ihnen die Barmherzigkeit nicht. Richer wurde Prediger in La Rochelle. De Lery, später französischer Pfarrer in Bern, hat eine wahrheitsgetreue „Geschichte der Seereise nach Brasilien, auch Amerika genannt", geschrieben (ursprünglich französisch-lateinische Ausgabe: Genf 1586). Die Kolonie war von kurzem Bestand. Villegaignon kehrte zurück, schrieb als leidenschaftlicher Gegner der Evangelischen und endete 1571 in großem Elend.

Das ist die kurze, traurige Geschichte der ersten, evangelischen Missionsunternehmung. Denn um eine solche handelte es sich in der Tat. Die Hoffnung, dem in der Heimat verfolgten Glauben ein Asyl in der neuen Welt zu bereiten, war nicht das Leitmotiv derjenigen, welche auf evangelischer Seite am Unternehmen in erster Linie beteiligt waren. Nicht ein ruhiges Genießen des Glaubens war das lockende Ideal; sondern dies war der Plan: es sollten in diesen fernen Regionen der Heiden lebendige, leuchtende, vom göttlichen Wort durchdrungene Kolonistengemeinden gebildet werden als Träger der eigentlichen Heidenmission, und der Blick auf die furchtbare, geistig-sittliche Verwahrlosung der Eingeborenen raubte den Predigern die Hoffnung auf eine große Ausbreitung des Reiches Christi nicht. Das Unternehmen aber ist durchaus mit dem Namen Calvins zu verbinden, da er als dessen geistiger Vater angesehen wurde. Ihm haben die von Genf entsandten Prediger ihre Anliegen ans Herz gelegt, ihn gingen sie um seine Fürbitte an, und er hat sich durchaus mit der Sache solidarisch gewusst, schrieb er doch nach deren tragischem Ausgang in Schmerz und Entrüstung von Villegaignon als einem „Hirnwütigen, der, von uns nach Amerika geschickt, daselbst die gute Sache in seiner Zügellosigkeit so schlecht verteidigt hat." (Brief Nr. 2814, an Farel, 24. Februar 1558.) Es war ein heroisches, von einem großen Glaubenseifer eingegebenes Unternehmen. Dass dasselbe scheitern musste, ist ja klar, auch wenn die Unlauterkeit und Unbrauchbarkeit eines Villegaignon nicht in Betracht gezogen wird. Auch die beste, treuste Führung hätte es nicht auf die Dauer zu halten vermocht angesichts des Abhängigkeitsverhältnisses, in welchem es sich zur katholischen Regierung Frankreichs befand; eine Kolonialmission war ja damals nur denkbar innerhalb der Konfession des Mutterlandes. Die erste – freilich verunglückte Missionstat der evangelischen Kirche darf diese Unternehmung immerhin genannt werden; sie ist ein Beweis für den heroischen Opfersinn und den starken Ausbreitungstrieb, welche von Calvin ausgingen.

Wir gehen über zu der Frage: *Wie dachte der Genfer Reformator von der Heidenmission?* Es ist nicht gerade vieles, was sich aus seinen zerstreuten Äußerungen zu dieser Frage ergibt, und sie treten nicht in erheblichem Maße heraus aus dem Rahmen reformatorischer Gesamtanschauung. Er teilt mit den andern Reformatoren das Staunen über die große Ausdehnung der Mission durch die Apostel selbst. Er redet zu Ps. 22. 28 davon, wie Christus gleich einem Blitz die Welt von Aufgang bis Untergang durchdrungen habe, um von allen Seiten die Völker in die Kirche herbeizuholen, und Ps. 110. 3 („Deine Kinder werden dir geboren wie der Tau aus der Morgenröte") legt er folgendermaßen aus: „Ich zweifle nicht daran, dass David hier Gott preist um der Mehrung des Volkes Christi willen. Die Kinderschar oder den Nachwuchs, der geboren werden soll, vergleicht er also mit dem Tau; denn er soll wachsen auf außerordentliche Weise. Jedermann ist erstaunt, die Erde befeuchtet zu finden, ohne dass man doch den Tau fallen sah – so wird, sagt David, Christo ein zahlloser Nachwuchs erwachsen, der die ganze Erde bedecken soll ... Dass dies aber nicht nur so unbesonnen angekündigt worden ist, zeigt die Erfahrung, denn es ist unglaublich, wie eine so große Menge in so geringer Zeit in Christi Reich gesammelt werden konnte, und dies einzig durch die Stimme des Evangeliums, während die ganze Welt wütend widerstand."

Calvin hat gelegentlich, wie auch Luther und Melanchthon taten, von dieser apostolischen Ausbreitungsarbeit in einer Weise geredet, dass man meinen könnte, er schreibe den Aposteln die zum Abschluss gebrachte Evangelisation des Erdreiches zu (diese Anschauung von der apostolischen Mission kennzeichnete die nachfolgende Orthodoxie, und vermöge derselben hat diese eine Wiederaufnahme der Ausbreitungsarbeit abgelehnt). So kann er z.B. sagen: „Nach Christi Auferstehung begannen die Grenzen des Reiches Gottes in die Weite und Breite unter alle möglichen Nationen ohne Unterschied ausgedehnt zu werden, und wurden nach Christi Wort die Gläubigen von allen Seiten gesammelt."

Immerhin hat Calvin anderswo wieder der Überzeugung Ausdruck gegeben, dass das Reich Christi seitdem und in der Gegenwart noch im Wachsen begriffen sei, so wenn er z.B. zu Jes. 45. 23 sagt: „Wenn Christus den Richterstuhl besteigen wird, um den Erdkreis zu richten, wird sich vollenden, was zu Anfang des Evangeliums zu werden begann und was vor unsern Augen bis heute im Werden begriffen ist" – oder zu Mal. 4. 3: „Wie das Reich Christi wohl begann in der Welt, als Gott wollte, dass das Evangelium überall ausgebreitet würde, und heute noch in seinem Laufe geht und noch nicht vollendet ist, so liegt auch das, was der Prophet hier sagt, noch nicht fertig vor."

Nirgends behauptet Calvin, die Apostel seien mit dem Evangelium bis an das Ende der Erde gekommen. Sie haben Arbeit begonnen, aber nicht vollendet, und sie geht fort. Aber durch wen? Das ist die Frage, in welcher die reformatorische und vollends die nachreformatorische, orthodoxe Theologie nicht zu derjenigen Klarheit durchgedrungen ist, welche zur Übernahme der Missionspflicht und -tat erforderlich war: sie konnte sich nicht entschließen, den apostolischen Auftrag seines außerordentlichen Charakters zu entkleiden und als permanente, große Aufgabe der christlichen Gemeinde zu erkennen. Freilich, die Orthodoxie hat Calvin überboten, indem sie direkt dogmatisierte, das Apostolat sei mit den Aposteln erloschen, weshalb die Kirche zur Heidenmission kein Recht und keine Befugnis hätte. Denn wenn er auch mit seinen Zeitgenossen festgehalten hat an der Meinung, das Apostolat pflanze sich nicht als Amt durch die ganze Geschichte der Kirche fort, so hat er doch wiederum hervorheben können, dass Gott noch immer Apostel erwecken könne und auch erweckt habe. Hören wir ihn darüber in seiner Institutio (1559. 2. 779 f.): „Als diejenigen, welche nach der Anordnung Christi mit der Leitung der Kirche betraut sind, werden von Paulus genannt: 1. Apostel, 2. Propheten, 3. Evangelisten, 4. Hirten, 5. Lehrer. Nur die beiden zuletzt Genannten bilden ein ordnungsgemäßes Amt in der Kirche; die andern drei Kategorien erweckte der Herr zu Beginn seines Reiches, und er erweckt sie auch etwa wieder, wenn die Not der Zeiten es erheischt. Welches die Funktion des Apostels sei, ergibt sich aus jenem Auftrag: Geht hin und predigt das Evangelium aller Kreatur (Mk. 16. 15). Nicht werden ihnen bestimmte Grenzen gesteckt; vielmehr wird der ganze Erdkreis bezeichnet als für den Gehorsam Christi zu eroberndes Gebiet; sie sollen wo immer sie können unter den Völkern das Evangelium ausbreiten und so sein Reich aufrichten ... Die Apostel also sind entsandt, damit sie den Erdkreis vom Abfall zum rechten Gehorsam gegen Gott zurückführten und sein Reich durch die Predigt des Evangeliums allenthalben aufrichteten, oder, wenn du lieber willst, damit sie als die ersten Erbauer der Kirche ihre Fundamente in der ganzen Welt legten."

Wir übergehen die Definition des Prophetenamtes. Die Evangelisten stellt Calvin als Helfer den Aposteln an die Seite, und er gelangte zu dem Ergebnis: „Jene drei Funktionen sind in der Kirche nicht zu bleibendem Bestand begründet worden, sondern für diejenige Zeit nur, in der Gemeinden da, wo zuvor keine gewesen oder wo sie von Mose zu Christus überzuführen waren, entstehen sollten. Ich leugne jedoch nicht, dass Gott auch nachher Apostel oder wenigstens an ihrer Statt Evangelisten von Zeit zu Zeit erweckt hat, wie z.B. in unsern Tagen geschehen ist. Denn solche Männer, welche die Kirche vom widerchristlichen Abfall zurückführten, taten not. Das Amt selbst jedoch heiße ich nichtsdestoweniger ein außerordentliches, weil es in den geordneten Kirchen keine Stätte hat." Der Apostel unterscheidet sich dadurch vom Pastor, dass er den Dienst am Wort und Sakrament nicht, wie dieser, innerhalb der Grenzen bestimmter Gemeinden, sondern in der weiten Welt vollbringt. Bei jenen Äußerungen über das Evangelistenamt seiner Zeit mag Calvin an den außerordentlichen Auftrag gedacht haben, welcher ihm selbst und seinesgleichen geworden war.

Es ist bemerkenswert, dass im Zusammenhang der Gedanken Calvins über die Ausbreitung des Reiches Christi seine Prädestinationslehre keine Rolle spielt. Es kommt ihm nicht in den Sinn, dieselbe auf irgend ein bestimmtes Volk anzuwenden und auf diese Weise zu erklären, dass es mit der Predigt des Evangeliums übergangen worden sei. Vielmehr findet er, wenn er an die Berufung der Völker zum Reiche Christi denkt, seinen Trost im Blick auf das Walten Gottes, welches sicher zu seinem Ziele kommt, ohne dass es der besondern Veranstaltungen bedürfe. „Nicht durch das Treiben der Menschen wird das Reich Christi gefördert oder gestützt; das ist vielmehr Gottes Werk ganz und gar, weshalb die Gläubigen nur dazu angewiesen werden, zum Lobpreis Gottes sich zusammenzufinden." (zu Ps. 118. 25). Damit lehrt Calvin jedoch nicht die Pflicht der christlichen Passivität. Wir wissen ja, dass der Ausbreitungstrieb in ganz Europa nirgends so, wie in Calvins Genf, eine Macht war, und so hören wir den Reformator zu Jes. 12. 4 und 5 folgendes sagen: „Daraus wird ersichtlich, wie stark in allen Frommen das Verlangen sein soll, dass Gottes Güte allen offenkundig werde, damit alle zu *einer* Verehrung Gottes gelangen. Dann zumal sollen wir in diesem Begehren entbrennen, wenn wir aus einer großen Gefahr, besonders aus der Tyrannei des Teufels und vom ewigen Tode befreit worden sind ... Wir werden gelehrt, dieses sei unsere Pflicht, dass wir überall unter den Völkern die Güte Gottes bekannt machen. Nicht aber sollen andere ermahnt und vorausgesandt werden, damit wir inzwischen untätig sitzen bleiben; sondern es geziemt sich, andern zum Vorbild voranzugehen."

Angesichts der Berufung der Heiden „darf das Evangelium nicht im Winkel verborgen bleiben, sondern es muss überall verkündigt werden".

Das ist ein Aufruf zur Missionsarbeit, eine Erinnerung an die Missionspflicht der Christengemeinde. Aber er ist – wie man es ähnlich auch bei Luther finden kann – ein sporadischer Ruf, der verhallt und nicht durchdringt, und als eine prophetische Stimme künftiger Zeiten, die seinen Inhalt verstehen werden, gilt. Sein Sinn ist über Calvins Bewusstsein hinausgegangen. Denn erst dann konnte er verstanden und betätigt werden, als die Gemeinschaft der Gläubigen ihres Rechts und ihrer Pflicht bewusst wurde, in freier Initiative die Mission an die Hand zu nehmen. Solches lag aber noch keineswegs im Gesichtskreis Calvins, hat er doch stark die Pflicht der christlichen Obrigkeit betont, die wahre Religion in ein noch ungläubiges Land ihrer Herrschaft einzuführen, wie denn auch die ersten größeren Missionsunternehmungen von evangelischer Seite die holländischen Regierungsmissionen waren.

Es ergibt sich: Calvin hatte es wohl vor Augen, dass die Völker der Erde insgesamt ins Reich Christi berufen seien; er sah dieses Werk noch nicht als vollendet an und erwartete seine Fortführung von Gott selbst durch den Bedürfnissen entsprechende Wiedererweckung außerordentlicher, apostolischer Persönlichkeiten; er konnte auch der christlichen Kirche ernsthaft ihre Pflicht zurufen, mit der Predigt des Evangeliums in alle Welt zu gehen. Aber es war ihm, wie seinen Zeitgenossen, verborgen, dass das apostolische Amt einen regulären Dienst sämtlicher Christen bedeute, und so fehlte für die konsequente Missionstat noch die Grundlage der Einsicht in ihr Recht und ihre Pflicht, weshalb seine Missionsaufforderungen gelegentliche Prophetenrufe waren für künftige Tage. Wir dürfen diesen Mangel reformatorischer Einsicht heute als eine göttliche Freundlichkeit, welche jene ersten Generationen evangelischer Christen erfuhren, beurteilen. Denn die Wege in die Heidenmission standen ihnen tatsächlich nicht offen., weil in der überseeischen Welt die katholischen Kolonialstaaten durchaus dominierten; darum hat der barmherzige Gott auch die reformatorische Christenheit nicht plagen wollen durch Enthüllung unlösbarer Aufgaben. Die Kirche Genfs zumal hatte alle Kräfte der Opferwilligkeit und Martyriumsfreudigkeit aufzuwenden, um ihrer Riesenaufgabe der Evangelisation in Europa nachzukommen.

Mit dem Pietismus sodann erwachte das eigentliche, evangelische Missionsleben. August Hermann Francke und der Graf Zinzendorf sind seine Väter geworden, und als der Rationalismus es in den Schoß der Brüdergemeine zurückdrängte, empfing es seine Neubelebung von England her durch die große Erweckung, welche mit den Namen Wesley und Whitefield verbunden ist; diese aber hatte wiederum durch den Pietismus ihre Antriebe empfangen.

Wir können nun im Zusammenhang unseres Themas die Frage aufwerfen, ob das mit dem Pietismus erweckte evangelische Missionsleben mit Calvin und seinem Lebenswerk und seinen Einflüssen irgendwelche ursächliche Beziehungen aufweise. Und solche sind nicht zu verkennen. Denn es ist bekannt, dass der Pietismus selbst, obwohl er die lutherische Kirche kräftig ergriff, seine Wurzeln stark im Calvinismus hatte. Es genügt ein Blick auf Speners Lebensgeschichte und auf sein Verhältnis zum reformiert gewordenen Jean de Labadie, um dieses wahrzunehmen. Die Christenheit Calvin'scher Herkunft hatte doch in anderem Maße als die lutherische denjenigen reformatorischen Grundsatz, welcher die Missionsarbeit möglich machte, in sich aufgenommen: die Erkenntnis des allgemeinen Priestertums der Gläubigen. Sie kannte von der Reformation her das Recht der Gemeindeglieder auf freie, mündliche Aussprache über das göttliche Wort, – darum war sie der Nährboden der Konventikel; sie hatte es nicht versäumt, mit dem Recht der Gemeindeglieder auf Arbeit an der Kirche zu rechnen, während die lutherische Pastoren- und Fürstenkirche der orthodoxen Zeit dieses gänzlich außer acht ließ. Und Calvins Charisma war es gewesen, der Kraft, welche in der Ruhe der Heilsgewissheit erlangt war, die Wege zur Arbeit an der Welt zu weisen; er hat die Überzeugung in seine Kirche hineingelebt und gepredigt, dass die Förderung des Reiches Christi eine allgemeine und persönliche Angelegenheit aller Glieder der Kirche sei. So ist zu sagen: Das evangelische Missionsleben der Gegenwart, welches dem Pietismus entstammt, wurzelt in demselben Maße im Calvinismus, als der Pietismus seinen Ursprung in diesem hat; mit dem Pietismus ist es im wesentlichen in calvinischem Boden entstanden, und wenn wir in diesen Monaten Calvins besonders gedenken, mögen die großen Anregungen nicht übersehen werden, welche, von seinem Lebenswerk ausgegangen, geschichtlich zum Missionsleben der evangelischen Christenheit geführt haben.

Calvin und die Mission (1909)

ERNST KOCHS

Pastor Ernst Kochs († 1953) war bis 1937 Pfarrer in Emden und veröffentlichte einige größere Studien über 400 Jahre Geschichte und Struktur der Reformierten Kirche in Ostfriesland am Ende des 18. und am Beginn des 19. Jahrhunderts.

Original von „Reformirte Kirchen-Zeitung" (Nürnberg) Band. 32 (1909), S. 322-324, dort ist die Quelle mit „Monatsblatt der Norddeutschen Missions-Gesellschaft" angegeben.

Das Jahr 1909 steht unter dem Zeichen des großen Reformators Johann Calvin, dessen Bedeutung für den Gesamtprotestantismus gar nicht hoch genug gewertet werden kann. Sollte er, der aus seiner tiefen Schrifterkenntnis und seiner reichen christlichen Erfahrung heraus in den bestehenden und entstehenden Kirchen so mannigfaltige Kräfte entbunden und der Christenheit seiner Zeit und aller Zeiten so unschätzbare Antriebe gegeben hat, für die vornehmste Aufgabe der Christenheit, die Ausbreitung des Königreichs Gottes unter den nichtchristlichen Völkern, gänzlich blind gewesen sein? Um die Antwort vorwegzunehmen: „Für die Mission im ganzen ist er ebenso blind gewesen, wie die übrigen Männer der Reformation." Wenn sich jedoch gerade bei Calvin wenigstens ein Ansatz zum Missionssinn und sogar zu praktischer Missionsübung findet, so fällt das gegenüber der bewusst ablehnenden Stellung der übrigen Reformatoren um so nachdrücklicher und erfreulicher ins Gewicht.

Dass die Reformatoren unserer Kirche sich einer Missionsverpflichtung weder theoretisch noch praktisch bewusst geworden sind, ist für den Missionsfreund eine immer aufs neue befremdliche Tatsache. Die Tatsache ist um so auffallender, als man doch in der zeitgenössischen katholischen Kirche einen neu erwachten Missionstrieb vorfand. Aber man dachte nicht daran, diese falsche katholische Missionsmethode nach evangelischen Grundsätzen umzugestalten, vielmehr war das Missionsinteresse in den Gedanken der Reformatoren vollständig ausgeschaltet. Das stand freilich den Reformatoren außer Zweifel, dass das Evangelium für alle Völker bestimmt sei und die Kirche eine unbeschränkte Ausdehnungsfähigkeit besitze. Aber man war der Überzeugung, dass die Aufgabe der Weltmission nicht nur auf die Apostel beschränkt gewesen sei, sondern auch tatsächlich durch sie und ihre Schüler in hinreichendem Maße gelöst sei. Und das konnte man im Ernste meinen, gerade in einer Zeit, als die Welt immer größer wurde, als die überseeischen Entdeckungen die Grenzen der bis dahin bekannten Welt so unermesslich erweiterten! Aber selbst das Auftauchen einer neuen, vom Evangelium völlig unberührten Welt vermochte die Reformatoren in dieser wunderlich beschränkten Meinung nicht zu erschüttern. Beza wenigstens weicht der durch die Entdeckung Amerikas auftauchenden Verlegenheit mit der naiven Bemerkung aus, dass doch sicherlich schon durch die Apostel wenigstens ein Geruch des Evangeliums bis nach Amerika gedrungen sein müsse; jetzt aber seien die Bewohner jenes Erdteils um ihres Unglaubens willen verworfen.

Man hat die Reformatoren damit entschuldigen wollen, dass ihnen der Weg zu den Heiden verschlossen gewesen sei. Gewiss waren 250 Jahre später, als das Missionsinteresse allgemein erwachte, die Türen viel weiter aufgetan; aber gerade in der Reformationszeit traten doch gewaltige Heidenländer in den Gesichtskreis der abendländischen Welt. Die katholischen Spanier und Portugiesen haben ihrer großen Kolonisationsarbeit sofort die missionarische folgen lassen. Die Reformatoren haben den Weg zu den Heiden aber nicht einmal gesucht. Dazu war doch die große Welt des Islam ihnen genugsam bekannt, aber der Türke kam ihnen nur als Gottesgeißel für die abtrünnige Christenheit und als Vorbote der antichristlichen Endzeit, niemals aber als Missionsobjekt in Betracht. Mit mehr Recht lässt sich darauf verweisen, dass sie über den ungeheuren Aufgaben der Evangelisation einer verweltlichten Christenheit keine Zeit und Kraft mehr zur Heidenmission fanden. Aber sie haben auch die Verpflichtung dazu nicht empfunden, und befremdlich muss es bleiben, dass sie bei ihrem sonst so eindringenden Schriftverständnis den durchgehenden Missionszug und Missionsruf des Neuen Testaments so verkennen konnten, dass sie durchgehends alle Stellen, die von dauernder Missionspflicht gegenüber den Heiden handeln, auf die verweltlichte und ins Heidentum zurückgesunkene Christenheit bezogen haben. Der einzige Gesichtspunkt, unter dem die Reformatoren eine Missionsverpflichtung für ihre Zeit anerkennen würden, liegt in der Linie des Rechtsgrundsatzes, dass ein christlicher Landesherr, sobald er etwa in heidnischen Ländern Kolonialeroberungen machen würde, damit nicht nur das Recht erwirkt, von seinen neuen Untertanen die Annahme seiner wahren Religion zu verlangen, sondern auch die Verpflichtung übernimmt, solchen rechten Gottesdienst bei ihnen einzurichten. Gerade mit letzterem Gedanken steht nun auch bezeichnender Weise der einzige Missionsversuch, den das ganze Reformationszeitalter aufzuweisen hat, in ursächlichem Zusammenhange.

Dass aber gerade Johann Calvin es ist, der zu diesem Missionsunternehmen seine Hand geboten hat, ist doch mehr als ein bloßer Zufall. Zwar unterscheidet sich auch Calvin in der Ausschaltung des Missionsgedankens aus seinem System nicht grundsätzlich von den übrigen Reformatoren, speziell der lutherischen Kirche. Auch er sieht den Missionsbefehl Jesu durch die Apostel und ihre Schüler erfüllt. In seiner Auslegung des Missionsauftrages Matth. 28 macht er allerdings die richtige Bemerkung, dass die Missionsverheißung des letzten Verses nicht auf die Apostel zu beschränken sei, sondern der Kirche aller Zeiten gelte, auch den schwachen und ängstlichen Seelen unter den Kirchenlehrern der Gegenwart. Aber leider zieht er daraus nicht die Konsequenz, dass dann auch der Missionsbefehl nicht auf die Apostel und ihre Zeit beschränkt werden darf. Bei der Auslegung von Matth. 24, 14 („es wird gepredigt werden das Evangelium vom Reich in der ganzen Welt zu einem Zeugnis über alle Völker und dann wird das Ende kommen") macht Calvin sich selbst den Einwurf, dass es doch auch Antipoden und eine ganze Menge weit entfernt wohnender Völker gebe, zu denen noch nicht der geringste Schall des Evangeliums gedrungen sei. Doch weit entfernt, aus dieser Tatsache die Verpflichtung zu dauernder Missionstätigkeit herzuleiten, begnügt er sich mit der Bemerkung, dass der Herr offenbar nicht an alle einzelnen Landstriche der Erde denke, auch keine bestimmte Zeit für die Ausbreitung des Evangeliums angegeben, nur den Tag seiner Wiederkunft als Schlusstermin für die Evangelisierung der Welt genannt habe. So weicht er auch an dieser Stelle aus, wo es doch fast kein Ausweichen gab. Bei Matth. 9, 38 („die Ernte ist groß") gibt er ausdrücklich zu verstehen, dass er ebenso wie die andern Reformatoren die verweltlichte Christenheit als das Missionsgebiet der Kirche ansieht: die Bitte um Arbeiter in der Ernte sei niemals zeitgemäßer gewesen, als in der Zeit der gegenwärtigen Verwilderung und Verwüstung der Kirche. Was endlich Calvins Lehre von der Prädestination betrifft, die dem Missionstrieb den Lebensnerv abzuschneiden scheint, so ist zu bedenken, dass er eine allgemeine Berufung durch die Wortverkündigung als Grundlage für die besondere Berufung ansieht. Damit hatte er auch die innere Ermächtigung, die Aufforderung zu bestimmter Missionsübung, als ihm dieselbe von anderer Seite nahegelegt wurde, mit freudigem Eifer aufzugreifen. Wie hätte der Mann mit dem weltweiten Horizont für seine reformatorische und evangelistische Tätigkeit auch Bedenken tragen sollen, im Einzelfalle auch einmal über die Grenzen der Christenheit hinauszugehen?

Zum Verständnis dieses höchst merkwürdigen und allerersten evangelischen Missionsversuches muss von vornherein darauf hingewiesen werden, dass er nicht selbständig, sondern nur als Nebenzweck eines Kolonisationsprojektes unternommen wurde, also nur als Anhängsel eines politischen

Aktes. Die treibende Kraft des ganzen Unternehmens war ein Mann von unlauterem Charakter, der Malteserritter Nikolaus Durand de Villegaignon, der es im Dienste der französischen Marine bis zum Vizeadmiral gebracht hatte, dann aber, weil er die Gunst des Königs verloren, aus seinem Dienste geschieden war. Um sich aufs neue beim König beliebt zu machen, unterbreitete er ihm unter Vermittlung und Fürsprache des Admirals Coligny den abenteuerlichen Plan, an der brasilianischen Küste eine französische Kolonie zu gründen, und damit ein gewisses Gegengewicht gegen die überseeische Alleinherrschaft der Spanier und Portugiesen herzustellen. Sobald es ihm gelungen war, den König für seinen Plan zu gewinnen, begann er, Ansiedler für die neue Kolonie anzuwerben. Er wandte sich zu diesem Zwecke an die bedrängten und verfolgten reformierten Landsleute mit der Verheißung, ihnen dort eine Zufluchtsstätte zu bieten, wo sie ungehindert ihres Glaubens leben könnten. Durch sein feierlich gegebenes Versprechen, in der neuen Ansiedlung den Gottesdienst genau nach der Genfer Kirchenordnung einzurichten, ließ sich wirklich eine beträchtliche Anzahl Reformierter bewegen, sich ihm zur Verfügung zu stellen, zumal er keinen Zweifel darüber ließ, dass er auch in seiner Glaubensüberzeugung den Reformierten nahe stehe, und dazu die Fürsprache Colignys auszubeuten verstand. Am 15. Juli 1555 schiffte sich Villegaignon mit seinen Kolonisten, Soldaten und allerlei Abenteurern ein und landete in der Bucht von Rio de Janeiro, ohne jedoch an der Küste festen Fuß fassen zu können. Er musste vor dem Widerstande der Eingeborenen sich auf eine benachbarte Insel zurückziehen, die er befestigte und nach seinem Gönner Coligny nannte. Schon bald zeigte sich in dem eintretenden Nahrungsmangel die Folge der Übereilung, mit der das abenteuerliche Unternehmen ins Werk gesetzt war. Die Reformierten aber hielten ohne Murren aus.

Um nun die Zahl der reformierten Ansiedler zu vermehren, sandte Villegaignon mit den heimkehrenden Schiffen Briefe an Coligny und Calvin, in denen er um weitere Sendung reformierter Landsleute und namentlich um reformierte Prediger bat, die die Ansiedler mit regelmäßiger Wortverkündigung versorgen und zugleich den Heiden auf der Insel und an der benachbarten Küste das Evangelium verkündigen könnten. Auf Colignys Empfehlung griff Calvin mit freudigem Eifer zu. Mit Dank gegen Gott begrüßte man in Genf die Ausbreitung des Reiches Jesu Christi in einem so entlegenen und unermesslich großen Lande und unter einem Volke, das ohne alle Gotteserkenntnis dahinlebte. Auf Befragen erklärten sich sodann Petrus Richter und Wilhelm Chartier bereit, falls die Gemeinde sie rechtmäßig dazu erwählte, als Prediger und Missionare hinauszugehen. Nach einer öffentlichen Auslegung der betreffenden (d. h. wohl auf die Mission bezüglichen) Schriftstellen wurden sie von dem Genfer Predigerkollegium feierlich abgeordnet und zu treuer Amtsführung ermahnt, worauf sie das Bekenntnis ablegten, die Fahrt nach Amerika antreten zu wollen, um das Evangelium dort auszubreiten. Am 19. November 1556 fuhren die Genfer nebst 200 neuen Ansiedlern hinüber.

Mit allen Ehren nahm sie Villegaignon im März 1557 in Empfang. Leider ist das ganze Unternehmen an der Niederträchtigkeit dieses elenden Menschen gescheitert, der gar bald seine Maske abwarf und sich als verkappter Römling entpuppte. Verfolgung und Bedrängnis aller Art, Vertreibung und Märtyrertum war das Los der meisten Ansiedler. So bewundernswert auch die Energie und Weisheit war, womit die Prediger die ersten schwierigen Vorarbeiten zum Missionswerk und die ersten Missionsversuche unternahmen, so war doch von dauernden Erfolgen keine Rede, weil der Gouverneur fünf der Ansiedler hinrichten ließ und die übrigen in die Heimat zurücktrieb.

So ist die Erstlingsblüte des späteren großen Missionsfrühlings der evangelischen Kirche dahingewelkt, ehe sie Frucht ansetzen konnte. Zu früh hatte sie sich hervorgewagt. Es war noch nicht Missionszeit. Im Reiche Gottes hat alles seine Stunde. Doch ist dieser misslungene Erstlingsversuch ein mächtiger Beweis, dass der jungen Reformationskirche Missionssinn und Missionstrieb nicht gänzlich gefehlt und sie für die Ausbreitung des Evangeliums unter den Heiden, als sie dazu aufgefordert wurde, auch große Opfer nicht gescheut hat. Dass aber das hoffnungsvolle Unternehmen sich mit dem Namen Johann Calvin verbindet, ist auch ein Beitrag zur Würdigung des großen Reformators in seinem Jubiläumsjahre.

Der Missionsgedanke bei Kalvin (1934)

ERNST PFISTERER

Studienrat Ernst Pfisterer, Bochum, war Calvinforscher (z.B. „Calvins Wirken in Genf").

Erschienen in Neue Allgemeine Missionszeitschrift 1934: S. 93-108.

Das Material zu dem vorliegenden Aufsatz ist einerseits entnommen der Institutio Kalvins, deutsche Übersetzung von Karl Müller, Neukirchener Verlag; andrerseits E. Doumergue, Jean Calvin, Les hommes et les choses de son temps, 4. Band, La pensée religieuse de Calvin, Lausanne 1910. Die Übersetzung der Zitate aus Doumergue stammt von mir. Außerdem habe ich herangezogen W. Schlatter, Kalvin und die Mission, Evangelisches Missionsmagazin, Neue Folge 1909, 53. Jahrgang; für Luthers Großen Katechismus die Ausgabe von Luthers Werken, herausgegeben von Buchwald u.a., 3. Auflage 1905.

I.

1. Das Heidentum kennt Kalvin nach diesem Material nur aus der Bibel und der antiken Literatur. Irgendeine Spur, dass er eine nähere Kenntnis der neuentdeckten heidnischen Völker hätte oder sich mit dem Islam befasst hätte, lässt sich nicht finden. Für den Franzosen Kalvin waren eben die Türken nicht die Realität wie für Luther und die Deutschen, deren Land aufs Schwerste durch sie bedroht war (Türken vor Wien 1529). Doch hat Kalvin ohne allen Zweifel sich mancherlei über die brasilianischen Indianer berichten lassen; denn Jean de Léry, einer der Teilnehmer an dem Villegaignonschen Abenteuer, von dem später noch zu reden sein wird, ist nach seiner Rückkehr aus Brasilien in Genf wieder seinem Schuhmacherhandwerk nachgegangen, hat 1559 geheiratet und ist erst nach 1560, offenbar in der Zeit der ungeheuren Nachfrage nach Pfarrern wegen des raschen Aufblühens der protestantischen Gemeinden in Frankreich, Pfarrer zuerst in Frankreich, dann in Bern geworden. Dass er sich an der nur zwei Monate dauernden Missionsarbeit unter den Topinambu-Indianern beteiligt hat, geht aus seinem Bericht über seinen Aufenthalt in Brasilien hervor, der sogar eine Liste von Wörtern der Eingeborenensprache enthält. Durch ihn hat also Kalvin Nachrichten über das Leben und Treiben heidnischer Völ-

ker erhalten, aber eine Widerspiegelung dessen lässt sich in dem vorliegenden Material nicht nachweisen.

2. Welche Gedanken Kalvin nun über das Heidentum hat, ergibt sich aus den folgenden Sätzen:

„Wir stellen als unbestreitbar fest, dass der menschliche Geist durch natürlichen Instinkt eine gewisse Ahnung von der Gottheit hat. Denn Gott erweckt in allen Menschen eine Art von Erkenntnis seines gottheitlichen Wesens, damit niemand sich mit Unwissenheit entschuldigen könne. ... Schon ein Heide (Cicero) hat gesagt, dass kein Volk so barbarisch und kein Stamm so verwildert sei, dass ihm nicht die Überzeugung von der Existenz eines Gottes tief im Herzen säße. Mögen manche Völker sich im übrigen wenig von wilden Tieren unterscheiden, so haben sie doch einen Samen von Religion nie ganz verlieren können. ... Wenn also, solang die Welt steht, kein Land, keine Stadt, ja kein Haus der Religion entbehren konnte, so ist dies ein stilles Zeugnis dafür, dass in alle Herzen eine Empfindung vom göttlichen Wesen gelegt ward" (Inst. I,3,1)

„Wo das ganze Leben von regelmäßigem Gehorsam erfüllt sein sollte, lebt man in allem seinem Tun im offenen Aufruhr gegen Gott und sucht ihn nur mit einigen Opfern zu besänftigen; wo man ihm mit heiligem Leben und Herzen dienen sollte, denkt man sich läppisches Spielwerk und nichtige Übungen aus, mit denen man ihn sich geneigt machen will; wo endlich die ganze Zuversicht auf ihm ruhen sollte, verlässt man sich auf sich selbst oder auf Kreaturen. Endlich verwickelt man sich in einen solchen Haufen von Irrtümern, dass die hellen Funken, unter deren Schein man etwas von Gottes Herrlichkeit hätte sehen können, durch die Finsternis der Bosheit erstickt werden und erlöschen. Bei alledem bleibt doch jener Same, der niemals mit der Wurzel ausgerottet werden kann, nämlich die Ahnung von irgendeinem göttlichen Wesen. Derselbe ist aber derartig verdeckt, dass er nur die bösesten Früchte trägt" (Inst. I,4,4).

„Der Menschengeist ist eben wie ein Labyrinth: nicht bloß jedes Volk, sondern beinahe jeder Mensch dichtet sich seinen eigenen Götzen. Denn zur Dunkelheit und Unwissenheit gesellte sich Frechheit und Übermut. Wie aus einem wüsten und weiten Schlund Gewässer hervorquellen, so ergoss sich geradezu ein Schwarm von Göttern aus dem Menschengeist. Welche Fülle von Aberglauben und Verkehrung, in der sich die schreckliche Blindheit des menschlichen Geistes kundtut!" (Inst. I,5,12)

„Man pflegt nicht in der Weise zu fremden Göttern abzufallen, dass man den höchsten Gott offensichtlich verlässt oder auf ihre Stufe herabrückt; sondern man lässt ihm seinen obersten Platz, umgibt ihn aber mit einem

Schwarm niederer Gottheiten, mit denen er sein Wirken teilen soll. Auf diese Weise wird die Herrlichkeit des göttlichen Wesens – wenn auch unvermerkt und trügerisch – zerteilt, so dass dem einen Gott nicht alles bleibt" (Inst. I,12,1).

3. „Bezüglich des Ursprungs der Götzenbilder wird allgemein für richtig gehalten, was im Buch der Weisheit (14,15) steht: man fing an, verehrte Tote abergläubisch zu verehren und zu ihrem Gedächtnis Bilder aufzustellen. Ohne Zweifel ist dies eine uralte Sitte, die viel zur Verbreitung des Götzendienstes beigetragen haben mag, die ich aber nicht für seine erste Quelle halten kann. Denn, wie aus den Büchern Mose hervorgeht, waren Götzenbilder früher im Gebrauch als jene Weihung von Bildern für die Toten, deren die heidnischen Schriftsteller öfter gedenken, aus einem gewissen Familienehrgeiz überhandnahm. Wenn z.B. Rahel ihres Vaters Götzen gestohlen hat, so lässt dies auf eine ganz allgemeine Verbreitung des Götzendienstes schließen. Man kann daraus ersehen, dass der Menschengeist von jeher, wenn ich so sagen darf, eine Werkstätte zur Herstellung von Götzen gewesen ist. Wie der Mensch seinen Gott im Herzen sich denkt, so will er ihn durch eine äußere Gestalt darstellen. Der Verstand erzeugt das Götzenbild, die Hand gebiert es. Der Ursprung der Götzenbilder ist der, dass die Menschen an Gottes Gegenwart nicht glauben, sie könnten ihn denn fleischlich greifen." Vgl. 2. Mos. 32,1ff. (Inst. I,11,8).

„Solcher Errichtung von Bildwerken folgte dann alsbald die Anbetung: da die Menschen Gott in den Bildern zu sehen glaubten, verehrten sie ihn auch in ihnen. Endlich ließen sie ihre Herzen und Augen ganz dadurch gefangennehmen, versanken immer tiefer in törichte Stumpfheit und behandelten ihre Bildwerke mit einer blöden Ehrfurcht und Bewunderung, als wäre selbst ein Stück der Gottheit in ihnen. Irgendein roher Aberglaube muss schon dahinterstecken, wenn ein Mensch einem Bildwerk göttliche Ehren darbringt, wobei es keinen Unterschied macht, ob es Gott selbst oder irgendeine Kreatur darstellt. Aus diesem Grund hat der Herr nicht bloß die Errichtung von Statuen verboten, sondern auch die Weihung von Steinen und sonstigen Denkzeichen, bei denen man Anbetung üben wollte. Aus demselben Grunde heißt es auch in dem Gebote: ‚Du sollst sie nicht anbeten.' Denn sobald man sich Gott unter sichtbarer Gestalt vorstellt, denkt man auch seine Kraft an dieses Bild gebunden. Die Menschen sind so stumpf, dass, wenn sie Gott nur erst gebildet haben, sie ihn auch an dieses Machwerk binden, – und Anbetung ist die unausbleibliche Folge. Ob sie dabei das Bild kurzweg selbst anbeten oder Gott in dem Bilde, macht keinen Unterschied. Wo man einem Bildwerk göttliche Ehren erweist, treibt man Götzendienst, mag die Theorie lauten, wie sie will. Und weil Gott eine abergläubische Verehrung nicht annimmt, raubt man ihm, was man den Götzenbildern gibt. Gegen dieses Urteil helfen keine Ausflüchte" (Inst. I,11,9).

4. Aber „trotz seines Falles und seiner Verkehrung ist der Menschengeist noch immer mit ausgezeichneten Gottesgaben bekleidet und geschmückt. Wenn wir bedenken, dass Gottes Geist die einzige Quelle der Wahrheit ist, so werden wir die Wahrheit selbst weder verwerfen noch verachten, wo sie sich auch findet, wenn anders wir nicht dem Geiste Gottes eine Schmach antun wollen: wer die Gaben Gottes geringachtet, verwirft und verschmäht ihn selbst." Nachdem Kalvin als Beispiel die Leistungen des Altertums auf den verschiedensten Gebieten (Recht, Politik, Philosophie, Literatur, Medizin, Mathematik) angeführt hat, schließt er mit den Worten: „Müssen wir also sehen, dass, mit der Schrift zu reden, der ‚natürliche' Mensch noch solchen Scharfsinn und solche Geschicklichkeit im Durchdenken irdischer Dinge besitzt, so wollen wir dadurch ermessen lernen, wie viele gute Gaben der Herr der Menschennatur noch gelassen hat, auch nachdem sie des wahren Gottes beraubt ward" (Inst. II,2,13-15).

Sind nun auch „alle guten Seiten, die im Leben der Ungläubigen und Götzenanbeter auftreten, Gaben Gottes", so sind diese Menschen doch nicht „einer Belohnung, sondern vielmehr einer Bestrafung" würdig, weil „ihre Werke durch die Unreinigkeit des Herzens von Anbeginn an verderbt sind" (Inst. III,14,3).

II.

1. Entsteht nun den Christen nicht die Aufgabe, nach Maßgabe der ihnen verliehenen Gaben die Heiden vor dieser Bestrafung zu bewahren? Kalvin antwortet darauf im Kommentar zum Galaterbrief: „Gott legt uns das Heil aller Menschen ohne Ausnahme ans Herz, wie Christus für die Sünde der ganzen Welt gelitten hat." So ist also Jesu Leiden für die Sünde aller Menschen die Grundlage für die Arbeit auch an den Heiden.

2. Nun gründet Kalvin die Verpflichtung des Christen den Heiden gegenüber nicht etwa auf den Missionsbefehl Matth. 28,19 oder Mark. 16,15, sondern auf seine Verpflichtung dem Nächsten gegenüber:

„Christus zeigt in der Erzählung von dem Barmherzigen Samariter, dass unter dem Nächsten auch jeder ganz fremde Mensch zu verstehen ist, so dass wir nicht etwa das Liebesgebot auf den Kreis unserer Verwandtschaft beschränken dürfen. Gewiss sollen wir Menschen, die uns besonders verwandtschaftlich nahestehen, auch mit besonderer Teilnahme unterstützen; dergleichen streitet nicht wider Gott, sondern ist durch Gottes Vorsehung also geordnet. Zugleich aber sage ich, dass man das ganze Menschengeschlecht ohne Ausnahme mit derselben Stimmung der Liebe umfassen soll; hier ist kein Unterschied zwischen Griechen und Barbaren, Würdigen und Unwürdigen, Freunden und Feinden; denn wir sollen die Menschen nicht an und für sich, sondern in Gott ansehen" (Inst. II,8,32).

Ganz besonders wichtig ist Kalvin die Erkenntnis geworden, dass allen Menschen Gottes Ebenbild in die Seele, aber auch in den Leib eingeprägt ist. Darum schreibt er: „Nach des Herrn Vorschrift sollen wir allen Menschen insgesamt Gutes tun, deren größter Teil dessen doch nicht wert ist. Die Schrift gibt eben die treffliche Regel, dass wir nicht auf Verdienste sehen sollen, sondern auf das allen Menschen eingeprägte Ebenbild Gottes, dem wir niemals zu viel Ehrerbietung erweisen können. So werden unsrer Liebe vor allem die Genossen des Glaubens empfohlen (Gal. 6,10), sofern durch Christi Geist in ihnen Gottes Ebenbild erneuert und wiederhergestellt ward. Aber welcher Mensch dir auch begegnen wird, der deiner Hilfe bedarf, du hast keinen Grund, dich ihm zu entziehen. Du sagst vielleicht, es sei ein Fremder; aber der Herr hat ihm einen Stempel aufgedrückt, der ihn zu deinem Verwandten macht: darum gebietet er (Jes. 58,7): ‚Entzeuch dich nicht von deinem Fleisch'" (Inst. III,7,7).

Welch größeren Liebesdienst könnte ein Christ dem, „der seiner Hilfe bedarf", erweisen, als dass er ihn zu dem führt, der auch für seine Sünde gestorben ist! So müsste schon, was bisher von Kalvins Worten angeführt worden ist, genügen, um zu zeigen, dass er jegliche Arbeit Innerer und Äußerer Mission, die im Geiste Christi geschieht, von ganzem Herzen begrüßt und unterstützt hätte.

Aber er hat sich noch viel deutlicher über diese Fragen ausgesprochen.

3. Der Ruf Gottes gilt allen Menschen, allen Staaten, allen Völkern:

„So viele Menschen es auf der Erde gibt, alle sind eure Nächsten. ... Gott hat nicht *eine Menschenrasse* erwählt, er hat nicht seinen Dienst in ein bestimmtes *Land* beschlossen, sondern die Wand ist zerbrochen, so dass es heute weder Juden noch Griechen gibt. ... Wenn ich mir gesagt habe: Da ist ein Mensch aus einem fremden Land. Welche Beziehungen bestehen denn zwischen uns, zumal da wir nicht ein verständliches Wort miteinander reden können? Und wenn ich das alles zu mir gesagt habe, was tut's? Wenn ich ihn dann betrachte und anschaue, so werde ich in ihm eine Natur sehen, die er mit mir gemein hat. ... Da ist doch ein und dieselbe Natur, durch die uns Gott zusammengefügt und gebunden hat. ... Versuchen wir also, soweit es an uns liegt, auch den Seelen solcher Menschen das Heil und ihren Leibern Gutes zu verschaffen" (Predigten über das Deuteronomium, Opera 28).

„Gott will alle retten, damit, soweit es an uns liegt, wir so das Heil allen verschaffen, die aus dem Reiche Gottes verbannt zu sein scheinen, in der Zeit, in der sie ungläubig sind. Alle, das will nicht heißen, jeden für sich, sondern *alle Staaten und Völker*. ... Wir dürfen also die Vatergüte nicht auf uns oder eine gewisse Anzahl von Menschen beschränken" (Predigten über den 1. Timotheusbrief, Opera 53).

4. Aber steht der Missionsgedanke nicht im Widerspruch mit der Erwählungslehre? Darauf antwortet Kalvin in dem Teil der Institutio, der die Erwählungslehre behandelt (Inst. III,23,12-14): „Weil wir nicht wissen, wer zur Zahl der Auserwählten gehört oder nicht, so müssen wir uns mit einem Sinn ausrüsten, der alle zur Seligkeit bringen will. Wir wollen suchen, jeden, der uns begegnet, zu einem Kind des Friedens zu machen; aber unser Friede wird nur auf den Kindern des Friedens ruhen (Luk. 10,6). So viel an uns ist, wollen wir sittliche Mahnungen austeilen wie eine heilsame Arznei, damit niemand sich oder andere ins Verderben bringe. Gottes Sache aber wird es sein, diese Mahnung für seine Auserwählten zu segnen."

Und ähnlich in einer der Predigten über den 1. Timotheusbrief: „Wir wissen nicht, ob es nicht Gott gefallen wird, ihnen (den armen Irrenden) Gnade zu erweisen (wenn wir für sie beten) und sie auf den Weg des Heils zu führen. Wir sollen sogar das hoffen, da sie alle nach dem Bilde Gottes geschaffen sind. Und da unser Heil aus nichts anderem als der reinen, unverdienten Güte Gottes hervorgeht, warum soll er nicht dasselbe an denen tun, die noch jetzt auf dem Wege des Verderbens sind, wie wir es gewesen sind?"

5. Jeder Christ, mag er auch nie mit Heiden in Fühlung kommen, so dass sie ihm „Nächste" werden, hat ihnen gegenüber dennoch eine Pflicht: die, für sie zu beten. Innerhalb der Auslegung der Anrede des Vaterunsers lesen wir (Inst. III,20,36-40): „Wir müssen die Liebe, die wir zum himmlischen Vater tragen, auch seinem Volk und seiner Familie beweisen. Darum soll ein Christenmensch seine Bitten darauf stimmen, dass sie allumfassend werden und allen gelten, die Brüder in Christo sind. Ja, wir wollen nicht einmal bloß an solche denken, die wir gegenwärtig als Christen kennen, sondern an *alle Menschen auf der ganzen Erde*; denn wir wissen nicht, was Gott über sie beschlossen hat; für uns aber ist es eine Regel der Frömmigkeit und Menschenliebe, dass wir das Beste für sie wünschen und hoffen."

„Wenn wir für die Gläubigen beten, so sollen wir auch Mitleid und Erbarmen mit den armen Ungläubigen haben, die noch in Irrtum und Unwissenheit wandeln, und wir sollen Gott bitten, dass er sie mit uns zu sich ziehe, auf dass wir alle eins seien" (Predigten über 1. Tim., Opera 53).

Ganz besonders deutlich spricht sich Kalvin über unsere Gebetsverpflichtung für die Ausbreitung des Reiches Gottes über die ganze Erde bei der Auslegung der zweiten Bitte aus (Inst. III,20,42): „Wir beten also diese Bitte nur recht, wenn wir bei uns selbst anfangen und begehren, von allem sündhaften Wesen gereinigt zu werden, welches Unruhe und Unreinigkeit in Gottes Reich hineintragen müsste. Und weil Gottes Wort das königliche Zepter seines Reiches ist, so ist der Inhalt dieser Bitte, der Herr möge alle Sinnen und Herzen dem freiwilligen Gehorsam gegen sein Wort unterwerfen. Das geschieht, wenn er durch das verborgene Wirken seines Geistes dem Worte Kraft gibt, so dass es die verdiente Anerkennung gewinnt. Danach sollen wir erst an die Gottlosen denken, welche mit verzweifelter Wut gegen Gottes Reich ankämpfen. Gott richtet sein Reich auf, indem er die ganze Welt sich zu Füßen legt, jedoch in verschiedener Weise: er bändigt die sich auflehnenden Gedanken, bei anderen aber bricht er den Stolz, der sich nicht bändigen lässt. Wir bitten, dass dies täglich geschehe, damit Gott seine Gemeinden sammle von *allen Enden der Erde*, dass er sie ausbreite und mehre, mit seinen Gaben ausrüste und die rechte Ordnung in ihnen festige, dass er auf der anderen Seite alle Feinde der reinen Lehre und des Glaubens niederschlage, ihre Pläne zerstöre und ihre Anschläge zunichte mache. In dieser Weise soll Gottes Reich seine täglichen Fortschritte machen, bis endlich bei Christi Wiederkunft seine Fülle erscheint, da nach dem Worte des Paulus (1.Kor. 15,28) Gott alles in allen sein wird."

Kalvin nimmt es mit dem Gebet für den Nächsten so ernst, dass er in einer Predigt über Daniel (Opera 41) ausruft: „Wenn wir für unsere eigenen Nöte Gott um Hilfe anrufen, so dürfen wir unsere Nächsten nicht vergessen; denn der, der nur an sich denkt, trennt sich damit von dem Leib unsers Herrn Jesus Christus, und wenn er sich von ihm getrennt hat, welche Verbindung soll er dann noch mit Gott haben?"

6. Dass schließlich auch der Missionsgedanke von dem Leitmotiv der Ehre Gottes beherrscht wird, das Kalvins ganzer Theologie eigentümlich ist, ist nur natürlich: In einer Predigt über Deut. 33,18-19: „Sie werden die Völker rufen", erläutert der Reformator die Stelle in folgender Weise: „Was wir von dieser Stelle festzuhalten haben, ist, dass wir versuchen, soweit es an uns liegt, alle Menschen der Erde zu Gott zu ziehen, damit er einmütig geehrt werde und ihm alle dienen. Und wahrhaftig! wenn wir

etwas Menschlichkeit in uns haben und sehen, dass die Menschen ins Verderben gehen, bis Gott sie unter seinem Gehorsam hat, müssen wir dann nicht von Mitleid bewegt werden, die armen Seelen aus der Hölle zu ziehen und sie auf den Weg des Heils zu führen!"

Schlatter zitiert die Erklärung zu Jes. 12,4 u. 5: „Daraus wird ersichtlich, wie stark in allen Frommen das Verlangen sein soll, dass Gottes Güte allen offenkundig werde, damit alle zu *einer* Verehrung Gottes kommen. Dann zumal sollen wir in diesem Begehren entbrennen, wenn wir aus einer großen Gefahr, besonders aus der Tyrannei des Teufels und vom ewigen Tode, befreit worden sind. ... Wir werden gelehrt", fährt Kalvin in überaus bedeutsamer Weise fort, „dieses sei unsere Pflicht, dass wir überall unter den Völkern die Güte Gottes bekannt machen. Nicht aber sollen andere ermahnt und vorausgesandt werden, damit wir inzwischen untätig sitzen bleiben; sondern es geziemt sich, andern zum Vorbild voranzugehen."

7. Wer soll aber den Missionsdienst ausrichten? Zunächst einmal der, der einem Ungläubigen Nächster wird. Der Schluss des eben angeführten Zitats zu Jes. 12 geht viel weiter. Enthält er nicht die unmittelbare Aufforderung, Missionsarbeit zu treiben? Schlatter bedauert es, dass die reformatorische (und vollends die nachreformatorische, orthodoxe) Theologie sich nicht entschließen konnte, den apostolischen Auftrag seines außerordentlichen Charakters zu entkleiden und als permanente große Aufgabe der christlichen Gemeinde zu erkennen. Hier liegt, was Kalvin betrifft – über die anderen Reformatoren kann ich nicht urteilen – eine Verwechselung zwischen Amt und Auftrag vor. Das Amt des Apostels, des Evangelisten, mit dem füglich das Amt eines Missionars mutatis mutandis gleichgesetzt werden darf, ist ein außerordentliches, „weil es in der regelmäßigen Organisation der Kirche keine Stelle hat" (Inst. IV,3,4-5). Stimmt denn das nicht? Erleben wir es nicht, wie, je geordneter und selbständiger die Missionskirchen werden, desto mehr innerhalb dieser Kirchen das Amt des Missionars vor dem des Pfarrers zurücktritt; denn „die Aufgabe der Apostel erkennt man aus Christi Befehl (Mk. 16,15): Gehet hin in alle Welt und prediget das Evangelium aller Kreatur. Es sind ihnen nicht bestimmte Grenzen gesetzt, sondern sie sollen den ganzen Erdkreis zum Gehorsam Christi leiten", während dem Pastor „eine bestimmte Gemeinde zugewiesen ward". Apostel (Propheten), Evangelisten „erweckte der Herr zu Anfang seines Reiches und erweckt sie noch jetzt zuweilen, wie es die Notwendigkeit der Zeit erfordert". Kalvin wiederholt noch einmal: „Diese drei Ämter wurden der Kirche nicht für alle Zeiten gegeben, sondern nur für die Zeit des beginnenden Baus. Doch leugne ich nicht, dass Gott auch

später zuweilen Apostel erweckt hat oder wenigstens Evangelisten, wie dies zu unserer Zeit geschehen ist."

8. So ist das Amt des Missionars ein außerordentliches, der Missionsauftrag dagegen ist dauernd. Wozu sollte denn sonst Kalvin bei der Auslegung der zweiten Bitte so eindringlich der Christenheit ans Herz legen, darum zu „bitten, dass dies täglich geschehe, damit Gott seine Gemeinden sammle von allen Enden der Erde, dass er sie ausbreite und mehre, mit seinen Gaben ausrüste und die rechte Ordnung in ihnen festige". Da steckt doch ein ganzes Missionsprogramm drinnen, anfangend damit, dass „von allen Enden der Erde" die Gemeinden gesammelt werden, endend mit ihrer Organisation: dass er „die rechte Ordnung in ihnen festige". Kalvin liegt also die Anschauung der späteren Orthodoxie, den Aposteln zuzuschreiben, dass schon sie die Evangelisation des Erdkreises zum Abschluss gebracht hätten, völlig fern, wie es sich ja auch aus einer Reihe anderer von mir angeführter Zitate klar ergibt. Zum Beweis, dass auch Kalvin gelegentlich dieser Anschauung gehuldigt habe, führt Schlatter das Wort an: „Nach Christi Auferstehung begannen die Grenzen des Reiches Gottes in die Weite und Breite unter alle möglichen Nationen ohne Unterschied ausgedehnt zu werden, und wurden nach Christi Wort die Gläubigen von allen Seiten gesammelt." In aller Bescheidenheit bin ich der Meinung, dass dieses Wort gerade das Gegenteil beweist; denn Kalvin schreibt doch ausdrücklich: die Grenzen *begannen* ausgedehnt zu werden! Die Gläubigen (ob im Urtext der Artikel wirklich steht, kann ich leider nicht feststellen) wurden von allen Seiten (also aus allen Himmelsrichtungen, nicht etwa Ländern) gesammelt. War es denn nicht genau so?

9. Julius Richter hat im ersten Band seiner Evangelischen Missionskunde die Gedankengänge, die ein Anpacken der Missionsarbeit innerlich hemmten, zusammengestellt: das Ende der Welt sei nahe; ein großer Teil der Menschheit, besonders die nichtchristlichen Völker, seien zur Verdammnis bestimmt; sie seien jetzt verstockt, weil sie zu den Zeiten Adams, Noahs und der Apostel das Evangelium nicht angenommen hätten; die Mission sei Angelegenheit der weltlichen Obrigkeit; schließlich bestehe nur eine allgemeine christliche Zeugnispflicht. Ist es nun zuviel gefragt, wenn ich auf Grund des vorgelegten Materials behaupte: diese Hemmungen sind sämtlich Kalvin unbekannt? Er hat sie, soweit sie aus dem Mittelalter stammen, überwunden. Das vorliegende Material erhält dadurch sein besonderes Gewicht, dass das Grundsätzliche zu dem ganzen Missionsgedanken Kalvins der Institutio entnommen ist, d.h. dem offiziellsten Dokument aus seiner Feder, an dem er während der ganzen Zeit seiner öffentlichen Wirksamkeit ständig gearbeitet hat; die übrigen Belege sind

gleichsam Erläuterungen zu der in der Institutio niedergelegten Gesamtanschauung.

Dass die Nähe des Weltendes den Tätigkeitsdrang der Christen hemmen solle, dafür findet sich hier nicht die geringste Spur, auch nicht dafür, dass nur die Obrigkeit für die Ausbreitung des Reiches Gottes zu sorgen habe. Sie hat in ihrem Teil mitzuhelfen; denn es ist die Aufgabe des irdischen Regiments, „die äußere Gottesverehrung zu erhalten und zu schützen, die gesunde Lehre der Frömmigkeit und den Wohlbestand der Kirche zu verteidigen" (Inst. IV,20,1-3). „Jeder gibt zu, dass kein Staat glücklich bestehen kann, der nicht zuerst für Frömmigkeit sorgt." „Gerade darum werden heilige Könige in der Schrift gelobt, weil sie den verderbten Gottesdienst gebessert und für einen reinen Zustand der Religion gesorgt haben. Darum ist es Torheit, der Obrigkeit die Fürsorge für die göttlichen Dinge abzusprechen und ihr nur die menschliche Rechtspflege zuzuweisen" (Inst. IV,20,9-13). Aber damit ist doch die Nächstenpflicht, die Gebetspflicht und die Pflicht der Bereitschaft, dem Rufe Gottes zu folgen, nicht ausgeschaltet.

Die Betonung der Erwählungslehre führt bei Kalvin genau zu den entgegengesetzten Folgerungen, als es bei der orthodoxen Theologie der Fall zu sein scheint. Ich erinnere noch einmal an die Auslegung der zweiten Bitte und der Anrede des Vaterunsers: Bei unserem Gebet „wollen wir nicht einmal bloß an solche denken, die wir gegenwärtig als Christen kennen, sondern an alle Menschen auf der ganzen Erde; denn wir wissen nicht, was Gott über sie beschlossen hat". Die Predigten erklären den Begriff „alle Menschen auf der ganzen Erde" durch Ausdrücke wie: „Alle, das will nicht heißen, jeden für sich, sondern alle Staaten und Völker. ... Wir dürfen also die Vatergüte nicht auf uns oder eine gewisse Anzahl Menschen beschränken", ferner: „Gott hat nicht eine Menschenrasse erwählt, sondern die Wand ist zerbrochen, so dass es heute weder Juden noch Griechen gibt." Folglich, „weil wir nicht wissen, wer zur Zahl der Auserwählten gehört oder nicht, müssen wir uns mit einem Sinn ausrüsten, der alle zur Seligkeit bringen will". So werden gerade durch die Erwählungslehre die Christen zur höchsten Aktivität aufgerufen, weil sie wissen, dass Angehörige aller Rassen und Völker, Länder und Staaten zur ewigen Seligkeit bestimmt sind. Dass man sich nicht hinter den Vorwand einer allgemeinen christlichen Zeugnispflicht verkriechen kann und darf, geht aus all dem Angeführten klar hervor.

10. Luther ist offenbar mehr in den mittelalterlichen Vorstellungen befangen; denn am Ende des Abschnittes „Von dem Glauben" in seinem Großen Katechismus schreibt er: „Darum scheiden und sondern diese Arti-

kel des Glaubens uns Christen von allen andern Leuten auf Erden. Denn was außer der Christenheit ist, es seien Heiden, Türken, Juden oder falsche Christen und Heuchler, ob sie gleich nur einen wahrhaftigen Gott glauben und anbeten, so wissen sie doch nicht, wie er gegen sie gesinnt ist, können sich auch keiner Liebe noch Gutes zu ihm versehen, darum sie in ewigem Zorn und Verdammnis bleiben; denn sie den Herrn Christum nicht haben, dazu mit keinen Gaben durch den Heiligen Geist erleuchtet und begnadet sind." Daneben steht aber die Erläuterung zur zweiten Bitte: „Derhalben bitten wir nun hier zum ersten, dass solches (Gottes Wort) bei uns kräftig werde und sein Name so gepriesen durch das heilige Wort Gottes und christliches Leben, beide, dass wir, die es angenommen haben, dabei bleiben und täglich zunehmen, und dass es bei andern Leuten einen Zufall und Anhang gewinne und gewaltiglich durch die Welt gehe, auf dass ihrer viel zu dem Gnadenreich kommen, der Erlösung teilhaftig werden, durch den Heiligen Geist herzugebracht, auf dass wir also allesamt in einem Königreich, jetzt angefangen, ewiglich bleiben."

Der junge Kalvin drückt sich in der Institutio von 1536 wie in dem Genfer Katechismus von 1537, der an dieser Stelle einfach eine Übersetzung der Institutio ist, ganz ähnlich wie Luther aus: „Wir bitten also, dass das Reich Gottes komme, d.h. dass der Herr von Tag zu Tag die Zahl seiner Gläubigen mehre, die seinen Ruhm in allen Werken feiern sollen, und dass er ständig den Zufluss seiner Gnadengaben über sie reichlicher ergieße, durch die er in ihnen mehr und mehr leben und regieren soll, bis dass er, nachdem er sie völlig mit sich verbunden hat, sie gänzlich erfülle." Ein solch scharfes Wort wie das Luthers über Heiden, Juden und Türken kann ich bei Kalvin nicht finden. So knüpft der Kalvin von 1536 an den Luther von 1529 an und entfaltet den Missionsgedanken immer klarer und reiner bis zur Institutio von 1559 und stößt dabei die ihn hemmenden Gedankengänge mehr und mehr ab. Kalvin, der Mann der zweiten Generation unter den Reformatoren, ist auch hier der „logische Luther", wie Doumergue einmal sagt. Und die Orthodoxie fällt in bereits überwundene Gedankengänge zurück.

III.

1. Diesen Anschauungen getreu hat Kalvin, als sich ihm die Gelegenheit zum Beginn einer Heidemissionsarbeit bot, zugegriffen: Der französische Maltheserritter Nikolas Durand de Villegaignon hatte 1555 eine Anzahl von Reformierten, denen er die Einführung der Genfer Kirchenordnung versprach, und den Abschaum der Pariser Gefängnisse in der Nähe des heutigen Rio de Janeiro angesiedelt. Erst mit einem zweiten Schub von

etwa 300 Reformierten, unter denen auch der anfangs erwähnte Genfer Jean de Léry war, kamen auch zwei Prediger, die durch die Vermittlung des damals noch katholischen Admirals Coligny von Kalvin entsandt wurden, um ihren Landsleuten zu dienen, aber auch, um unter den Indianern zu arbeiten. Doch nur zu bald entpuppte sich Villegaignons hinterhältiger und unlauterer Charakter. Die Reformierten zogen sich von der Insel, auf der die Kolonie eingerichtet war, auf das gegenüberliegende Festland zurück, fanden bei den Eingeborenen freundliche Aufnahme und begannen ihre Missionsarbeit. Aber schon nach zwei Monaten, am 4. Januar 1558, verließen sie den brasilianischen Boden endgültig und erreichten nach den furchtbarsten Entbehrungen und Strapazen am 26. Mai die heimische Küste. Vier von ihnen, die schon in den ersten Tagen der Seefahrt von dem seeuntüchtigen Schiff mit einem Boot zum Festland zurückgerudert waren, fielen in die Hände Villegaignons und wurden von ihm wegen Ketzerei getötet. Das ist in kurzen Zügen die überaus schmerzvolle Geschichte der ersten evangelischen Missionsunternehmung und der ersten evangelischen Missionsmärtyrer. Das ganze kolonisatorische Unternehmen brach ebenfalls sehr schnell zusammen. Villegaignon selbst starb 1571 plötzlich, von den Protestanten verflucht, von den Katholiken verachtet.

Die wichtigste Frucht für den Protestantismus dürfte gewesen sein, dass dadurch Coligny in Fühlung mit Kalvin kam.

2. Musste nicht Kalvin, wenn er nach seiner nüchternen Art prüfte, warum dieser erste Missionsversuch so rasch scheiterte, diese Erfahrung als einen Fingerzeig Gottes ansehen, dass es nicht sein und seiner Zeit Beruf sei, die frohe Botschaft über die Weltmeere zu tragen? Und wahrlich! durfte Kalvin es nicht als eine ganz besondere Freundlichkeit seines Gottes ansehen, dass er gerade in den dem Villegaignon-Abenteuer unmittelbar folgenden Jahren in Kalvins Heimatland eine ungeahnt und unerwartet reiche Saat aufgehen ließ? Über 2500 Gemeinden sollten mit Predigern versorgt werden! Das Feld war reif zur Ernte, aber wo sollte er all die Schnitter herbekommen, um die Ernte einzubringen? So hat Kalvin die Freuden und die Leiden einer Missionsleitung im reichsten Maße auf seinem Missionsfeld, innerhalb der europäischen Christenheit, erfahren.

Was die Heidenmission angeht, so musste er erkennen: sein und seiner Zeit Auftrag war es, die Stellung vorzubereiten, von der aus zur gottgegebenen Zeit der Angriff in die weiteste Ferne vorgetragen werden konnte. Zu Kalvins Lebzeiten war die Stellung noch zu schwach, als dass er es, zumal nach dem ersten Misserfolg, hätte wagen dürfen, den Befehl zum Angriff zu geben. Die Tatsache, dass in Genf je eine französische, englische, niederländische und italienische Flüchtlingsgemeinde bestand –

und ähnlich war es in Straßburg, Frankfurt, Wesel –, spricht Bände, wie ungefestigt die Verhältnisse der kalvinistischen Kirchen noch in den letzten Lebensjahren des Reformators waren.

Für diese Wartezeit ist es bedeutsam, dass Kalvin neben die Nächstenverpflichtung die Gebetsverpflichtung für die Ungläubigen setzt. Durch das Gebet wurde in dem Betenden das Bewusstsein der Verantwortung den Heiden gegenüber wachgehalten, in ihm die Aufmerksamkeit gepflegt, ob nicht Gott die Gebete erhöre und die Wege ins Heidentum hinein öffne, und des Betenden Wille gestärkt, wenn Gottes Ruf mitzuhelfen an ihn ergeht, ihm zu folgen. Da nun das Gebet für die Rettung der Ungläubigen allen Christen anbefohlen ist, ist die Verantwortung für die Heiden auf die denkbar breiteste Grundlage, soweit es die Menschen betrifft, gestellt: die ganze Christenheit ist die Trägerin der Verantwortung. Sie soll darum auch die Reservearmee bilden, aus der Gott zu seiner Zeit die Kämpfer an die Front ruft, während die Zurückbleibenden sie mit ihren Gebeten stützen und tragen.

So ist der Kalvinische Missionsgedanke aus der Zeitlage entstanden und weist doch weit über sie hinaus. Dadurch sind die Seinen auf den Tag zubereitet worden, an dem sie die Arbeit unter den Heiden und Mohammedanern aufnehmen sollten. Schon dreißig Jahre nach Kalvins Tod brach dieser Tag an.

3. Im härtesten Kampf mit den Spaniern hatten sich die Nordniederländer ihre politische Freiheit errungen, und damit hatte der Kalvinismus eine unumstrittene Heimat, eine feste Stellung gewonnen, von der aus Gott der evangelischen Christenheit die Bahn zu den Heiden erschloss.

Im Sommer 1595 gelang es nämlich den Niederländern, die Ozeansperre der niedergehenden katholischen Mächte, der Spanier und Portugiesen, zu durchbrechen und auf Java zu landen. Schon auf der zweiten Reise nach der malaischen Inselwelt wurden von den Prädikanten, die die Seeleute zu betreuen hatten, die ersten Eingeborenen getauft. Für die Missionsarbeit, die sich in der Folgezeit in Niederländisch-Indien unter dem Schutz der Ostindischen Kompanie und ganz von ihr abhängig entwickelt hat, ist (nach Schlunk, Niederländisch-Indien als Missionsfeld) wesentlich, dass man keinen Unterschied zwischen der Evangelisationsarbeit unter den Europäern und der Missionsarbeit unter den Heiden macht, dass demnach die Prädikanten nicht nur ihre Europäergemeinden, sondern obendrein die Eingeborenengemeinden zu bedienen hatten. Diese Art, die Missionsarbeit aufzuziehen, ist, wie mir scheint, nichts anderes als die Umsetzung des Kalvinischen Missionsgedankens von der Nächstenverpflichtung in die

Praxis. Gerade diese Art der Missionsarbeit hat aber gezeigt, dass der Missionsgedanke einer Erweiterung und Vertiefung durch den Missionsbefehl bedurfte. Und Kalvin wäre sicherlich der letzte gewesen, der sich dagegen gestemmt hätte, schreibt er doch selbst, dass Gott noch jetzt zuweilen, wie es die Notwendigkeit der Zeit erfordert, Evangelisten erweckt. Trotz aller Schwachheit und aller Mängel sind doch durch Gottes Gnade durch die Männer, die unter dem Einfluss des Kalvinischen Missionsgedankens das Heil den Ungläubigen Insulindes brachten, Früchte für die Ewigkeit entstanden: „Die Übersetzung der Bibel ins Hochmalaische steht noch heute auf den Molukken in höchstem Ansehen"; „die von der Kompanie gestifteten Christengemeinden gehören noch heute zum Teil zu den guten Gemeinden der neueren Missionsarbeit."

Calvin and Missions (1936)

CHARLES E. EDWARDS

Charles E. Edwards came from Ben Avon, Pittsburgh, PA, and is otherwise unknown. Probably he edited Devotions and prayers of John Calvin (Baker Book House, 1976).

Originally published in The Evangelical Quarterly vol. 8 (1936), pp. 47-51. Reprinted with permission by the editor and Paternoster Press, Exeter, Great Britain.

Some writers seem to have unjustly criticized Calvin, concerning an alleged lack of zeal for foreign missions. It would be far easier to turn the criticism against many modern Calvinists, who-have vastly more information, equipment, opportunities and resources, for their manifest lukewarmness. Good answers have been offered to justify Calvin and the other Reformers, and these should be emphasized. Prior to the defeat of the Spanish Armada in 1588, after the first Reformers had passed away, the sea power of the world was in the hands of those who opposed the Gospel. An illustration of the situation was seen in the disastrous ending of the evangelical colony that Admiral Coligny sent to Brazil. Calvin apparently did everything for it that was in his power. Of late years; do sensible people condemn the Bible Societies for not sending colporteurs to Soviet Russia, or missionary societies for not attempting to enter some Moslem lands where imprisonment or death might promptly arrest the missionary ? With shame and sorrow we confess that many professed Calvinists have not a spark of Calvin's zeal for the Gospel. The Reformation was itself a missionary movement, on a grand, international scale; and for more than a century it had to fight for its life. In some lands it suffered losses which have never been regained. Our foreign missions, so glorious in results, are expensive; and it is a strange ignorance or forgetfulness which imagines that Reformers, generally poor in purse, could commandeer the funds needed for such an enterprise.

In various aspects, evangelical missions in Latin America, also missions among French, Italians or Slavs in the United States or Canada, resemble the Reformation, confronting the same errors, using the same Scriptural methods, and obtaining similar conversions and results. Three goodly volumes were published, being reports of Commissions, presented to the Congress on Christian Work in Latin America, Panama, February 1916. Representatives of fifty organizations from twenty-two countries assembled there. Interdenominational missionary conferences were held in New York City in 1854 on the occasion of the visit of Rev. Alexander Duff to the United States; another, in Liverpool in 1860; and a far larger one in 1888 in London. In New York City a really ecumenical one in 1900 was attended by some seventeen hundred delegates and six hundred foreign missionaries. A great advance was seen in the World Missionary Conference in Edinburgh, in 1910. But Latin America was excluded here, through the influence of some German Societies, and some elements of the Church of England. The advocates of mission work in lands nominally Christian said that millions and millions of people there are practically without the Word of God and do not really know what the Gospel is. How interesting, that a modern missionary conference, on a technicality, would seem to exclude the Reformation, and the work of John Calvin !

It ought to be an edifying stimulus to all missionaries and their supporters, to gather from Calvin's writings some revelations of his missionary zeal. In his exposition of the Lord's Prayer (*Institutes*, Book III, Chap. XX, 41, 42) he says, "As the name of God is not duly hallowed on earth, it is at least our duty to make it the subject of our prayers." "God sets up his kingdom, by humbling the whole world, though in different ways, taming the wantonness of some, and breaking the ungovernable pride of others. We should desire this to be done every day, in order that God may gather churches to himself from all quarters of the world, may extend and increase their numbers, enrich them with his gifts, establish due order among them." Also, note some comments: Isa. xii. 4, "declare his doings among the people", "He means that the work of this deliverance will be so excellent, that it ought to be proclaimed, not in one corner only, but throughout the whole world." Mic. iv. 3, "A law shall go forth from Zion, that is, it shall be proclaimed far and wide; the Lord will show, not only in one corner, what true religion is, and how he seeks to be worshipped, but he will send forth his voice to the extreme limits of the earth." And the last verses of Romans, "He again refers to the end, mentioned in the beginning of the first chapter, for which the gospel is to be preached,– that God may lead all nations to the obedience of faith."

Calvin's lectures on Jeremiah, Ezekiel, Daniel and the Minor Prophets were followed by appropriate prayers. Here follows a portion of his prayer after commenting upon Mic. vii, 10-14, "May we daily solicit thee in our prayers, and never doubt, but that under the government of thy Christ, thou canst again gather together the whole world, though it be miserably dispersed, so that we may persevere in this warfare to the end, until we shall at length know that we have not in vain hoped in thee, and that our prayers have not been in vain, when Christ evidently shall exercise the power given to him for our salvation and for that of the whole world." And in conclusion of comments on the last verses of Malachi i, his prayer, in part: "O grant, that we may seek true purity and labour to render our services approved by thee by a real sincerity of heart, and so reverently profess and call upon thy name that it may be truly acknowledged as fulfilled in us, which thou hast declared by the prophet, – that undoubtedly thy name shall be magnified and celebrated throughout the whole world, as it was truly made known to us in the very person of thine only-begotten Son."

In the volume of Dr. B. B. Warfield's articles, *Calvin and Calvinism* (p. 14) we read, "Calvin was the great letter-writer of the Reformation age. About four thousand of his letters have come down to us, some of them of almost the dimensions of treatises, many of them also of the most intimate character in which he pours out his heart. In these letters we see the real Calvin, the man of profound religious convictions and rich religious life, of high purpose and noble strenuousness, of full and freely flowing human affections and sympathies. Had he written these letters alone, Calvin would take his place among the great Christians and the great Christian leaders of the world."

And these letters reach representatives of the three great families of Christendom: Latin, Slav, and Teutonic. Being a Frenchman, of the Latin race, we need give no illustrations of his profound missionary influence upon France. We may mention, however, his noble messages to heroic men, women and students of France, upon the eve of their martyrdom. Nor will we quote his letters to Italian co-workers. Turning to the Slavs, the Poles were and still are an important branch of that European family. In 1549 King Sigismund Augustus of Poland accepted from Calvin the dedication of his commentary on Hebrews, where he says: "Your kingdom is extensive and renowned, and abounds in many excellences; but its happiness will then only be solid when it adopts Christ as its chief ruler and governor, so that it may be defended by his safeguard and protection; for to submit your sceptre to him is not inconsistent with that elevation in which you are placed, but it would be far more glorious than all the triumphs of the world." In 1555 Calvin wrote to Nicholas Radziwill, one of the most distinguished of the Protestant nobles of Poland: "It is my wish that the kingdom of Christ should flourish everywhere, yet at the present moment Poland deservedly occupies my thoughts with a very special anxiety. For from the time that the light of a purer doctrine began to shine upon it, this happy beginning has at the same time inflamed my desire with the hopes of a better progress. Unquestionably you see that it is a work of immense difficulty to establish the heavenly reign of God upon earth. You see with what indifference that cause is treated, which ought not only to occupy the chief place among our cares, but even absorb all our thoughts." In closing a letter to the Waldenses of Bohemia, Calvin said, "We pray our Heavenly Father to govern you continually by his Spirit, to shield you with his protection, to enrich you with his gifts, and to bless all your holy labours."

And Calvin was interested in the Teutonic peoples, and had such friendly relations with Germans, for instance Melanchthon, that we here omit quotations from that correspondence. But so large a proportion of his followers to-day speak English, that it is apropos to quote from his missionary messages to them. To John Knox he writes: "It was a source of pleasure, not to me only, but to all the pious persons to whom I communicated the agreeable tidings, to hear of the very great success which has crowned your labours. But as we arc astonished at such incredible progress in so brief a space of time, so we likewise give thanks to God whose extraordinary blessing is signally displayed herein."

His letter to the precocious boy-king, Edward the Sixth, deserves remembrance: "It is indeed a great thing to be a king, and yet more over such a country, nevertheless! have no doubt that you reckon it beyond comparison better to be a Christian. It is therefore an invaluable privilege that God has vouchsafed you, sire, to be a Christian king, to serve as his lieutenant in ordering and maintaining the kingdom of Jesus Christ in England."

In dedicating a new edition of his commentary on Isaiah to Queen Elizabeth, he wrote: "It is not so much my object to be favoured with your countenance in my personal labours as humbly to entreat, and by the sacred name of Jesus Christ to implore, not only that through your kindness all orthodox books may again be welcomed and freely circulated in England, but that your chief care may be to promote religion, which has fallen into shameful neglect. And if this is justly demanded from all kings of the earth by the only begotten Son of God, by a still more sacred tic docs he hold you bound, most noble Queen, to perform this duty, for when even you, though a King's daughter, were not exempted from that dreadful storm which fell with severity on the heads of all the godly, by the wonderful manner in which he brought you out safe, though not unmoved by the fear of danger, he has laid you under obligation to devote yourself and all your exertions to his service. So far are you from having any reason to be ashamed of this deliverance that God has given you large and abundant grounds of boasting by conforming you to the image of his Son, on whom the prophet Isaiah bestows this among other commendations, that from prison and from judgment he was raised to the loftiest height of heavenly dominion." And to Bucer he wrote: "I pray that the English may make a stand for the genuine purity of Christianity, until everything in that country is seen to be regulated according to the rule which Christ himself has laid down."

All the works of Calvin show his genius, but the *Institutes* was his masterpiece. The first editions appeared some four centuries ago, and celebrations will take place. But should there not be some good and permanent results from these celebrations ? Look again at the vast field of foreign missions. Why should not plans be formed to obtain funds for the translation of the *Institutes* in perhaps a score of missionary languages ? Our missions will be infantile, immature, unless they arc furnished with adequate Christian literature. And here we have a work that has been commended by a great chorus of critics in each of these centuries. Do we wish to see something like the Reformation in a score of modern peoples ? By the blessing of God such a republication may be a powerful assistance, supplying the native preachers with the Scriptural teachings that they need. Calvin was the first to give a systematic form to the ideas of the Reformation. Enemies called the *Institutes* "the Koran of the heretics". Reyburn says, "What Newton's *Principia* is to science, that Calvin's *Institutes* is to theology." And millions, even hundreds of millions, may yet be won to Christ through Calvin's gospel.

Calvinism and the Missionary Enterprise (1950)

SAMUEL M. ZWEMER

Samuel Marinus Zwemer (1867-1952), nicknamed The Apostle to Islam, was an American missionary, traveler, and scholar. After being ordained to the Reformed Church ministry, he was a missionary at Busrah, Bahrein, and at other locations in Arabia from 1891 to 1905. He also traveled widely in Asia Minor, and he was elected a fellow of the Royal Geographical Society of London. In 1929 he was appointed Professor of Missions and Professor of the History of Religion at the Princeton Theological Seminary where he taught until 1951. He was influential in mobilizing many Christians to go into missionary work in Islamic Countries. Beside editing 'The Muslim World' for 37 years (1911-1947) he wrote appr. 30 influential books.

© *Theology Today*. Originally published in *Theology Today (Princeton, NJ) 7 (1950)*, pp. 206-216. Reprinted with permission from the publisher (http://theologytoday.ptsem.edu).

I. Calvin and Missions

It was the Roman Catholic Church historian and missionary professor, Joseph Schmidlin of Münster, who asserted that all the Reformers, Luther, Zwingli, Melanchthon, and Calvin were not conscious of the missionary idea and displayed no missionary activity. Whatever may be true of Luther's attitude toward the Jews, the Turks, and the pagans of his day (and there is much to be said), Calvin stood in a class by himself in this respect. This has been clearly shown by two German scholars in articles that appeared in 1909 and 1934. The first was by the great theologian Schlatter of Tubingen entitled "Kalvin und die Mission" in the *Evangelische Missionsmagazin* (Vol. 53) and the other by Asst. Professor Ernst Pfisterer of Bochum in *Die Allgemeine Missionszeitschrift* under the title "Der Missionsgedanke bei Kalvin" (March, 1934). Both of these writers agree that Calvin recognized the missionary obligation of the Church both in theory and practice.

Schmidlin asserts that Calvin did not recognize such obligation nor its practical fulfillment. He confined his missionary ideas, says Schmidlin, to commonplaces and declared missions superfluous. Schmidlin calls "the two lone Protestant missionary undertakings of the Reformation Era" a failure. That of Gustav Wasa among the Lapps "was not really to pagans and that of the French emigrants in Brazil was a mere colonizing venture." A different, although tragic, story is told regarding these three hundred Calvinists who came to Brazil and attempted successfully to preach to the Indians in 1558 but of whom a number were killed as heretics by the Roman Catholic Governor Villegainuous.

As regards Melanchthon a recent monograph does justice to this great Reformer, but grants that neither he nor Luther had the missionary spirit or vision of John Calvin.[46] We learn from the introduction that there was general ignorance of Islam in Europe for 500 years after the Hejira (A.D. 622). Dante the poet puts Mohammed with Judas and Beelzebub in the lowest inferno. Historians and theologians generally were ignorant not only of the origin of Islam but of its teaching. Whatever accounts we have of this world-religion are unhistorical, uncritical, and unsympathetic. The very titles of the books written during this period are indicative of the general attitude, for example: *Confutation Improbatio, Cribratio Alchorani, Notationes contra Mahometi dogmata.*

At the time of the Reformation there was a slight change for the better. Luther was deeply interested in Islam, the religion of the Turks. His writings have been the subject of special studies in this respect by Vossberg, Holston, Simon, and Barge. Melanchthon was a careful student of all that Luther wrote on the subject. Melanchthon's viewpoint is, however, of greater importance because he was a historian as well as a theologian. The material for Kahler's study consists of Melanchthon's letters, commentaries, poems, and especially a number of introductions that he wrote to books by various writers dealing with the Turks and Islam. We have an account of Mohammed's life, of Islam as a sect, and of the Turks as representing the political power of this religion. Melanchthon points out that Islam is a heresy based on fiction. The Moslem errs in his knowledge of God, in his denial of the person and offices of Christ, in the doctrine of the Holy Spirit, and especially in his soteriology. He accuses Islam of Eudaemonism and Hedonism, and states that it is the enemy of true culture because of its social ethics in regard to marriage and slavery. The concluding section (pages 105-164) gives a summary of Melanchthon's position on the history of religions. The author holds that Melanchthon, while emphasizing the abso-

---

[46] *Melanchthon und der Islam: Eine Beitrag zur Klärung des Verhältnisses zwischen Christentum und Fremdreligionen in der Reformationszeit,* by Manfred Kohler. Leipzig: Leopold Klotz Verlag, 1938.

lute character of Christianity, portrays his ignorance of the real strength of Islam and its vital elements. He does not rid himself of medieval indifference to the missionary call and intolerance of all kinds of "heresies." Neither Melanchthon nor Luther in spite of their partial knowledge of this non-Christian religion was ever stirred in his heart to propose missions to Moslems.

John Calvin lived in the sixteenth century, not in the nineteenth. We cannot expect of him a world-view and world vision like that of William Carey. But he was not blind or deaf to the heathen world and its needs.

Calvin's knowledge of the pagan nations was taken from the Bible and classical literature. There is no proof that he had ever come in touch with the newly discovered world of Asian and African paganism. The Turks, of whom Luther writes frequently, were not on his horizon. He was, however, in direct contact with the Indians of Brazil through a missionary adventure of which we will speak later.

In a recent volume of special study on Calvin and his views of the Kingdom and the Church by Dr. Karlfried Frohlich, we learn of the broad horizon that was part of Calvinism.[47]

Calvin visualizes the struggle for that Kingdom as a conflict between Christ and Satan. He is, therefore, fond of all the Bible language in the Old and New Testament that deals with such a struggle between light and darkness, between sin and grace.

There is a most interesting excursus on the contrast between Calvin and Ignatius Loyola which touches Calvin's place in the history of missions. The author calls attention to the fact that these two men were contemporaries. Calvin and Loyola both felt that they were champions for the glory of God in this world. Both were men of action. Both brought their ideas as a complete sacrifice for the attainment of that end, the victory of Christ. Both of them had an aristocratic view of such a glorious mission. The reformer of Geneva and the nobleman of Spain were men of iron will. The one exerted it in Roman-Protestant Europe, and the other in every part of the world where he sent his missionaries, especially the Far East. The author points out the enormous difference, however, in the vision of these two men. Ignatius sees visions and dreams; Calvin bows himself under the mighty will of God. The prayer-idea of the Spaniard is meditation; of Calvin it is the free expression of the heart's desire for communion with God.

---

[47] *Gottesreich, Welt und Kirche* (München, 1930).

The spiritual writings of Ignatius were written for an inner circle; Calvin wrote for the whole Christian public (pp. 70-74).

In another portion of his book Frohlich speaks of Calvin's cosmopolitan correspondence and how he kept in touch with the Reformation in every part of Europe. He writes to someone in Great Britain, "God has created the entire world that it should be the theater of his glory by the spread of his Gospel." In these words he shows his longing and desire for the spread of the mission of the Church and its message everywhere. His letters to John Knox in Scotland, to the Polish king Sigismund, to friends of the Reformation in England, Italy, France, and the Netherlands, testify to the outreach of his ecumenic soul.

In 1538 Calvin actually proposed in a letter to Bullinger a plan for a general synod of all Protestant Churches to meet together for consultation to strengthen each other and to agree on the proper attitude toward the power of the State. The author adds, "This great idea was never realized. History has not conferred on him the honor, but the idea continued to live as a heritage for later generations, for Calvin believed that the Kingdom of Christ should be extended not only inwardly but outwardly in every part of the world, for this is the will of God."

The result of his correspondence and his efforts can be seen in the strong character of Reformers such as John Knox and Coligny, in Oliver Cromwell and the heroes of the Netherlands. It was the spirit of Calvin that made them advocates of the extension of the Kingdom of Christ in their attempts for colonial expansion.

Calvin's view of the heathen world is based upon two doctrines – that of man's creation in God's image and that of common grace. In the former he teaches that by creation all men have a knowledge of God and a germ of religion (*Inst*. I, 3: 1). But sin has darkened this gleam of truth. The soul of man is a labyrinth. Man made his own gods and superstitions (*Inst*. I, 5: 12). Nevertheless, the heathen mind retained a knowledge of a High-god (*Inst*. I, 12: 1). This is very like the idea vindicated in our day by one of the greatest anthropologists, Wilhelm Schmidt in his six-volume work, Der Ursprung der Gottesidee, in contrast to the common evolutionary view of the origin of religion.

Calvin at the very outset of his Institutes (I, 3: 1-2) lays down a great missionary principle, namely, man's natural instinct for God. "The human mind by natural instinct possesses some sense of Deity – God hath given to all some apprehension of his existence which he frequently and insensibly renews." Men universally know that there is a God and that he is their

Maker. Nothing human is alien to God's divine purpose in the gift of his Son. He so loved the world that his Son died "not for sinners only but for the sin of the world." "The worship of God," says Calvin, "is the only thing which renders man superior to brutes and makes them aspire to immortality." Again, "The seeds of religion are sown by God in every heart although we scarcely find one man in a hundred who cherishes what he has received."

The primal instinct is obscured by ignorance and wickedness. It is the doctrine of common grace in Calvin that explains the character of those seekers after God in heathendom whose ardent desire for light and whose good works remain in mystery if the gulf between fallen man and God is unbridgeable. Even as regards the final destiny of the unbeliever Calvin is not harsh and negative but positive and full of restraint. In Book 3, 25: 12 he deals with Immortality and Resurrection and uses those remarkable words: "How great and severe is the punishment, to endure the never ceasing effects of his wrath! On which subject there is a memorable passage in the ninetieth psalm: that though by his countenance he scatters all mortals, and turns them to destruction, yet he encourages his servants in proportion to their timidity in this world, to excite them, though under the burden of the cross, to press forward, till he shall be all in all."

Calvin goes on to describe the origin of idolatry as a desire to form with human hands an image of God as conceived by a warped imagination (*Inst.* I, 11: 9). Yet in spite of all departure from truth and righteousness, the heathen mind and heart still bear traces of common grace in natural endowments and gifts of genius; "we learn from this how many good gifts the Lord has left in human nature even after it was deprived of the knowledge of the true God" (*Inst.* II, 2: 13-15). As one reads Calvin, one is astonished at the breadth and depth of his teaching regarding common grace. This is in accord with the true missionary spirit and distinguishes Calvinism from an extreme Barthianism which finds no points of contact and no bridge between Christianity and the non-Christian faiths. The doctrine of common grace is that of faith in the soil of the human heart.

"Down in the human heart crushed by the Tempter ... Feelings lie buried that grace can restore."

The call of the Gospel is for all men, says Calvin ("Sermons on Deut.," *Opera*, 28). God desires all men to be saved and to come to the knowledge of the truth – "all states and all peoples" ("Sermons on I Tim.," *Opera*, 53). Nor is the duty of evangelism to all the world hemmed in or contradicted by the doctrine of predestination (*Inst.* III, 23: 12-14). "We do not know," writes Calvin, "whom God has elected nor where his elect dwell."

Moreover we are in duty bound to pray for the heathen, "for all people in the whole earth" (*Inst.* III, 20: 36-40). This comes out clearly in his exposition of the second petition of the Lord's Prayer. The same thought is emphasized in a powerful sermon on Daniel (*Opera*, 41) where he exclaims, "When we think and pray only about our own needs and do not remember those of our neighbors, we cut ourselves loose from the body of Christ Jesus our Lord and how can we then be joined to God."

Calvin also sees as the goal of all missions the Glory of God. To draw souls out of hell and put them on the way of salvation is to glorify God ("Sermon on Deut.," *Opera*, 33: 18-19). The same thought occurs in a sermon on Isaiah 12: 4-5. "This is our duty, everywhere to make known among the nations the goodness of our God."

Dr. Julius Richter in his Science of Missions (*Missionskunde*) gives the following five reasons why the early Reformation period was so barren of direct missionary effort: The idea was current that the end of the world was at hand; the non-Christian world was considered as under condemnation and destined to perdition. The heathen were hardened because they rejected the preaching of Noah and that of the Apostles; only the secular power could enter heathen lands; and there is only a general and not a particular duty to preach the Gospel. All this is true, but did Calvin offer these reasons? No. There is very little in his writings to show such tendencies. He arose above his age and above his contemporaries. Pfisterer takes up each of these medieval views of the contemporary Reformers and demonstrates that Calvin was not of their company. His missionary outlook, ideals, and theory were far in advance of those of Luther (see article by Pfisterer, pp. 104-106). Such sharp words as Luther used of Turks, Jews, and the heathen are not found in Calvin.

When we come to the pragmatic test in regard to foreign missions, Calvin was the only Reformer who actually planned and organized a foreign mission enterprise. It was an effort by colonists to Brazil and its pagan Indians in 1555 by Calvinist refugees from Geneva and France. Through it Admiral Coligny came into touch with Calvin, and his life and influence was one of the by-products of this mission; born out-of-due-time and destroyed by Roman Catholic persecution.

Gaspard de Chatillon Coligny, admiral of France and Protestant leader, was in touch with Calvin in 1558 when the colony went to Brazil. He advocated religious toleration in France but was *le heros de la mauvaise for-*

tune as sole leader of Protestantism. He was killed in the massacre of St. Bartholomew. His daughter became the wife of William the Silent, Prince of Orange.

At the close of the eighty years war in 1595, the Dutch Calvinists also sent out mission preachers, in this instance to the East Indies. At Ceylon and on other islands they established a work that has continued fruitful until the present day. They translated the entire Bible into Malay, and that book is still a witness of their missionary zeal.

There were two religions locked in combat for Western Asia and North Africa. But some of the Reformers themselves felt that Islam with all its errors and its Arabian fanaticism was closer to the truth than the medieval papacy. The Dutch in their struggle with Spain chose for their motto *Liever Turksch dan Paapsch* – Rather the Turk than the Pope! I was told that one can still read these words and the symbols that accompany them on the carved pillars of a church at Middelburg. Islam was long considered a Christian heresy, and so, some think, should be our approach today.

In one of his letters Erasmus actually proposed that, "The best and most effectual way to overcome and win the Turks would be if they should perceive those things which Christ taught and expressed in his life shining in us. For truly it is not meet nor convenient to declare ourselves Christian men by this proof or token if we kill very many but rather if we save very many. Nor if we send thousands of heathen people to hell, but if we make many infidels faithful. To my mind it were best before we should try with them in battle, to attempt to win them with epistles and some little books."

II. Calvinism and Islam

It is remarkable that as far back as 1871 in an address on Calvinism delivered as Rector of St. Andrews, the historian James Anthony Froude, called attention to the strange parallel between the Reformation in Europe under Calvin and that in Arabia under Mohammed. Islam indeed, as Bancroft remarks, is the Calvinism of the Orient. It, too, was a call to acknowledge the sovereignty of God's will. "There is no god but Allah." It, too, saw in nature and sought in Revelation the majesty of God's presence and power, the manifestation of his glory transcendent and omnipotent. "God," said Mohammed, "there is no god but he, the living, the self-subsistent; slumber seizeth him not, nor sleep; his throne embraces the heavens and the earth and none can intercede with him save by his permission. He alone is exalted and great." It is this vital, theistic principle that explains the victory of Islam over the weak, divided, and idolatrous Christendom of the

Orient in the sixth century. "As the Greek theology," so Froude remarks, "was one of the most complicated accounts ever offered of the nature of God and his relation to man, so the message of Mahomet, when he first unfolded the green banner, was one of the most simple. There is no god but God; God is King, and you must and shall obey his will. This was Islam, as it was first offered at the sword's point to people who had lost the power of understanding any other argument; your images are wood and stone; your metaphysics are words without understanding; the world lies in wickedness and wretchedness because you have forgotten the statutes of your Master, and you shall go back to those; you shall fulfill the purpose for which you were set to live upon the earth, or you shall not live at all" (Froude, *Calvinism*, p. 36).

He then goes on to say, by way of correction: "I am not upholding Mahomet as if he had been a perfect man, or the Koran as a second Bible. The Crescent was no sun, nor even a complete moon, reigning full-orbed in the night of heaven. The morality of it was defective. The detailed conception of man's duties inferior, far inferior, to what St. Martin and St. Patrick, St. Columba and St. Augustine, were teaching or had taught in Western Europe. Mahometanism rapidly degenerated. The first caliphs stood far above Saladin. The descent from Saladin to a modern Moslem despot is like a fall over a precipice. But the light which was in the Moslem creed was real. It taught the omnipotence and omnipresence of one eternal Spirit, the Maker and Ruler of all things, by whose everlasting purpose all things were, and whose will all things must obey" (Froude, *Calvinism*, pp. 37-38).

Yet Calvinism and Islam had much in common. Both are opposed to compromise and all half-measures. Both were a trumpet call in hard times for hard men, for intellects that could pierce to the roots of things where truth and lies part company. Intolerance is sometimes a virtue. The very essence and life of all great religious movements is the sense of authority; of an external, supernatural framework or pattern to which all must be made comfortable.

Calvinism and Islam were neither of them systems of opinion but were attempts to make the will of God as revealed (in the Bible, or according to Mohammed in the Koran) an authoritative guide for social as well as personal affairs, not only for Church, but for State. They both believed in election and reprobation, dependence on God's will, not on man's.

Calvinism and Islam have at their very core the principle of a claim of finality and universality, and it is this principle that is the very basis of a missionary religion. Paul's theology and soteriology made him a missionary and drove him across all racial barriers, compelling him to set forth Christianity as final and triumphant. The strongest plea for missions is the will of God for the whole world. We can only have a passion for the glory of God when we acknowledge his sovereignty in every realm of life.

If singleness of aim is a mark of leadership, Calvin and Mohammed were both born leaders. As Barth expresses it: "Calvin first had a theme and then thought of its variation; first knew what he willed and then willed what he knew." The same might be said of Mohammed. The genius of spiritual conquest is the consciousness that God is commanding the battalions, that the issue is not uncertain, and that the goal is God's eternal glory. More than a century ago, James Montgomery, a true Calvinist, closed his great missionary hymn, beginning, "Oh Spirit of the Living God," with the stanza:

"God from eternity hath willed All flesh shall His salvation see; So be the Father's love fulfilled The Saviour's sufferings crowned through thee."

Our American statesman, John Hay, a century later, interpreted in the same Calvinistic fashion the prayer, "Thy will be done," in his great hymn, beginning, "Not in dumb resignation we lift our hands on high."

With God's sovereignty as basis, God's glory as goal, and God's will as motive, the missionary enterprise today can face the most difficult of all missionary tasks – the evangelization of the Moslem world. God in his sovereign providence and by his Holy Spirit has led the Reformed faith geographically to the very heart of the Moslem world. For more than one hundred years the Churches of the Reformed tradition were the only ones that went to its cradle and its strongholds in the Near East. They, more than any other branch of the Church, were pioneers in the world of Islam. Familiar names come to memory: Jessup, Post, Van Dyck, Dennis – in Syria; Shedd and his colleagues – in Persia; Lansing, Hogg, Watson – in Egypt; Forman, Wherry, Ewing – in North India; Keith Falconer, John Young, Peter Zwemer, Henry Bilkert, George Stone, Mrs. Thorns, Sharon Thorns, Mrs. Harrison, Mrs. Mylrea, John Van Ess (to mention only a few of those who have passed on to their reward) – in Arabia.

It is still true, as Professor Lindsay stated at the meeting of the Reformed and Presbyterian Alliance in Glasgow, that "the Presbyterian Churches do more than a fourth of the whole mission work abroad done by all the Protestant Churches together." The Calvinistic Churches entered the world of Islam earlier and more vigorously than any other group. The first missionary to the Turks was a Reformed preacher, Venceslaus Budovetz of Budapest. He was born in the year 1551, and belonged by his religion to the

Unitas Fratrum, which was a branch of the Hussite Church in Bohemia. He was very faithful and a zealous member of the Church. Having spent more than ten years in Western Europe at Protestant universities, especially Reformed, and in travels, he became a very strong and convinced Calvinist, and became acquainted with some of the most renowned evangelical scholars and religious leaders of his time (see *The Moslem World*, vol. XVII, pp. 401 ff. for a sketch of his life and influence by Professor Josef Soucek of Prague).

Among these friends were Theodore Beza of Geneva, the French Reformed lawyer Philip Mornay du Plessis, the Basel Reformed theological professor, Crynaeus, and also one of the Lutheran theologians, David Chytraeus, who had part in composing the famous Lutheran book of symbols, *The Formula of Concord*.

Vaclav Budovec lived in Constantinople from 1577 to 1581. He sought opportunity to win back apostates and to preach to the Turks; but he was staggered by the power of Islam. "I have been not a little in temptation," he wrote, "seeing how these ungodly Turks prosper and that the noblest parts of the earth where God himself walked in human body ... have been conquered by them in an incredibly short time." In one of his letters sent to his son in later years, he mentions the fact that he actually did win one Turk for Christ. Budovec wrote a number of books in the Czech language, one of them being called *Anti-al-Koran*. It is a defense of the Christian faith and a refutation of Islam. This book is very rare, but copies are found in the University and other private libraries in Prague. Here we have the first Christian apologetic written by the Reformation Church for Moslems.

Nor can we forget that the Reformed Churches of South-Eastern Europe were the bulwark against the invasion of Islam for centuries. Again we note that in Java and Sumatra the Reformed Churches of the Netherlands have had more converts from Islam than any other mission in any part of the world. Over 62,000 living converts from Islam are connected with the various missions in Java alone. These missions cover territory which has a population (almost solidly Mohammedan) of nearly forty million souls.

As regards America, it is not without providential significance that when the world of Islam faces a crisis and affords the Church a new opportunity, Reformed and Presbyterian bodies together have the strongest and widest work in five of the great lands of the Moslem world: Egypt, Syria, Iraq, Persia, and Arabia. "The union of the United Presbyterian, the Reformed, and the Presbyterian Church," said the late Dr. Robert E. Speer, "would bring a new joy and faith to the Church which today has responsibility for the strongest mission work in the world for the evangelization of Mohammedans."

God's own hand has indeed led the children of the Covenanters, of the Huguenots, and of the Dutch into the very heart of the world of Islam. Its old historic cities are mission stations of our Churches: Alexandria, Cairo, Khartum, Beirut, Damascus, Aleppo, Bagdad, Busrah, Mosul, Teheran, and Tabriz. The Arabian mission of the Reformed Church and the South Arabia Mission of the Scottish Church have marched around Islam's Jericho, and their trumpet gives no uncertain sound. The walls of Arabian intolerance and fanaticism have already fallen before the medical missionary pioneers of these Churches. But there are whole provinces of Arabia still unoccupied and vast Moslem areas in Africa and Asia where the missionary has never entered. This is the missionary challenge to the Calvinists of today. A challenge to dauntless faith and indiscourageable hope and a love that will not let go. Think of Afghanistan, and all western and Southern Arabia; of Russian Turkestan, parts of Siberia, Bokhara, and the Crimea, of Central Asia, of Tripoli in Africa, the French Sudan. Here is a population of nearly forty-five millions! All these are a call to action for those who yearn to see the victory of the Cross over the Crescent.

Calvin's Missionary Message: Some Remarks about the relation between Calvinism and Missions (1950)

JOHANNES VAN DER BERG

Johannes van den Berg, D.Th., emeritus Professor of Church History, born 1922 (Rotterdam), Reformed minister 1947-1959, Professor at the Free University Amsterdam (1959-1976), at Leiden University (1976-1987). Has published on 17th, 18th and 19th century church history. Special fields of interest: Anglo-Dutch ecclesiastical and theological relations, predestinarianism; Jewish-Christian relations and polemics; millenarianism; Protestant Enlightenment.

Originally published in The Evangelical Quarterly vol. 22 (1950), pp. 174-187. Reprinted with permission by the editor and Paternoster Press, Exeter, Great Britain.

It is a somewhat dangerous undertaking to associate a theological system, which is the spiritual property of only a part of the Church, with the great work in which all Christians take part – especially when we not only look for a historical connection, but also try to understand the meaning of Calvinism for to-day's missionary work. The danger of bringing the lofty missionary task into the often clouded sphere of theological controversy looks to be anything but imaginary.

To avoid all misunderstandings and misconceptions it is necessary to state clearly what is the meaning of the words "Calvinism" and "missions". When we rate these notions at their true value, it appears that there is a much closer connection between them than we could surmise and that Calvinism, not in spite of its main characteristics, but as a fruit of its core and essence, has given rise to a rich development of missionary activity.

It is almost impossible to give a clear and at the same time exhaustive definition of Calvinism. In a general sense we can say that Calvinism is that complex of theological thinking and Christian activity which finds its deepest roots in Calvin's rediscovery of the comprehensive meaning of the Gospel, It takes different forms according to the various circumstances in which it develops, but it always retains those characteristic elements which we already find in the works of Calvin himself – a passionate desire not only for the salvation of souls, but also for the honour of Him who saves poor sinners by His electing grace and who asks complete obedience to His sovereign Will in all spheres of life. It was not Calvin's wish to form a new school of theological thought – he only wanted to return to the pure sources of the Gospel and to show that the Lord and Saviour has His holy claims on all the complex relations in which man knows himself to be placed. We make a caricature of Calvinism if we lay too much stress on the differences between Luther and Calvin: the soteriological line, the emphasis on the salvation of souls, is with Calvin as strong as with Luther.[48] Calvin's doctrine is not a cold and passionless system of moral codes, bound together by an abstract doctrine of predestination – on the contrary, all the works of Calvin tremble with wonder at the great mystery of Cod's saving grace, and the *Soli Deo Gloria,* which is indeed one of the "distinctive ideas" of Calvinism, is deeply rooted in the *Sola Gratia.* God will be honoured on the broad front of life by those who know themselves to be saved by His free grace and His eternal love.

When we now turn to the meaning of the word "missions", we have to remember that the missionary obligation has never and nowhere been more clearly expressed than by our Lord Himself in the missionary command of Matt, xxviii. 19, 20: "Go ye therefore, and teach all nations, baptising them in the name of the Father and of the Son and of the Holy Ghost, teaching them *to* observe all things whatsoever I have commanded you." This command of our Lord contains three elements: the nations must be brought to Christ and made His disciples (personal conversion), they have to be baptised-in His name (formation of the Church) and they must sit at His feet to learn the meaning of His commandments for the whole of their existence (development of Christian life). All missionary work has a soteriological character: its chief end is to bring men into communion with the Saviour, it aims at personal conversion. Hut at the same time it is comprehensive and totalitarian: not only the soul of the sinner has to be saved, but his whole life and all the relations in which he stands have to be brought under the command of his Saviour, who is also his King.[49] So we see that the soteriological and the theological line, the notion of the salvation of the soul and that of the honour of our God and King, form an indivisible unity – not only in the thinking of Calvin, but also in the Gospel itself, as becomes clear to us when we pay attention to the missionary command of Matt, xxviii.

---

[48] Cf. G. C. Berkouwer, *Geloof en Rechtvaardiging* (1949). pp. 55-60.
[49] Cf. J. H. Bawinck, *The Impact of Christianity on the Non-Christian World* (1949), pp. 18-23.

It is the rediscovery of that scriptural unity, which is the principal meaning of the Calvinistic Reformation. Those Christians, who call themselves *issus de Calvin,* who want to belong to the spiritual progeny of that great Reformer, know that there is a relation between their Calvinism and the missionary obligation of the Church. They are often put to shame by the zealous ardour of fellow-Christians whose theological opinions they cannot share but who nevertheless have been more fully aware of the urgency of Christ's command than they have been themselves – and because of all this they have to speak with great modesty and deep humility. But yet they know that the vision which Calvin has shown them is not alien from the spirit of the Gospel, but has sprung from the only source for theological thinking and missionary activity alike, God's holy Word. They are aware that their knowledge is partial and defective and that they have often used the light which God had given them in a wrong way, but they are also aware of the immense implications of the message which Calvin, by the grace of God, derived from the rediscovered and reopened Bible, and it is with that message that they want to serve the Church Universal in the fulfilment of its missionary task.

But as soon as all this begins to engage our attention, we aced before a very difficult problem. One of the most are remarkable and mysterious facts of church history is the – at first sight – rather negative attitude of the Reformers with regard to the missionary obligation of the Church. It looks as if the rediscovery of the Gospel did not lead to a new zeal to spread the message of Christ throughout the world. The loud call for missions which rings through the New Testament found a very weak echo in the works of the Reformers, As we shall see, the lack of missionary *activity* is easy to explain – but much more difficult is the question, why the missionary *ideal* takes such a comparatively small place in the Reformers' thought. In this respect there is more harmony than difference between the great Reformers, though of course with each of them the problem has another accent and aspect. So though we only look for the missionary element in Calvin's thinking, we often have to speak about the opinions of the Reformers in general.

It appears that with Calvin the thought that the Gospel has to spread throughout the world and has to take its course to the ends of the earth is very dear; less clearly, however, does he sec in what manner this must happen; and the practical application of the missionary ideal is almost completely lacking.

A variety of explanations have been given to elucidate this difficult problem, We will consider some of them, and ask ourselves if they are sufficient to answer the questions with which we are confronted. From the Roman Catholic side a number of reasons have been brought to the fore. In the first place it has been said, that because the Reformers abandoned the Catholic conception of the Church, there remained no one who had a right to send out missionaries.[50] This explanation, however, docs not hold, since the Reformers, and especially Calvin, had a very clear notion of the Church, which proved afterwards to be of the utmost importance for the development of the cause of missions. Calvin only purified and restored the concept of the Church and it is not to be wondered at that as a result of this purification the idea of missions had to find a new foothold. This explains the initial hesitation with regard to the ecclesiastical foundation of missions, which hesitation, however, was very soon overcome by the inherent forces of the Calvinistic conception of the Church.

It has also been remarked that the abandoning of the ascetic ideal of the Middle Ages robbed the Reformers of one of the strongest stimuli for missionary activity.[51] Now it is an undeniable fact that, from the times of the fro-Scottish Missions down to the period of the missionary activity of the Jesuits, asceticism was a very important missionary motive, in connection with the doctrine of the meritoriousness of good works. But here, too, a purification was needed: the. asceticism of the Roman Catholic Church had to give way to a not less heroic preparedness to make great personal sacrifices for the sake of the Redeemer, who does not ask for merits but only for gratitude. Also in this point the foundation of missions had to be laid on a deeper level.

A well-known Roman Catholic argument against the Reformation, especially with regard to the propagation of the Gospel, is that the elimination of the monastic orders left a disastrous vacuum which could not properly be filled.[52] Indeed, the orders have done much for the cause of the Gospel throughout the world, and the lack of them created a real problem for a time after the Reformation, Hut this fact was only a practical hindrance to the fulfilment of the missionary task, and least of all a reason to have no feeling for the missionary obligation itself.

The Jesuit author H. de Lubac, who deals with the missionary attitude of the Reformers in a more understanding way than Galm does, tries to ex-

---

[50] M. Galm, *Das Erwachen des Missionsgedankens im Protestantismus der Niederlande* (1915), p. 8.
[51] M. Galm, *op. cit.*, pp. 8-9.
[52] M. Galm, *op. cit.*, p. 8.

plain our problem partly from mediaeval ideas.[53] Already in the time of R. Lullus there was some opposition to missions, which sprang from a combination of eschatological and quietistic-mystical motions. But Pfisterer has already clearly shown[54] that Calvin was not only free from the influence of these mediaeval ideas, but even overcame these ideas by his clear insight into Scripture, and so blazed the trail for a better understanding of the missionary task,

A really important check to the full unfolding of the missionary idea was the Reformers' fear of the idea of "apostolic succession". It is a great pity that by this fear, justifiable as it is in itself, the clear view on the missionary obligation was darkened. It was a strong argument of the Reformers against the hierarchy of the Roman Catholic Church, that the office of the twelve Apostles was only a *munus extraordinarium* with a temporary character. But in the heat of the debate they were in danger of forgetting that the task of the Apostles to spread the Gospel and to proclaim the message of Jesus Christ is the task of the Church as a whole, whose Apostolate it is to go out into the world with the apostolic *kerygma*. Because of all this the missionary command of Matt, xxviii. remained in the shadow of theological discussions. Still we have to remember that the opinion of the Reformers on this point was not yet quite settled – Calvin[55] as well as Zwingli[56] and Bucer[57] left open the possibility of a temporary renewal of the apostolic office in the Church. Calvin's view on the Apostolate was not so narrow as to leave no room at all for the missionary command, though it was certainly a hindrance in finding the right form for the fulfilment of it. I would even venture to say that if the Reformers had had a broad opportunity for missionary activity, their onesided understanding of the Apostolate, due to the fact that no missionary problems were under discussion, would certainly have been corrected by their own dominant theological conceptions. Moreover we must not mistake Calvin's opinion on this point for that of the later Lutheran orthodox divines, who went so far as to assert that the missionary command had already been fulfilled by the Apostles themselves. Calvin never expressed this thought; he only sees a *beginning*

---

[53] H. de Lubac, *Le fondement theologique des Missions* (1940), p. 60.
[54] E. Pfisterer, „Der Missionsgedanke bei Kalvin", *Neue Allgemeine Missionszeitschrift* (1934), p. 103.
[55] *Institutio IV*, iii. 4.
[56] Cf. P. Drews. „Die Anschauungen reformatorischer Theologen über die Heidenmission", *Zeitschrift für praktische Theologie* (1897), p. 221.
[57] Cf. P. Drews, *op. cit.*, p. 215.

of the spreading of God's Kingdom throughout the world during the times of the Apostles (*post Christi resurrectionem fines regni Dei longe lateque ... prorogari coeperunt*[58]), Beza was the first Reformed theologian who contended that the Apostles really had brought the *odor Evangelii* to the ends of the earth, even to America![59] He uses this assertion as an argument in his controversy with Saravia about the apostolic succession. We must, however, not forget that it was Saravia who had unhappily linked the missionary command to his defence of the Anglican system of Church government; that Beza's argument has not found much approval among those Calvinistic divines who were interested in missionary questions, and that even Beza did not quite deny the duty of the Church to spread the Gospel among the Gentiles.[60] So we can say that the Reformers' misunderstanding of the apostolic function of the Church sometimes hushed, but never choked, the missionary voices which we hear in their works.

It is a popular misunderstanding that Calvin's doctrine of predestination was a hindrance to the outgrowth of the missionary ideal. The reverse is true – this doctrine is not a stimulus for passivity, but calls man to high activity[61] combined with a deep and humble feeling of dependence, as Calvin himself clearly expresses in his *Institutio* when, appealing to the works of Augustine, he vehemently denounces the caricature which even in his time was made of the doctrine of election.[62] With great approval he quotes the words of Augustine: "Because we do not know who belong to the number of the elect and who do not belong to it, we have to be in such a mood that it would be our desire that all were saved. So it will happen that we exert ourselves to make every one whom we meet a partner of the peace [of God]." It is a noteworthy fact that many defenders of the doctrine of predestination were at the same time zealous advocates of the missionary cause – e.g. Augustine, Bucer,[63] Carey, Kuyper and many others.[64] They derived their doctrine of predestination from the great Apostle to the

---

[58] Quoted from P. Drews, *op. cit.*, p. 290. Calvin says this in his commentary on Ps. cx.

[59] Cf. P. Drews, *op. cit.*, p. 307.

[60] As even M. Galm concedes, *op. cit.*, p. 35.

[61] Cf. E. Pfisterer, *op. cit.*, p. 104.

[62] *Institutio III*, xxiii. 12-14.

[63] Cf. J. N. van der Bosch, *Zendingsgedachte uit den tjid der Hervorming* (1941), p. 29.

[64] With most of these men the doctrine of free grace was only a barrier against a too human conception of the missionary task and methods.

Gentiles, as Carey already remarked in his *Form of Agreement:* "Nevertheless we cannot but observe with admiration that Paul, the great champion of the glorious doctrines of free and sovereign grace, was the most conspicuous for his personal zeal in the work of persuading men to be reconciled to God."[65]

So it appears that we can only very partially explain from theological motives the lack of missionary fervour with Calvin and the other Reformers. These motives are found on the margin of the Reformers' thinking and would therefore never have been able to darken the clear view of the missionary obligation which one could expect to have resulted from the rediscovery of the Gospel, if there had not been a hindrance on quite another level. Not the inward attitude of the Reformers, but the outward circumstances were the most serious obstacle in the way of missionary thinking. The Reformers had no contact with the heathen world. Almost all the lands where missionary work was possible were under the control of Roman Catholic countries, Moreover the hands of the Reformers were tied by the heavy struggle with the Roman Catholic Church, in which the existence of the Reformation was at stake. Is it any wonder those Churches which were always in danger of being persecuted and destroyed, which had to build up their ecclesiastical life from the ground and which, moreover, had no contact whatever with the world outside, dominated as it was by the Roman Catholic powers, had no clear vision of the missionary exigencies and possibilities? I am convinced, that the main cause of the alleged lack of missionary zeal with Calvin and the other Reformers lies in the outward circumstances: the missionary ideal remained as it were a subterranean stream, unable to reach the sea of the Gentile world, and hindered in its speed by theological objections, which were according to Kenneth Scott Latourette perhaps partly an unconscious outgrowth of the external difficulties.[66]

But all this must not lead us to close our eyes to the fact that the stream of missionary zeal never quite disappeared from the Reformers' thought, With Calvin this stream is much greater than one is superficially inclined to suppose. Not only does the universal meaning of the Gospel take a dominant place in his works, especially in his commentaries on the proph-

---

[65] A. H. Oussoren, *William Carey, especially his missionary principles* (1945), p. 274, see also p. 127.
[66] K. S. Latourette, *A History of the Expansion of Christianity*, III (1939), p. 25.

ets and in his exposition of the Lord's Prayer[67] – he also insists that the Christian community has to pray for the conversion of the heathen and to draw all nations of the earth to God.[68] It is true that his thoughts on this subject were rather dim – but that they were not merely theoretical speculations is proved by his part in the undertaking of De Villegaignon, which we have to see as a really missionary enterprise, of which the Genevan Reformer was the spiritual father.[69] It is moving to read how the emigrants, even after the treason of De Villegaignon, tried to go on with their missionary work on the inhospitable coast of Brazil, and it shows how true it is what Latourette says: "Protestantism proved missionary wherever it had clone contact with non-Christians."[70]

Summarising we may say that we find in the works of Calvin the latent presence of a strong missionary zeal, which was sometimes dimmed by theological misunderstandings, but which was mainly prevented from reaching full development by the very difficult circumstances of the Calvinistic Reformation during Calvin's lifetime. That Calvin's fundamental recognition of the missionary duty of the Church did not lead him to a pica for organised missionary work[71] is no wonder – such a plea could only find a hearing in a later period under more favourable circumstances. We may yet add that Calvin's missionary ideal, of which we see faint and sometimes even clear glimpses in all his works, circles around the two main poles of his thinking: the theological one of the glory and praise of God and the soteriological one of the Christian compassion to save souls from hell and to lead them on the path of salvation.[72]

Only if the theological and the soteriological line are equally emphasised and form a harmonious unity, does the missionary idea find a sphere in which it can come to full growth when the time has become ripe for it. This becomes clear, if we focus our attention on the development of missionary

---

[67] Cf. the quotations from Calvin given by C. E. Edwards, "Calvin and Missions", *The Evangelical Quarterly*, viii (1936), pp. 48-49.

[68] Cf. a sermon on Deut. xxxiii. 18-19, quoted by E. Pfisterer, *op. cit.*, p. 101, and the commentary on Isa. xii. 4-5, quoted by W. Schlatter, „Calvin und die Mission", *Evangelisches Missions-Magazin* (1909), pp. 48-49.

[69] Cf. W. Schlatter, *op. cit.*, pp. 333-338.

[70] K. S. Latourette, *op. cit.*, III, p. 27.

[71] At least as far as we know: his letters to the Brazilian emigrants are lost.

[72] Both elements we find in a striking juxtaposition in a passage quoted by E. Pfisterer, op. cit., p. 101, from a sermon on Deut. xxxiii. 18-19, which we have already mentioned.

zeal and thought in the history of Calvinism. The first Calvinist whom we meet as an ardent champion of the Church's obligation to obey the missionary command of our Lord is the Canterbury Canon A. Saravia, from whom had appeared in 1590 a treatise about the diverse grades of the ministers of the Gospel, Already from the full title[73] of the book it appears that Saravia did not aim in the very first place at a defence of the missionary command; as we have already seen above, the chief object of his work was to defend the episcopal system of Church government against the attacks of the Presbyterian Calvinists, to whom he had once belonged during his ministry and his professorship in Holland,[74] So his plea for missions was neutralised by the fact that it was embedded in a plea for a system against which the majority of Calvinists had a strong antipathy.

Of much more importance for the awakening of a practical missionary interest was the work of J. Heurnius: *De legatione evangelica ad Indos capessenda admonitio,* which appeared in 1618. This treatise is not so much a systematic exposition as a *cri de cœur,* in which the latent missionary current bursts out with great vigour, l'he main hindrances had disappeared: no longer were the hands of the Reformed tied by heavy persecutions, no longer was the way to other parts of the world barred by the Roman Catholic powers, it could no longer be said that there was no contact whatever between the Calvinistic part of Western Europe and the Gentile world, By the relations between Holland and the-East Indies the floodgates for the missionary stream were opened – now the pure water of the Gospel could flow through them, driven forward by a Calvinism which had escaped the dangers of orthodoxy and scholasticism in consequence of its full emphasis on personal piety and salvation, It is worth while to note that just those theologians who were strongly interested in soteriological questions and in whom the tender piety of the Canons of Dordt had become flesh and blood, were at the same time the most enthusiastic advocates of the Church's missionary obligation. The cry of Heurnius was not a solitary voice: W. Teellinck wrote his *Ecce Homo* and J. van Lodensteyn his *Beschouwinge van Zion,*[75] A. Walaeus gave solid missionary instruction in his Seminary at Leiden, J. Hoornbeek proved himself a scholarly advocate for the cause of missions in several of his works, and the great theologian

---

[73] *De diversis ministrorum Evangelii gradibus, sicut a Domino fuerunt instituti, et traditi ab Apostolis, ac perpetuo omnium ecclesiarum usu confirmati.*

[74] Cf. M. Galm, *op. cit.*, p. 34.

[75] "Contemplation of Sion." Both works are a defence of the missionary cause.

of that time, G. Voetius,[76] paid very much attention to missionary questions in his *Disputationes* as well as in his *Politica Ecclesiastica*. How unjust it is to denounce the missionary zeal of these Dutch theologians as mere "propaganda", as nothing but a desire to increase the influence of the Reformed Church, appears already from the fact that next to the plantation of Churches Voetius sees the conversion of the heathen as an independent missionary purpose. Here again we find the soteriological line, though Voetius, as a good Calvinist, does not neglect the theological line: *"causa finalis ultima et suprema est gloria el manifestatio gratiae divinae"*.[77]

Galm has rightly observed the relation between the stress on personal piety, which we find with the above-mentioned theologians, and their plea for missionary activity.[78] But quite wrongly he reduces their theological attitude, from which their missionary zeal resulted, to catholicising tendencies. It cannot be denied that in the elaboration of their missionary ideas they underwent the influence of Roman Catholic authors; but their missionary attitude itself was quite definitely not a result of Roman Catholic influences.[79] The elements in their thought which Galm ascribes to catholicising tendencies, among which what he calls the ascetic element takes the first place, can easily be traced to the influence of Calvin and the other Reformers, who knew themselves to be the heirs apparent of the rich treasures of the old Christian Church.

That the stream of Dutch missionary activity silted up at last is due to internal and external circumstances which prevented the progress of the newly awakened missionary enthusiasm in Church and State. The missionary stream was stopped at its source by the decay of Dutch Calvinism, which fell into scholasticism on the one hand and mysticism on the other by a one-sided emphasising of the theological or the soteriological line. And the stream which could still flow on in spite of those hindrances could not reach its goal because of the counter-currents of indifference and even hostility with which the East India Company met the missionary work during the second half of its existence.[80] But the voices of the seventeenth-

---

[76] Cf. for a list of Voetius' missionary treatises, H. A. van Andel, *De Zendingsleer van G. Voetius* (1912), pp. 21-37.

[77] Quoted from H. A. van Andel, *op. cit.*, p. 143.

[78] M. Galm, *op. cit.*, p. 143.

[79] Cf. H. Kraemer, „De plaats van den Zendeling", in *De Kerk in Beweging* (1947), pp. 213, 214.

[80] Cf. C. W. Th. Baron van Boetzelaer van Asperen Dubbeldam, *De Protestantsche Kerk in Nederlandsch-Indie* (1947), passim.

century Dutch advocates of the cause of missions had not sounded in vain: the effects of the stimuli which they gave can still be seen in the remains of the old Dutch mission-work in the East, and the echo of their words awakened later generations – was not Carey most probably influenced by Heurnius's *Admonitio*, when he wrote his *Inquiry*?[81]

Meantime there were other entirely or partly Calvinistic countries for which the gates to the heathen world opened themselves: when the missionary stream in Holland silted up, a brook began to trickle from England and Scotland to the Thirteen Colonies, which became the forerunner of a mighty stream of missionary activity, expanding itself from Great Britain to all parts of the world, Already in the *Larger Catechism of Westminster* that ripe fruit of Calvinistic thinking, we see something of that broad vision, when we are taught to pray that the fullness of the Gentiles be brought in.[82] And according to the *Directory for the Public Worship of God*, given by the Westminster Assembly, the minister has "to pray for the propagation of the Gospel and Kingdom of Christ to all nations, for the conversion of the Jews, the fullness of the Gentiles, the fall of Antichrist and the hastening of the second coming of our Lord".[83]

These prayers found their echo in many hearts. As a century before in Holland, voices were now raised in England and Scotland advocating the cause of missions. In 1723 a book by a Scottish minister, Robert Millar of Paisley,[84] appeared: *The History of the Propagation of Christianity and Overthrow of Paganism*. With him we find the same characteristic element as with the Dutch theologians of the former century: he asks for a reformation at home, "that a holy warmth of sincere piety may so burn in our hearts, as would prompt us to spend and be spent for promoting the Kingdom of Christ in every part of the world". Missionary zeal always springs up in those circles where a deep piety prevails; God's honour can only be sought by souls who have tasted the sweetness of His saving grace. About twenty years later, under the influence of the Cambuslang Revival, a number of Scottish ministers came together to form a "Concert of Prayer",[85]

---

[81] M. Galm, op. cit., p. 49, quoting from J. R. Callenbach. Justus Heurnius (1897), pp. 85ff. See for the influence of Heurnius' work in Denmark and Germany M. Galm, op. cit., pp. 38, 49, 77, 80.

[82] Answer 191.

[83] From the "Publick Prayer before the Sermon".

[84] Cf. J. Foster, "A Scottish Contributor to the Missionary Awakening", International Review of Missions (1948), pp. 138 ff.

[85] Cf. J. Roster, "The Bicentenary of Jonathan Edwards' Humble Attempt", *International Review of Missions* (1948), pp. 375 ff.

which helped to blaze the trail for the great missionary awakening at the end of the eighteenth century. It pleased God to kindle the fire of missionary zeal in Calvinistic Scotland, when in Calvinistic Holland it had almost been extinguished.

Now the question remains: was this missionary awakening, seen from a human point of view, a fruit of Calvinism, or was it quite other factors which called it into life? It is impossible to give a clear answer to this question because of the utter complexity of the religious situation in the eighteenth century. In addition to the influence of Methodism, which was in its turn strongly influenced by German Pietism and Moravianism, there was also the influence of the "Great Awakening" in America, a revivalist movement "which had its deepest roots in Calvinistic theology".[86] The Moravian Zinzendorf, the Methodist Wesley, the Calvinist Edwards – they all stand at the cradle of the great missionary awakening. But that their stimuli found such an eager response on Calvinistic soil proves once again that missionary zeal was present in Calvinism, ready to spring forward when a broadening of the horizon coincided with a deepening of the spiritual life. The co-operation between a deep sense of God's free and sovereign grace and a fervent desire to glorify God all over the earth yielded rich fruits for the cause of missions, as we see in England and in Scotland: Carey and his partners as well as Duff and his fellow-workers may be called Calvinists in a broad and yet very deep sense.

From Great Britain the missionary ideals were brought to new life in Holland: the tree of missions flowered again, richer than ever before, on the old Calvinistic soil. We cannot say that all branches of Dutch missionary activity are equally rooted in Calvinism – but on the whole Dutch missions have never been able to disavow their Calvinistic origin. A splendid effort to combine Calvinistic and missionary thinking we find in a lecture which A. Kuyper gave at the first missionary Congress of the Reformed Churches[87] at Amsterdam in 1890, in which lecture[88] he tried to find a Calvinistic foundation for the missionary task of the Church. The same Calvinistic foundation was sought in the missionary Report of the Synod of the Reformed Churches, held at Middelburg in 1896. It is a pity that in the Report the soteriological line sometimes disappears behind the theological one, which gives to some turns of phrase a rather chilly effect[89] – but by

---

[86] A. Keller, Amerikanisches Christentum Heute (1943), p. 44.
[87] Separated from the Dutch Reformed Church in 1886.
[88] Edited by Prof. Bavinck under the title *Historisch Document* (1940).
[89] Cf. H. A. van Andel, *op. cit.*, p. 150.

the missionary work itself this one-sidedness soon was corrected, and on the whole the thoughts, expressed in lecture and Report, have been of the utmost importance for the cause of missions not only in the Netherlands, but also in the American Churches of Dutch origin.

We have come to the end of our historical survey, in which only some crucial points in the development of Calvinistic missionary thinking could be mentioned. If we venture to draw a conclusion from it we would say that Calvinistic missionary activity was at its height when there was perfect harmony and unity between the theological and the soteriological line in Calvinism. Where the theological line is emphasised at the expense of the soteriological, there looms a secularised Calvinism, which in its desire to fight "the wars of the Lord" on the broad front of life[90] loses its passion for souls, but on the other hand a one-sided stress on soteriology leads to a sterile mysticism which is quite passive with regard to the missionary task. The unity of these two lines can only be realised, if we remember and apply the wise words of Solomon: "in the multitude of people is the king's honour" (Prov. xiv. 28).

So it appears that a living Calvinism has a message for the missionary work of to-day. It derives that message from the Word of God: our charter of salvation, the programme for the task of our life. On a mural painting[91] in the missionary centre of the Reformed Churches at Baarn we see the old Calvin standing behind a young, modern missionary. Ages lie between them, but still they are one: for over the young man's shoulder Calvin's old hand points to the open book which the missionary holds in his hand: the Bible, the only medicine which can cure us from our self-made ideas and our arbitrary conceptions by showing us something of our Lord's holy Will and Plan. If missions threaten to become secularised, that Bible calls them back to the core of its message: the free grace of our Lord Jesus Christ, of which they have to give a joyful testimony. But if they are in danger of losing sight of their task on the broad front of life, it reminds them of the totalitarian character of the message of Christ: "teaching them to observe all things whatsoever I have commanded you". The man of the comprehensive approach is warned against the great danger of forgetting the essential task of the Church: to bring the people, the heathen, the lost sheep into the fold of Jesus – but the Pietist who thinks that he is ready if man's soul has been saved has to be reminded of the fact that a good shepherd not only brings his sheep into the fold, but also tries to cure its wounds with tender

---

[90] Cf. J. H. Bavinck. *Onze Werk Zendingskerk*, passim.
[91] A work of the Dutch painter Marius Richters, made in 1947.

care. The Calvinistic missionary does not ask the nations to throw away their cultural heritage, because he knows of God's common grace – but much less will he try to preserve it as if it were an order of creation, because he knows that the Word of God is an aggressive and revolutionary power in this world, for Christ has come to make all things new. He is on his guard against an airy optimism, with regard to the results of his work, because he knows that it is God who works both to will and to do *of His good pleasure* (Phil. ii. 13), but at the same time the doctrine of God's electing love protects him against despondency and pessimism: it is not of him that willeth, nor of him that runneth, but of *God that showeth mercy*.

Lastly, the doctrine which Calvin drew from the pure fountain of God's holy Word must bring us to deep humility and to great activity alike. Humility: Calvin's soteriology is one confession of our own impotence to do any good, to bring any soul to conversion, and one hymn of praise on God's sovereign grace. The conversion of the nations is never our work; it is only the work of God. But – and this is the other line, which runs through all the works of Calvin – God wants to use us as His instruments, He calls us, He sends us, we are under His command, His name must be glorified by our poor words and our still poorer deeds. And this is the scriptural summary of all that Calvin teaches us: "faithful is He that calleth you, who also will do it" (1 Thess. v. 24).

The Missionary Dynamic in the Theology of John Calvin (1964)

CHARLES CHANEY

Dr. Charles Chaney spend his life within the Southern Baptist Convention, among other positions as president of the Southern Baptist Home Mission, as president of the Southwest Baptist University (1983-86) and as dean of its Redford School of Theology.

Originally published in Reformed Review Vol. 17 (1964), No. 3 (March), pp. 24-38. Reprinted by permission of the editor of the Reformed review.

Introduction

One of the perpetual problems facing the Protestant missiologists is the apparent lack of a salient doctrine of the mission of the church in the theology of the Reformers. None has experienced more poignant embarrassment nor been more acutely aware of this hiatus than the descendants, both theological and ecclesiastical, of John Calvin.

The purpose of this study is twofold. First, the aim of this paper is to reexamine the concept of the mission of the church in Calvin's theology. Opinion has been divided as to whether there really is such a concept in Calvin's thought. Gustav Warneck, a sympathetic observer, said categorically that there was no recognition in Calvin of the church having a duty to send out missionaries.[92] He averred that the only missionary responsibility found in Calvin's thought was in regards to the duty of the magistrate to introduce the true religion in all his subjects.[93] Warneck's views have generally been adopted by other writers of Protestant missionary history.

On the other hand, especially in the last decade, there have been several scholarly defenses of Calvin's missionary ideas. Samuel M. Zwemer has averred that the very principles on which the modern missionary move-

---

[92] Gustav Warneck, *Outline of a History of Protestant Missions from the Reformation to the Present Time*, trans, by George Robson (New York: Fleming H. Revell Company, 1901), p. 19.
[93] *Ibid.*, p. 20.

ment had its origin are to be found in Calvin's theology.[94] The ablest exegete of Calvin's missionary concepts, in recent years, has been Johannes van den Berg. He maintains that Calvin's aversion to the claim of apostolic succession on the part of the Roman Catholic clergy "darkened" Calvin's understanding of the apostolic function of the church.[95] However, this alone was not sufficient to explain his lack of missionary fervor. "The main cause of the alleged lack of missionary zeal with Calvin ... lies in the outward circumstances" in which he lived.[96]

Calvin's thoughts on this subject will be re-examined in this paper.

The second aim in this study is to attempt to discover what particular doctrines of Calvin provided the missionary dynamic in the thought and practice of his spiritual descendants who were in the forefront of the rise of the Protestant world mission. It cannot be denied that men, classified theologically as Calvinists, have been in the vanguard of this movement. From the ill-fated missionary attempt of the French Calvinists in the Brazilian colony of Villeganon, in 1557,[97] to the popularization of the society method at the turn of the nineteenth century, men in the theological lineage of Calvin have been particularly prominent.

It is true that other factors have played an important part in the Protestant missionary awakening. However, Calvinism has provided not only much of the muscle and sinew of the movement, but it has also contributed much in basic motivation and fundamental principles. J. van den Berg has said:

> The Moravian Zinzendorf, the Methodist Wesley, the Calvinist Edwards – they all stand at the cradle of the great missionary awakening. But that their stimuli found such an eager response on Calvinistic soil proves once again that missionary zeal was present in Calvinism.[98]

The questions of this paper are: Did the seed of missionary zeal and concern find fertile soil in Calvinism because of Calvin's own thought or did it take root there because of the milieu of a different age? and, If Calvin's

---

[94] Samuel M. Zwemer, "Calvinism and the Missionary Enterprise," *Theology Today*, v. VIII (1950), pp. 206-216.

[95] Johannes van den Berg, "Calvin's Missionary Message," *The Evangelical Quarterly*, XXII (1950), p. 179.

[96] *Ibid.*, p. 180.

[97] The most recent account of this first Protestant missionary endeavor is G. Baez-Camargo, "The Earliest Missionary Venture in Latin America." *Church History*, v. XXI (1952), pp. 135-144.

[98] J. van den Berg, *op. cit.*, p. 185.

thought did house prolific missionary ideas, which ones had particular significance to the early Protestant missionary leaders?

I. Calvin's Missionary Principles

In order to answer the first question, it will be necessary to let Calvin speak for himself. However, it should be noted, as van den Berg has pointed out, that Calvin's references "to the missionary task of the church are scanty and vague"[99]. Nevertheless, the references are sufficiently numerous and clear to provide adequate documentation for at least an outline of missionary principles to be found in Calvin's theology.

The Calling of the Gentiles

The foundation of Calvin's missionary ideas was the calling of the Gentiles. In Calvin's thought, with the calling of Abraham God began to restrict himself to one people, the Jews.[100] However, through the prophets, God announced that the day would come in which he would extend his mercy and grace to all the peoples of the world.[101] God's reign over Israel through the Kingdom of David was but a portent of that greater Kingdom which was to come. In Calvin's exposition of Isaiah 2:4, he explained the calling of the Gentiles in these terms:

> Since ... God had not taken more than one nation to be the subject of his reign, the Prophet here shows that the boundaries of his Kingdom will be enlarged, that he may rule over the various nations. He likewise notices, indirectly, the difference between the Kingdom of David, which was but a shadow and this other Kingdom, which would be far more excellent. At that time God ruled over his own people by the hand of David, but after the coming of Christ, he began to reign ... in the person of his only-begotten Son ... He confirms the calling of the Gentiles, because Christ is not sent to the Jews only, that he may reign over them, but that he may hold his sway over the whole earth.[102]

The expression most used in Calvin's writings to explain this wonderful fact, that God had extended his reign to all mankind, was the Pauline metaphor of the broken wall. The gifts of the Holy Spirit were given "that all

---

[99] J. van den Berg, "Calvin and Missions," *John Calvin, Contemporary Prophet*, ed. J. T. Hoogstra (Grand Rapids: Baker Book House, 1959), p. 167.

[100] Commentary on Psalms 22:28, *Works* (Edinburgh: The Calvin Translation Society, 1844-1856), v. 8, p. 386.

[101] Commentary on Micah 4:1-2, *Works*, v. 28, p. 259.

[102] Commentary on Isaiah 2:4, *Works*, v. 13, pp. 98-99.

men might call upon the name of God, that we might all, be made partakers of the covenant of salvation which appertained only to the Jews, until the wall was broken down."[103]

With the coming of Christ, the wall had been broken down, the Gentiles had been grafted into the body of God's people, and the mercy of God had been given a "place indifferently amongst all nations."[104] The vessels of God's glory were henceforth to be partly taken from among the Gentiles and partly from among the Jews.[105]

The calling of the Gentiles is significant to Calvin's missionary ideas because of two reasons. First, the fact that Gentiles were included under God's reign meant that God would be gathering his people from all the earth. Calvin commented:

> Because the doctrine of the Gospel, by which God hath gathered to himself a Church indiscriminately out of all nations, proceeded from Mt. Zion, he justly says that they will come to it, who having, with one consent or faith, embraced the covenant of eternal salvation, have been united into one church.[106]

Second, the calling of the Gentiles also meant that the Gospel would be proclaimed to the Gentiles without distinction,[107] and, thus, all men would be invited to partake of God's salvation. Calvin said:

> There is no people and no rank in the world that is excluded from salvation; because God wishes that the gospel should be proclaimed to all without exception. Now the preaching of the gospel gives life; and hence ... God invites all equally to partake salvation.[108]

In Calvin's thought, as will become clearer below, the calling of the Gentiles was the fundamental missionary principle because it made a world-wide mission of the church both a possibility and a duty.

---

[103] *Divers Sermons of Master John Calvin, concerning the Divinitie, Humanitie. and Nativitie of our Lorde Jesus Christe* (London: Printed for George Bishop, 1581), p. 173.

[104] Commentary on Romans 9:25, *Works*, v. 38, p. 274.

[105] *Ibid.*, p. 272.

[106] Commentary on Isaiah 2:3, op. cit., p. 94.

[107] *Ibid.*, p. 97.

[108] Commentary on 1st Timothy 2:4, *Works*, v. 43, pp. 54-55.

The Progress of the Kingdom

A second important missionary principle in Calvin's thought was the progressive extension of the Kingdom of Christ throughout the world. Calvin used the metaphor of the royal sceptre often to express this concept. "Christ's Kingdom shall be vastly extended, because God would make his sceptre stretch far and wide."[109]

Calvin's view of the Kingdom was one of certain conquest. He said:

> Though the Kingdom of Christ is in such a condition that it appears as if it were about to perish at every moment, yet God not only protects and defends it, but also extends its boundaries far and wide, and then preserves and carries it forward in uninterrupted progress to eternity.[110]

With the coming of Christ, his Kingdom was only begun in the world.[111] "Yet it ought to be observed, that while the fullness of days began at the coming of Christ, it flows on in uninterrupted progress until he appears the second time for our salvation."[112]

The church has a part in this "uninterrupted progress." The church participates in the Kingdom. Calvin lamented, then exhorted:

> Would that Christ reigned entirely among us! For then would peace also have its perfect influence. But since we are widely distant from that peaceful reign, we must always think of making progress ...[113]

T. F. Torrance has pointed out the missionary significance of this participation in the Kingdom by the church.

> It is because of this participation in the Kingdom of Christ, in the heavenly peace, that the church can engage in its arduous task of extending that Kingdom on earth. And so throughout his works Calvin made it a point to teach the combination of the *medkatio vitae futurae* with the unceasing activity of the Church on earth in the growth and extension of the Kingdom.[114]

---

[109] Commentary on Psalm 110, *Works*, v. 11, p. 300.
[110] Commentary on Isaiah 9:7, *Works*, v. 13, p. 313.
[111] Commentary on Micah 4:3, *Works*, v. 28, p. 265.
[112] Commentary on Isaiah 2:2, *Works*, v. 13, p. 92.
[113] Commentary on Isaiah 2:4, *Ibid.*, p. 102.
[114] T. F. Torrance, "The Eschatology of the Reformers," Eschatology, eds. T. F. Torrance and J. K. S. Reid, Scottish Journal of Theology Occasional Papers. No. 2, Edinburgh: Oliver and Boyd, Ltd., 1952, p. 55.

The Gathering of the Church

A third missionary principle in Calvin's theology is his concept of the gathering of the church. At the same time in which the church participates in the extension of the Kingdom, the church is being gathered. Indeed, Calvin, speaking of the "spiritual and internal condition of the church," said, "the actual building of the Church is nothing less than the Kingdom of God."[115]

Further, wherever the word was sincerely preached and the sacraments correctly administered, one could rest assured that the church had reality.[116] For it was impossible, in Calvin's thought, for these two to exist without producing fruit and experiencing prosperity.[117]

The church was gathered only by the effectual word of God, when God himself teaches his people.

> There is no other way of raising up the church of God than by the light of the word, in which God himself, by his own voice, points out the way of salvation. Until the truth shines, men cannot be united together, so as to form a true church.[118]

After the completion of Christ's public ministry, the gospel was to be offered to all people. Calvin remarked, "But as the wall is broken down, the Gospel promulgated, we have been gathered together into the body of the church."[119]

The agents of this promulgation were the Apostles. "The Apostles ... were like the first architects of the Church, to lay its foundations throughout the world."[120] The Holy Ghost appeared in the manner he did on the day of Pentecost "to shew that hee woulde be in the mouthes of the Apostles, and woulde give them whatsoever was requisite for the executing of their office and commission."[121]

Calvin understood that the gospel had been preached to the whole world during the ministry of the Apostles. He spoke of Christ penetrating "with amazing speed, from the east to the west, like the lightening's flash, in

---

[115] Commentary on Micha 4:1-2; *Works,* v. 28, p. 257.
[116] *The Institutes*, IV, i, 9.
[117] *Ibid.*, IV, i, 10.
[118] Commentary on Micah 4:1-2, *Works,* v. 28, p. 257.
[119] Commentary on Psalm 110. *Works,* v. 11, p. 301.
[120] *The Institutes*, IV, iii, 4.
[121] *Divers Sermons,* p. 172.

order to bring into the church the Gentiles from all parts of the world."[122] However, Calvin did not mean by this that every particular people and tribe had had the gospel preached to them. This meant, rather, that no group was excluded from God's mercy. God now had presented "himselfe to all the worlde ... to great and small, as well to the Gentiles now, as to the Iewes before."[123]

Calvin knew quite well that not even the slightest report concerning Christ had reached the "Antipodes" and other distant nations. He maintained that the preaching of the gospel to the whole world in the time of the Apostles did not "absolutely refer to every portion of the world."[124]

He affirmed:

> The Kingdom of Christ was only begun in the world, when God commanded the Gospel to be everywhere proclaimed, and ... at this day its course is not as yet completed.[125]

The office of the apostle was an extraordinary ministry, not intended to be perpetual in the church. But Calvin avowed that God might still call others to that office when the necessity of the times required it.[126] In fact, Calvin confessed that God had occasionally raised up apostles even in his own time.[127]

Whether or not God did or would call and send out other apostles, Calvin insisted that still each individual Christian should have a part in the gathering of the church. Commenting on Isaiah 2:3, Calvin said:

> By these words he first declares that the godly will be filled with such an ardent desire to spread the doctrines of religion, that everyone, not satisfied with his own calling and his personal knowledge, will desire to draw others with him ... This points out to us also the ordinary method of collecting a church, which is, by the outward voice of men; for though God might bring each person to himself by a secret influence, yet he employs the agency of men.[128]

---

[122] Commentary on Psalms 22:28, *Works*, v. 8. p. 386.
[123] *Sermons of M. John Calvin on the Epistles of S. Paule to Timothie and Titus*, (London: Imprinted for G. Bishop and T. Woodcoke, 1579), p. 150.
[124] Commentary on Matthew 24:14, *Works*, v. 33, p. 129.
[125] Commentary on Micah 2:1-4, *Works*, v. 28, p. 265.
[126] *The Institutes*, IV, iii, 4.
[127] *Ibid.*
[128] *Works*, v. 13, p. 94.

For Calvin, God was still gathering his church. He would continue so to do until the gospel had reached the fartherest bounds of the earth.[129] There was a possibility that God might raise up special successors to the Apostles for this assignment, but as each individual shared his own calling and knowledge with others, he became God's agent in this task.

Personal Christian Responsibility

This introduces the fourth missionary principle in Calvin's theology. Christians are responsible, under God, to share the gospel of Christ with all men, everywhere.

Quotations from Calvin on this subject are very numerous. It will be advantageous to have the words of Calvin himself illustrate this principle which was such a vital part of his understanding of the Christian life.

A desire for the salvation of the world blazes, at times, from Calvin's works. He thought that this compassion should have been the experience of every true Christian and that it should have moved each Christian to do his best to bring others to Christ. He said:

> The desire which ought to be cherished among all the godly ... is, that the goodness of God may be made known to all, that all may join in the same worship of God. We ought especially to be inflamed with this desire ... after having been delivered from the tyranny of the devil and from everlasting death.[130]

> The character then of faith has also this in it – that the elect, while themselves obey God, desire to have many associates in this obedience, and many fellow-disciples in true religion.[131]

> Faith then only produces its legitimate fruit when zeal is kindled, so that everyone strives to increase the Kingdom of God, and to gather the straying, that the church may be filled. For when any one consults his own private benefit and has no care for others, he first betrays more clearly his own inhumanity, and where there is no love the Spirit of God does not rule there. Besides, true godliness brings with it concern for the glory of God. It is no wonder then that the Prophet, when describing true and real conversion, says that each would be solicitous about his brethren, so as to stimulate one another,

---

[129] Commentary on Matthew 24:14, *Works*, v. 33, p. 129.
[130] Commentary on Isaiah 12:4, *Works*, v. 23, p. 403.
[131] Commentary on Zechariah 8:20-23, *Works*, v. 30, p. 231.

and also that the hearts of all would be so kindled with zeal for God, that they would hasten together to stimulate his glory.[132]

As this last reference indicates, the Christian, according to Calvin, ought also to be motivated to bring all to the worship of the true God by his desire to bring glory to God. Calvin spoke in this manner many times.

We must endevour, as much as is possible, that God may be honored, and that the world may be gathered unto him, and we ourselves must come foremost.[133]

We ought also to consider the honour which he bestows upon us, then he condescends to make use of our services for extolling and spreading the glory of his nature, though we are altogether useless and of no value.[134]

Further, in Calvin's thought, the Christian should be motivated not only by compassion and a desire for God's glory, but also because such is the duty of the Christian both to God and to all the nations of the world.

God has deposited the teaching of his salvation with us, not for the purpose of our privately keeping it to ourselves, but of our pointing out the way of salvation to all mankind. This, therefore, is the common duty of the children of God.[135]

It is our duty to proclaim the goodness of God to every nation. While we exhort and encourage others, we must not, at the same time, sit down in indolence.[136]

But that seeing it is sayde of Zebulon and Isachar, who being placed in the borders or outleets of Jewry were mingled with the Gentils and heathenfolke, that they should not forbeare to provoke their neighbors to serve God: we also ought to followe that which is sayd heere of them. And specially let us put this in practice when we be among ye unbeleevers which would faine infect us with their corruptions, and bring us into a mislyking of God's service, to plunge us into their idolatrie ... Let us labor as much as in us lyeth, to winne them to God and to the Gospell of our Lorde Iesus Christ.[137]

This is the reason why Saint Paul useth this argument (1 Tim. 2:3-4). That God woulde have all the worlde to be saved: to the end that as much as lyeth

---

[132] *Ibid.*, p. 227.

[133] *The Sermons of M. Ioan Calvin upon the fifth books of Moses called Deuteronomie* (London: for George Bishop, 1583), p. 221.

[134] Commentary on Isaiah 12:1, *Works*, v. 23, p. 397.

[135] Commentary on Daniel 12:3, *Works*, v. 25, p.

[136] Commentary on Isaiah 12:5, *Works*, v. 13, p.

[137] *Sermons on Deuteronomy*, p. 220.

in us, we should also seeke their salvation which seeme to be as it were banished men out of the Kingdome of God.[138]

So then, seeing it is God his will [sic] that all men should be partakers of that salvation, we must have a care to drawe poore, seelie and ignorant creatures to us, that we may come altogether to this inheritaunce of the Kingdom of heaven.[139]

And, thus, we see in fewe words, that Saint Paules meaning is, to wit, that foreasmuch as God will have his grace to be knowen of al ye world, and hath commaunded his Gospell to be preached to all creatures, we must as much as lieth in us, procure the salvation of all them whiche are at this day straungers from the faith, and seeme ulterly to be deprived of the goodnesse of God, that we may bring them to it.[140]

Hence, it is evident that there was in Calvin's thought the basic principles of a missionary theology. Calvin had a Gospel that was offered to all the world. He was participating in the extension of a Kingdom that would include people from every language and land. The Kingdom would continue to grow, in spite of all opposition, until it reached the farthest bounds of the earth. Calvin's God was still calling his people to himself and would continue to do so until Christ's second coming. God's people were gathered into his church. They were also gathered by his church. For each Christian had the responsibility, "as much as in him lieth," to share the gospel with the whole world.

II. Calvin's Missionary Influence

The question now arises: if this were Calvin's thought, why then did he do and speak so little about this fundamental task of the church?

Calvin's lack of significant action and expression in this area was the result of many forces and circumstances. Two such forces, which contributed to his lack of positive action, became dynamic influences in the stimulation of missionary activity two centuries later.

Calvin's Doctrine of Election

First, Calvin's doctrine of election does seem, in at least one aspect, to have somewhat stifled missionary effort in his own day. However, in the

---

[138] *Sermons on Timothy*, p. 148.
[139] *Ibid.*, p. 149.
[140] *Ibid.*, p. 159.

later years of missionary awakening this same aspect became a mighty and important force.

This is not to say that Calvin was discouraged from missionary activity because his doctrine of election made such activity unnecessary. This charge has too often been made. Instead, the gracious election of God was a stimulus to activity, not a hindrance. Calvin was very insistent that the gospel must be offered to all.[141]

However, God's election was expressed, not only in the area of personal salvation or reprobation, but also in the area of determining what nations would have the gospel at particular times. In answering the charge that God would be inconsistent with himself if he invited all without distinction to salvation and yet only elected a few, Calvin said:

> And he who, forbidding Paul to preach in Asia, and leading him away from Bithynia, carries him over to Macedonia, shows that it belongs to him to distribute the treasure in what way he pleases.[142]

It was not in God's will and plan for all nations to hear the gospel at the same time.

> It was not his will that all should know the Gospell at the first blowe. And thereupon, there were some countries where he would not suffer Saint Paule to preach, as in Bithynia and Phrygia.[143]

Yet this did not mean that God would not, at some time, establish his word among those people. The implication was, rather, that God would be certain so to do. Speaking of those who had not as yet been made partakers of salvation, he said:

> We must not ... forget that God has made us all to his image and likeness, that we are his workmanshipe, that he may stretch foorth his goodnesse over them whiche are at this day faare from him, as we have had good proofe of it.[144]

> Now the same God who has already made us partakers of salvation may sometimes extend his grace to them also. He who hath already drawn us to him, may draw them along with us. The Apostle takes for granted that God will do so, because it had been foretold by the predictions of the prophets, concerning all ranks and nations.[145]

---

[141] *The Institutes*, III, xxiii, 14.
[142] *Ibid.*, III, xxiii, 10.
[143] *Sermons on Timothie*, p. 152.
[144] *Ibid.*, p. 160.
[145] Commentary on 1st Timothy 2:4, *Works,* v. 43, p. 55.

The proclamation of the gospel was, in Calvin's thought, God's work. It could be done only as God provided the opportunity, only as God opened the door. He spoke thus of Paul's metaphor of the open door:

> Its meaning is, that an opportunity of promoting the Gospel had presented itself. For as an opportunity of entering is furnished when the door is opened, so the servants of the Lord make advances when an opportunity is presented. The door is shut, when no prospect of usefulness is held out. Now as, on the door being shut, it becomes us to enter upon a new course, rather than by further efforts to weary ourselves to no purpose by useless labor. So where an opportunity presents itself of edifying, let us consider that by the hand of God a door is opened to us for introducing Christ there, and let us not withhold compliance with so kind an indication from God.[146]

In Calvin's own day, God opened very few doors to other peoples and lands. Only one real opportunity presented itself to Calvin. In 1556, he helped to get a party of colonists together to establish a settlement and Protestant refuge in Brazil. Included in the group were several ministers. One of the purposes of the colony and duties of the ministers was "to indoctrinate the savage and to bring them to the knowledge of their salvation."[147] This door soon closed with failure and martyrdom.

Several decades after Calvin's death, many doors began to open. Staunch Calvinists became some of the first to respond to these opportunities. The understanding that, in God's plan, the time had come for these nations to hear the gospel took on great significance. Andrew Fuller, long after the Protestant missionary movement was begun, expressed this significance:

> If we have any authority from Christ to preach at all ... weare doubtless warrented and obliged, by this commission to embrace any opening in any part of the earth, within our reach to the imparting of the word of life to them that are without it.[148]

Though there is no clear, cut statement of such in Calvin's works, one gets the impression that he concluded that it was not in God's plan for the pagan nations to be entered with the gospel in his day, for the doors did not open. He was confident that in time God would open those doors.

---

[146] Commentary on 1st Corinthians 2:12, *Works,* v. 40, p. 155.
[147] Quoted in G. Baez-Camargo. *op. cit.*, p. 135.
[148] Andrew Fuller, "God's Approbation Necessary to Success," *The Complete Works of Andrew Fuller*, ed. Joseph Belcher (Philadelphia: American Baptist Publication Society, 1845), I, 186.

This concept that mission work was God's work and that it is carried on where he so directs became fundamental to the rise and development of the Protestant missionary movement.

Calvin's Eschatology

A second factor in Calvin's theology which seems to have discouraged missionary activity in his own day was his eschatology. However, this too became a mighty force a few generations later in both arousing a slumbering church and in executing a mission to the heathen.

These two factors are closely related.

> For Calvin predestination and eschatology were two doctrines, neither of which could be expounded without the other. Predestination is the *prius*, eschatology the *posterius* of the Christian faith ...[149]

Calvin was horrified by the apocalyptic fanaticism of his time. He did not preach any such hope of a near end. For Calvin, it was a mistake to think that the gospel would be fulfilled with one mighty stroke. The Kingdom, he insisted, would have a progressive growth. Therefore, Calvin's interpretation of the signs of the time was more a philosophy of church history than an eschatological interpretation of the end.[150]

In Calvin's thought, there were to be three periods between the coming of the Holy Ghost on the day of Pentecost and the final manifestation of Christ. The first was the period of proclamation of the gospel to the whole world. This had been fulfilled before his day. This gracious invitation to salvation was offered to the world by the Apostles, Calvin interpreted each of Christ's commissions to carry the gospel to the world in this light. However, even though this period had been completed (not literally as noted above), still the end did not come.[151]

The second period before the final consummation was the period of the manifestation of the man of sin, the Antichrist. Before the end could come, Calvin avowed, the world would fall into apostasy and the Antichrist would obtain a footing in the church.[152] This did not take place immediately after the ascension of Christ because it was withheld "until the career

---

[149] Torrance, *op. cit.*, p. 57.

[150] Heinrich Quistorp, *Calvin's Doctrine of the Last Things*, trans. Harold Knight (London: Lutterworth Press, 1955), p. 114.

[151] Commentary on Matthew 28: 14, *Works*, v. 33, p. 130.

[152] Commentary on 2nd Thessalonians 2:2-10, *Works*, v. 42, p. 326.

of the gospel could be completed, because a gracious invitation of salvation was first in order."¹⁵³

Calvin believed that his own day was in the period of the worst manifestation of the Antichrist. For he contended that "it is not one individual that is represented under the term Anti-Christ, but one Kingdom which extends itself through many ages."¹⁵⁴

This kingdom had been possessed by Satan "that he might set up a seat of abomination in the midst of God's temple." The apostasy would be so great "that the vicar of Satan would hold supreme power in the church, and would preside there in the place of God."¹⁵⁵

These things, Calvin averred, had been fulfilled in the papacy. He said:

> Seeing then it is certain that the Roman Pontiff has imprudently transferred to himself the most peculiar properties of God and Christ, there cannot be a doubt that he is the leader and standard-bearer of an impious and abominable kingdom.¹⁵⁶

The third period was yet to come. It was to be a period of prosperity and fertility for the church. He said:

> For though the church be now tormented by the malice of men, or even broken by the violence of the billows, and miserably torn in pieces, so as to have no stability in the world, yet we ought always to cherish confident hope ... that the Lord will gather his church.¹⁵⁷

Speaking of the dark and cloudy weather of the days of tribulation he said:

> But as soon as the end shall have been put to those distresses, a day will arrive when the majesty of the Church shall be illustriously displayed.¹⁵⁸

Calvin's eschatology came to be of prime importance in later missionary activity. It was the eschatological context of later Calvinism that held together all the motives and goals of the early missionary enterprise.¹⁵⁹

---

[153] *Ibid.*, p. 333. See also p. 338.
[154] *Ibid.*
[155] *Ibid.*, p. 327.
[156] *The Institutes*, IV, vii, 25.
[157] Commentary on Matthew 24:30, *Works*, v. 33, p. 148.
[158] *Ibid.*, p. 146.
[159] See R. Pierce Beaver, "Eschatology in American Missions," *Basileia*, eds. Jan Hermelink and Hans Jochen Margull (Stuttgart: Evang. Missionsverlag GMBH, 1959), p. 61.

Cotton Mather held to the same type of epochal eschatology as that of Calvin. Mather believed that his day was on the brink of the third epoch.[160] He said:

> It is probable that the Holy Spirit will be again bestowed on the church for its enlargement, in operations similar to those which, in the first ages of Christianity, were granted for its plantation. The Holy Spirit ... will come and abide with us, and render this world like a 'watered garden.'[161]

However, it was Jonathan Edwards, with *An Humble Attempt to Promote Explicit Agreement and Visible Union of God's People in Extraordinary Prayer*, who sponsored a Calvinistic eschatology that was to have permanent influence on Protestant missions.[162] Expounding Zechariah 8:20-22, also one of the great missionary passages in Calvin's commentaries, he said:

> In this chapter we have a prophecy of a future glorious advancement of the church of God ... that last and greatest enlargement and most glorious advancement of the church of God on earth.[163]

The purpose of the *Humble Attempt* was to point out the method by which "this glorious advancement of the church should be brought on." This was to be accomplished

> by great multitudes in different towns and countries taking up a joint resolution, and coming into an express and visible agreement, that they will, by united and extraordinary prayer seek to God that he would manifest himself, and grant the tokens and fruits of his gracious presence.[164]

Therefore one of the contributions of Calvin to the Protestant missionary movement was his sure conviction that God would, in his own time and way, gather his church from the four corners of the world.

---

[160] See Ernst Benz, "Pietist and Puritan Sources of Early Protestant World Missions," *Church History*, v. 20 (1951), pp. 42-50, for discussion of this and for quotations from Mather's unpublished letters.

[161] Cotton Mather, *Essays to Do Good* (a new edition; Boston: Lincoln and Edmands, 1808), p. 135.

[162] R. Pierce Beaver, "American Missionary Motivation Before the Revolution," Reprinted from *Church History*, Vol. XXXI (June, 1962).

[163] *An Humble Amen*, Part II, Section 1.

[164] *Ibid.*, p. 358.

Calvin's Concept of the Glory of God

In reference to Calvin's contributions to the Protestant missionary enterprise, mention must be made of his emphasis on the glory of God. This has been so often discussed that only a brief reference is necessary here. To bring glory to God, in Calvin's thought, was the sole aim and goal of life. Everything the Christian did was to contribute to God's glory.

Quotations could be multiplied both from Calvin and his theological descendants. The fact that the glory of God was the prime motive in early Protestant missions and that it has played such a vital part in later missionary thought and activity can be traced directly to Calvin's theology.

Christian Compassion

Cotton Mather pointed out long ago that it was "a pity for the dark souls" of the Indians that moved John Eliot to begin his mission to them.[165] Christian compassion was second only to the glory of God as a motive in the early American missionary motivation.[166]

The theology of John Calvin is especially rich soil from which Christian compassion can grow. Calvin held that, in spite of the terrible consequences of the sin of Adam, there still remained a remnant of the knowledge of God in man, This remnant knowledge had two sources. First, it was to be found in "the seeds of religion," which God had planted in man's heart.[167] These "seeds" were: the innate sense that there is a deity and the persuasion that this deity ought to be worshipped.[168]

The second source of the remnant of the knowledge of God left to man was the glory of God's manifestation of himself in his creation.[169]

However, without the direct revelation of God's word to man, neither of these was sufficient to bring men to a true and correct knowledge of who God is or of how he should be worshipped. For the knowledge of God to be found in creation, because of man's sin, was able only to establish guilt. It was not sufficient alone to bring man to the true worship of God.[170]

---

[165] Cotton Mather, *Magndia Christi Americana* (Hartford: Andrus Roberts and Burr, 1820), I, 502.
[166] Beaver, "American Missionary Motivation," op. cit., p. 2.
[167] *The Institutes*, I, iv, 1.
[168] Commentary on Romans 1:20, *Works*, v. 3S. p. 27.
[169] *The Institutes*, I, v. 1.
[170] *Ibid.*, I, vi, 1.

As for the seeds of religion, when they sprang up in a man's heart, they were so corrupted by the man's depraved imagination that they produced no "good and fair crop."[171] In fact, as they did spring up, man, ignorant of the true God and correct worship of him, substituted a god created in his own mind and worship perverted by his own imagination.[172]

Therefore, for Calvin, all false religions were a result of man's sin, a vile perversion of that which God had planted in the heart of man. All worship and religious systems were abortive efforts to come to God. Without God's word correct knowledge and worship were impossible.

This meant that there was no ground for hope at all for the heathen, except by the preaching of the gospel. The heathen were, indeed, blind, helpless, and pitiful. To be aware of their condition was enough to move one to compassion and a desire for their salvation.

Thus, Calvin's theology, with its concept of a remnant knowledge of God which was insufficient to bring men to salvation uninstructed by God's special revelation in the word, provided not only the view that God had some point of contact with man, but also became a force in kindling Christian compassion.

III. Conclusions

The conclusions of this study have been evident in the discussion. It is the judgment of this author that Calvin's theology did have the basic principles necessary for a mission theology. Calvin was hindered from doing or saying a great deal about the mission of the church by his theological understanding of the circumstances of his own time and situation. At least two of the factors which, thus, colored his thought and deterred his action, became factors of importance in promoting the world mission of the church in the thought of later Calvinists.

Calvin's concept of the glory of God became a mighty motivating force in later missionary thought and action. His theological understanding of the other religions of the world provided both an entree for the gospel message and a stimulus to Christian compassion.

---

[171] *Ibid.*, I, v, 15.
[172] *Ibid.*

The Missionary Flame of Reformed Theology (1976)

DR. EDMUND P. CLOWNEY

Edmund Prosper Clowney, BA, BTh, MST, DD (1917-2005) was president of Westminster Theological Seminary 1966-1984 as well as Professor of Practical Theology and later the theologian-in-residence of Trinity Presbyterian Church (part of the Presbyterian Church in America) in Charlottesville, Virginia.

Originally published in Harvey M. Conn (Ed.). Theological Perspectives on Church Growth. Presbyterian and Reformed Publ.: Phillipsburg (NJ), 1976. Pp. 127-149. This shorter version was published by Presbyterian Network Vol. 1 (October 1987) pp. 15-22. Printed by permission of the publisher.

The Presbyterian vision of the mission of Christ's church has been condemned because of the doctrine of predestination. This doctrine cuts to the very nerve of missions. John Calvin has been quoted as saying that missions is only the work of God and therefore man has no responsibility in it. This is true, but Calvin then exhorts that man must sow the seed diligently precisely because God will bring the fruit. As this new Association forms, missions will play a critical role in its reason for existence and its growth. What then is the true reformed view of missions?

The whole Bible bears God's own witness that salvation is of the Lord, that apart from the new birth of the Spirit a man cannot even see the kingdom of God, much less enter it. Paul's cry of joy in the predestinating will of God sums up salvation: *"For of him, and through him, and to him, are all things: to whom be glory for ever. Amen"* (Rom. 11:36).

Reformed theologians have not learned enough from the great apostle to the Gentiles, but they and the whole church of the reformation have rightly shared Paul's vision of the triumph of God's electing grace in salvation. What is the missionary flame of reformed theology? What hope does it bring in the confusion and challenge of Christian mission in the last decades of this century?

Three of those themes burn within us as we reflect on the world mission of Christ's church in our day: the glory of God, the grace of God and the kingdom of God, based always on the word of God. There is no separate theology of missions to be added to reformed theology as an appendix, but there is a missionary depth and heart to the very doctrines that are most precious and central to the reformed faith.

The Glory of God – The Goal of Missions

We may begin by looking at the end – the climax of Paul's doxology and the final purpose of God's plan of salvation, and indeed of all things – the glory of God. "For of him, and through him, and unto him are all things. To him be the glory for ever. Amen" (Rom. 11:36).

Paul writes in awe as he reflects on the divine mystery, the theology of the mission of God. No mission problem was more acute for the apostle than his calling to proclaim the gospel among the Gentiles. Daily he bore the reproach of being a renegade, of betraying his own people to curry favour with the heathen. He was driven to reflect on the ways of the Lord as he saw his own people rejecting their Messiah and the Gentiles entering by faith into the number of the true people of God. The answer given to Paul by the inspiration of the Spirit is a magnificent vision of God revealed across the panorama of the history of redemption in the Old Testament. The glory of God is not an abstract principle for the apostle, but the purpose of every day's labour in his mission.

Paul understood that the Lord who chose to be glorified in him is the Lord who works all things according to the counsel of his will. He has not cast off his people whom he foreknew. There remains a remnant according to God's electing grace. Moreover, God's dealings with Israel and the nations in the past hold the clue to his purposes of mercy in the present. When Israel was judged of old, blessing flowed to the Gentiles, not simply in spite of Israel's failure, but as a result of God's judgment upon that failure. In Paul's day, when branches were broken off the olive tree of the people of God, the Gentiles as wild olive branches were grafted in.

But the story cannot end there. God is able to graft in again the natural branches and Paul ministers the gospel to the Gentiles in the fervent hope that as they enter into the blessings of the kingdom of God, the sons of the kingdom may be aroused to jealousy and come streaming in. "For as ye in time past were disobedient to God, but now have obtained mercy by their disobedience, even so have these also now been disobedient to God, that by the mercy shown to you they also may now obtain mercy" (Rom. 11:30).

These are the profound meditations that move Paul to adore the sovereign grace of God's plan of salvation. In his missionary task he is leading in the worship of God. Gentiles who had been barred from God's altar are now led in by the apostle, to offer not the sacrifices of bulls and goats, but their bodies as living sacrifices in the spiritual temple composed of living stones (cf. Rom. 12:1,2; Eph. 2:22; 1 Pet. 2:5). The songs of Gentile praise ascend to God as the prophets and psalmists had promised (Rom. 15:9-12; Ps. 18:49; Deut. 32:43; Isa. 11:10), and Paul, the apostle to the Gentiles, ministers in this great service of worship by the preaching of the gospel.

Further, Paul's gospel ministry is drawn into the most immediate union and fellowship with the Lord he serves. Christ himself is a minister of the circumcision, not in the sense that he ministers to them but in the sense that he takes up their ministry. The goal and fulfillment of the saving mission of the Son is that the name of the Father might be glorified in the eternal song of the redeemed (Rev. 15:3,4).

Now, we may ask, what practical result does this exalted aim have in dealing with the concrete problems of missions today? Does it change our perspective with reference to church growth? Does it offer guidance on the demand for a moratorium on North American and European missionaries? Does it direct us with respect to political implications of the missionary message?

In our efforts to strengthen the cause of missions are we aiming at God's glory or at worldly success? Jesus ministered to great multitudes, but they were progressively alienated by his message and they left him to die alone on the cross – that death in which God was supremely glorified. The doxological goal of missions must serve first the purpose of heart searching, but we dare not ignore its implications for the issues in debate.

On the one hand there is the sobering realization that God's name is vindicated and his glory revealed in his judgments as well as in his blessings. Paul clearly reflects on this, not only in Romans 9-11 but in the whole epistle. The revelation of the righteousness of God preached by Paul has two sides – the justifying righteousness that is the gift of God's grace through faith in Jesus Christ and the retributive righteousness that is God's judgment, also given in Jesus Christ (Rom. 1:17,18). Jesus came to Nazareth to preach, not because he judged Nazarenes to be 'winnable', but because the glory of God demanded that the gospel declaration be made in the town where Christ was brought up. Paul's repeated preaching in the synagogues was not a policy pragmatically determined by its success nor was it a means of recruiting Gentile proselytes of Judaism to serve as the nucleus for a Christian congregation. Rather Paul presented the gospel to the Jew first in order to honour the promises and plan of God, even if the result was a witness against the rebellious to be remembered in the day of judgment (Acts 13:46-47).

On the other hand, Jesus declares that His Father is glorified when His disciples bear much fruit (John 15:8). To seek the glory of the Father is to have fellowship in the mission of the Son, who could rejoice that the mysteries of the kingdom were hidden from the wise and prudent and revealed unto babes, for so it was well pleasing in the Father's sight (Luke 10:21). But that same Son of God pointed his disciples to the harvest and called them to be fishers of men only after he had filled their nets with fish. Men may prefer a simpler or more one-sided motivation, but Jesus knew the awesome glory of his Father's sovereign grace and reflected that glory in all of his ministry.

The doxological mode in missions goes beyond a certain optimism in the expectation of response. Rather it praises God for the assurance of the gathering in of all the sheep of Christ to the eternal fold. The Psalms celebrate God's triumphs, past, present and future, and summon the nations to join in the song. "But ye are an elect race, a royal priesthood, a holy nation, a people for God's own possession, that he may show forth the excellencies of him who called you out of darkness into his marvelous light" (1 Pet. 2:9). In a world of death, the church sings the joy of Christ's resurrection; in a world of despair, the church sings the sure hope of Christ's return.

The Grace of God the Source of Missions

The doxology of missions is a rainbow of praise arching over the throne of God. The end of that rainbow is the glory of God but its beginning is the grace of God. If all things are unto him, all things must also be of mm. All is to God's glory because all is of God's grace.

The Bible records, not man's search for God, but God's search for man. The initiative in salvation is always his. God calls to Adam in the garden after man's first transgression, and God seeks for worshipers in the whole history of redemption. Jesus grounds his final mission in his Father's electing purpose. He has other sheep that are not of this fold, and them also he must bring. They are his sheep because they have been given him of the Father; they are his because he gives his life for them. He must and will bring them, for they will hear his voice (John 10:27). God's choosing of his sheep and God's drawing diem to his Son (John 6:44) are the basis in Christ's own understanding for his death on the cross and his lifting up to glory.

The high mystery of God's choosing of his own in Christ before the foundation of the world (Eph. 1:3-5) silences us with wonder. This Scriptural doctrine is subject to constant and railing attack by those who judge it with the mind of the flesh. Sadly, it is sometimes defended in a strangely similar manner. But God has a purpose in drawing aside the veil, in permitting us to hear the very prayer of the Son to the Father. The purpose is that we might not glory in ourselves but in the mercy of our saving God. Significantly, the word of God does not present God's electing grace as a barrier but as an encouragement to missions. When Paul is tempted to leave Corinth in discouragement, Christ appears to him in a vision to inform him "I have much people in this city" (Acts 18:10). Christ's other sheep were not at that point evident to the apostle, but the fact that the Lord's elect were to be found in that seamy and sophisticated seaport gave Paul assurance in continuing his mission. Because Christ's grace is sovereign, it is sure.

Dealing with those who refuse the gospel is one thing. The time comes when the heralds of the kingdom must shake off the dust of their feet against those who will not hear the message (Matt. 10:14). But precisely because God's election is gracious and sure we dare not categorize populations as devoid of God's elect. To be sure, advocates of church growth have not proposed in principle that we abandon resistant populations, but only that we put a higher priority on efforts to reach receptive populations. Nevertheless, to suggest that the presence or absence of God's elect in a people can be determined by sample receptivity to the gospel overlooks the biblical emphasis on the hiddenness of God's elect. Indeed, even receptivity may be misleading. Because Jesus knew men's hearts he did not trust himself to the enthusiasm of the crowd that professed to believe in his name (John 2:23-25).

The Calvinistic preacher who told William Carey that if God willed the conversion of the heathen he could do it without Carey's help gives us a dismaying example of how to abuse a biblical truth by an unbiblical application. The biblical doctrine of election cannot be used to excuse our disobedience to Christ's missionary command. Neither can it be used to provide heavenly endorsement for our strategic planning. It remains as God's witness to his sovereignty; it humbles our pride and offers another assurance – the assurance of the triumph of God's will and God's way in the full ingathering of his harvest.

But if church growth writers in their zeal for evangelism have sometimes been tempted to computerize God's election they have rightly resisted the universalism of contemporary theology which would vaporize God's election by making it unquantifiable. The universalist position is persuasively argued by those who maintain that the election church is the servant church. It does not differ from the world by being a company of the saved; rather, it differs not in status but in function. The church is chosen to announce to the world that every man is elect in Christ.

Missionary as this theology may appear in terminology, it destroys the real meaning of missionary endeavour. God's calling is not just to service but to sonship. God redeems his people from bondage in Egypt that he might bear them on eagle's wings to himself (Exod. 19:4). The mystery of God's electing love cannot be explained in terms of some ulterior motive. God tells Israel that he has not chosen them because they are more in number than other people. No, he has set his love upon them because ... he loves them! (Deut. 7:7, 8). God has set his people upon his heart, written their names upon his hands, rejoiced over them as a bridegroom over a bride. He chooses them not simply or finally to use them, but to possess them -that he might be their God and they his people.

God's free grace, God's sure grace, is the foundation of salvation. God's grace not only has a fixed point of origin with him, it also has a fullness that is of him: the fountain of grace becomes a river of mercy. That is, God not only plans salvation in electing grace; he also executes his plan. In the fullness of time God's grace triumphs in a way that surpasses anything we could imagine. At the cross of Calvary God gave his only begotten Son to accomplish the mission of his love.

Apostolic mission theology preaches Christ crucified. Contemporary theologies of mission must be tested by that apostolic-zeal. The triumph of God's grace at the cross is still the despair of every humanist. To the Jews the cross was a stumbling block, and to the Greeks, foolishness (1 Cor. 1:23). How can the arrest, torture and death of Jesus be regarded as God's victory rather than his defeat? Only when the cross is seen as God sees it and as Jesus takes it. Paul preached Christ crucified as the sin-bearer, the one who was made to be sin for us that we might be made the righteousness of God in him (11 Cor. 5:21). Only if sin, not suffering, is the fundamental human problem does the cross bring salvation.

At the cross the measure of God's love is revealed in the price that the Father paid. All the love of the Father through eternity is given to his beloved Son (John 1:18). The Father so loves the Son that he gives him the world (John 3:35). Nothing that the Son asks of the Father will be refused. Yet in the mystery of God's saving love he gives his only begotten Son for a sinful world. Confused and overwhelmed by that mystery (can the Father love sinners more than his Son?) we can only say that grace means that

God loves guilty sinners more than himself. The Son of the Father willingly gives himself, laying down his life for his friends. Yet the Father also gives his Son – and if he delivers him up for us all, "how shall he not with him also freely give us all things?" (Rom. 8:32).

When the gospel is secularized or politicized it is simply destroyed. The Lord of love calls us to take up our cross and follow him. Those who call men in Christ's name must promise what he promised: persecution, hatred, family strife, suffering – and eternal life.

Jesus said, "And I, if I be lifted up, will draw all men unto me" (John 12:32). John tells us that the 'lifting up' of which Jesus spoke was the lifting up of the cross, the lifting up of his death. Our zeal to reach the lost in our generation springs from the conviction that men are eternally lost without Christ, and that the crucified and risen Christ draws them by faith to himself.

The crucified, risen, ascended Christ is the Lord who sends his disciples to the nations. The Spirit he gives is the inbreathing of his own risen life and power (John 20:22). Because Christ's victory is accomplished, the fulfillment of his purposes is not only assured in the future but realized in the present. Just as the Christian's victory over sin is gained by appropriating the finished work of Christ – because we are raised with Christ, we walk in newness of life – so, too, the mission of the church is fulfilled by faith as the church recognizes and acts upon the reality of Christ's present authority and dominion in heaven and earth. "Go ye therefore, and make disciples of all nations ..." The gift of the Spirit as the promise of the Father not only provides power for witnessing but also seals the actuality of the fulfillment of God's purpose in extending saving blessing to the nations.

The doctrines of grace are not only the key to the sanctification of the believer, they are the key to the evangelization of the world. That is because grace and faith forever go together. We triumph over the bondage of sin in our lives as we recognize what Jesus Christ has accomplished in our place on the cross and on the throne; we triumph over the bondage of sin in the world as we recognize that what Jesus Christ has accomplished on the cross and the throne redeems all his people from every nation. The distorting of this truth in the unbiblical universalism of 'ecumenical' theology must not blind us to the universalism of Christ's resurrection triumph. Paul's opponents argued that his doctrine of justification by faith would lead to license rather than holiness. Paul knew better. Faith reckons to be true what is true: when Christ died, we died; when he rose, we rose. So, too, Paul's doctrines have been seen as a threat to missions. But we should know better. Reformed missions reckons that to be true which is true. Christ has all power in heaven and earth, and nothing can separate him from those the Father has given him. He sends us to summon those whom he will bring – those other sheep who must be brought to the one flock, the one Shepherd.

But what is the attitude of those who, like Jesus, understand the Father's heart of compassion and share his joy over one sinner that repents? Those who know the meaning of grace will not only join in the feast for sinners, they will join in the search for sinners. Mission is demanded by Jesus' revelation of the love of the Father for sinners.

The Kingdom of God the Power of Missions

The glory of God, the grace of God, the kingdom' of God – in the New Testament these themes are interwoven in the fabric of the gospel. The biblical concept of the kingdom centers upon the divine King. It means the rule of God rather than the realm of God. Jewish nationalism had appropriated the Old Testament promises as a divine charter for the kingdom of Israel; Jesus restored the theocentric meaning of Old Testament eschatology by proclaiming the kingdom of God.

The whole history of salvation in the Old Testament declares that salvation is of the Lord. Ernst Bloch, the Marxist philosopher of the future, canonizes the category of the *'possible'* to quicken human hope. But God reveals Himself as the God of the *'impossible'*. Again and again the situation of the people of God becomes so desperate that deliverance is no longer possible. It is then that God saves – when Israel is in helpless slavery in Egypt, or pinned against the Red Sea by the chariots of Pharaoh, or crushed by the Midianites in the land of the promise. Indeed, God's great promises of the future are set against Ezekiel's vision in captivity – dead, dry bones filling the valley.

Mission theology is kingdom theology; but kingdom as defined by the person, the work, the calling, of the King. Christ's kingship and the program of his kingdom are foolishness to the kingdoms of this world.

Christ's royal victory is final and ultimate and therefore spiritual. He would not lead a Jewish war of liberation against the Romans but he went alone to the cross to conquer Satan – by dying on the cross! Christ's final victory is radically spiritual. Judged by worldly standards the cross is Satan's final victory and Christ's defeat. But in reality Satan is crushed by the atoning death of God's Son.

Christ is victorious. He has ascended and now rules in the power of his kingdom. The purposes of his kingdom are fulfilled on earth as men are brought back from darkness to become sons of light. Yet Christ will come again and after the judgment will form a new earth where perfect righteousness will be joined to perfect blessedness.

Missions requires us to understand the present and the future of Christ's kingdom design. Because Christ not only brings salvation but is salvation we may never conceive of salvation apart from the relation of persons to him. Liberation cannot define salvation, for biblical salvation does not consist in what we are delivered from but in whom we are delivered to. In uniting us to himself Christ does not promise that we will be delivered from suffering in this life. To the contrary, he calls us to his fellowship of suffering. Neither does Christ call us to bear the sword to bring in his kingdom by executing judgment in his name. The day of judgment will come soon enough, and God will avenge every injustice and judge every transgression.

Yet through suffering and forebearing, we wait for God's judgment; we do not enforce our own. We nevertheless participate in Christ's spiritual triumph – not by weapons of the flesh but by those weapons that are mighty before God to the casting down of strongholds and everything that is exalted against Christ (11 Cor. 10:4-6).

Church growth is kingdom growth by the power of the Holy Spirit. The advocates of church growth have rightly recognized that the secularizing of the gospel in the theology of liberation changes the meaning of salvation and thereby destroys the gospel. That insight needs to be renewed and deepened. The theology of secular hope has been set before the church ever since Satan offered Jesus the kingdoms of this world without the cross. But the dynamic of biblical church growth flows from the nature of Christ's kingdom.

Church growth writers have often reminded us of the bonds of human community, warning against ignoring these ties as we would claim men and women for the kingdom. The apostle Paul was sensitive to the customs and cultures of Jews and Greeks; he was willing to conform to these traditions, to bring himself in bondage to diem, as he says (1 Cor. 9:19,22), in order that he might win those who followed diem. But Paul's own position was one of freedom; his voluntary conformity did not represent abandonment of his liberty in Christ, only a willingness to serve Christ in the gospel (v.23). The liberty in which Paul serves is the liberty of a citizen of heaven, a new creature in Christ Jesus.

The gospel brings men into that liberty and forges a new fellowship, the fellowship of the Spirit-filled people of God. Again the key to our understanding is in Jesus Christ himself. The true circumcision are the people who worship by the Spirit of God, glory in Christ Jesus and have no confidence in flesh (Phil. 3:3). The ties that join those born of the Spirit to Jesus Christ free diem from the dominion of any earthly structure. Christians conform to social structures for the Lord's sake, but that very qualification is the sign of their deepest freedom.

The Christian's ultimate loyalty belongs to Jesus Christ alone. He is not a nationalist of an earthly state who finds in Christ the religious resources to enable him to fulfill his calling as a political being. He is a citizen of the heavenly polis who sustains his civic responsibilities here as a stranger and an alien; he has no abiding city but seeks after that which is to come (Heb. 13:14).

Through centuries of conflict the church has learned (we may hope!) the biblical lesson that the community of the people of God cannot be identified with the political state. But now the church must learn that it has an identity, a 'theopolitical' form of the community of Christ's kingdom in the world. Those who were once aliens, strangers from the covenant and the commonwealth, are now fellow-citizens with the Old Testament saints, members of the commonwealth, God's covenant people.

The form that the church takes cannot be an indifferent matter. The Holy Spirit who filled and fills the new people of God directed Christ's apostles as they established his assembly in the world. The New Testament provides form with freedom; among the 'all things' of Christ's commandments to be taught to the nations is the pattern of fellowship in worship, edification and witness that Christ has appointed for his people. Church growth is church growth – the building up in the world of the new people of God according to the word and will of the Spirit.

Here is an urgent concern. If our growing understanding of sociology outstrips our grasp of biblical theology, we may seek to build Christ's church from the wrong blueprints. Concretely, it is evident that in our efforts to respect sociological structures in evangelism we may unintentionally deny the biblical doctrines of the unity and catholicity of Christ's church. Christ's teachings are an offense to the mind of the natural man, and Christ's community is a rebuke to the tribalism, ethnocentricism and prejudice of the world's social orders.

Jesus predicts that the gospel will divide men, cutting between husband and wife, parent and child, brother and sister. More than that, Christ demands of everyone who follows him that he write off in advance every other tie: "If any man cometh unto me, and hateth not his own father, and mother, and wife and children, and brethren and sisters, yea and his own life also, he cannot be my disciple" (Luke 14:26).

The exclusive bonds that unite us to Christ bind us together in the body of Christ. The unity of that fellowship must be proclaimed as part of the gospel and manifested if the church is to be presented as a pure virgin to Christ. The point at which human barriers are surmounted is the point at which a believer is joined to Christ and to his people. The sacrament of baptism does not seal the union of the believer with Paul, Cephas or Apollos but with Christ. Christ is not divided and we cannot sanctify in his name the social barriers that wall up the Babylons of human pride.

The church can be a city set on a hill that cannot be hid only as it manifests in its life before the world the transforming reality of the community of the Holy Spirit. The church reaches out to every strata and segment of human society: Peter is called as an apostle to the Jews and Paul to the Gentiles. But if Peter breaks church fellowship to accomodate himself to Jewish prejudice, he must receive deserved rebuke (Gal. 2:14). If the life of the new community is divided by the barriers of the old, the power of the gospel and of the kingdom of Christ is denied.

How does all of this affect the Presbyterian Association in England? This Association is not just a vision to say that a denomination got lost in the shuffle of British history and ought to be put back into the picture. No, what is it that is really wanted? You may say a more biblical structure of church government; to that I say, 'Amen!' but that is not all. It is biblical doctrine subject to the word of God. In talking to the Ephesian elders, Paul said that he held nothing back in preaching the gospel. The doctrines that Paul taught were not always popular doctrines. Paul could have preached only portions of that doctrine, but that would not have made a strong church, a church that would hear and heed the preaching of all the fullness of the doctrine that the word of God teaches. In the world in which we live, we need to be drawn back to hear the word of our Creator-God, the Redeemer-God who is also the Saviour-God. The vision of this Association should not be simply to propogate a denomination or to replicate churches where people have enjoyed fellowship in the past. The mission of this Association must be to be truly biblical in the fullness of the teaching of the word of God, to exalt the grace of God and to exalt the kingship of Jesus Christ as the only Saviour in the power of the Holy Spirit. The glory of

God, the grace of God, the kingdom of God all based on the word of God – these are the great themes of reformed theology, and these are the themes that must be central for the theology of missions. This is not strange, of course, for reformed theology rightly perceived the central themes of Scripture. The theology of Scripture is missionary theology, for the Son of Man came to seek and to save that which was lost. All the themes of Scriptural theology center upon the Lord the Saviour. In the confusion of the contemporary world and the crisis of the world mission of the church, biblical theology brings us to the Lord himself: "This is my Son, my chosen: hear ye him" (Luke 9:35).

Calvin's Missionary Thought and Practice (1990)

MARK POGSON

Mark Pogson (1963*). He was born in the UK and took a four year course at Lebanon Missionary Bible College (later Northumbria Bible College) and completed a London University BD (Hons.) external degree. After a period of practical training in the UK, he studied at Government College, Lahore and the Punjab University, Urdu. In Pakistan he worked with students and with the Cathedral Church, Lahore where he was ordained into the Church of Pakistan. After serving for seventeen years in Pakistan, he moved to Switzerland where he is now based, with his wife and three children.

Originally published in Banner of Truth Issue 318, March 1990, 18-21. Reprinted by permission of the Banner of Truth Trust, Edinburgh (www.banneroftruth.co.uk).

It is all too often said that John Calvin had no interest in mission. Such statements are normally made out of an unintentional ignorance, a popular myth being repeated. In some cases, however, it is because the standard of judgment is not entirely fair, it being based on modern missionary activity or organisation. D. H-W. Gensichen has asked valid questions: 'Could it be that the modern form and structure of missionary activity was not the only possible norm for missions? Should not modern missionary conceptions and practices be examined in the light of the Reformation, rather than the attitude of the Reformers in the light of what had come to be considered as the only legitimate standard for missions?'[173] These are valid questions and while we shall not attempt to answer them directly, they should nonetheless be kept in mind.

In Calvin's thought the church assumes an importance which is often not to be found in today's understanding of mission.[174] He writes of the church: 'There is no other way to enter into life unless this mother conceive us in

---

[173] D. H-W. Gensichen, 'Were the Reformers Indifferent to Mission?' in *History's Lessons for Tomorrow's Mission* (World Student Christian Federation; Geneva, n.d.), 119-127.

[174] Cf. Wm. Clark, *The Conception of the Mission of the Church in Early Reformed Theology with special reference to Calvin's Theology and Practice in Geneva* (unpublished dissertation, New College, Edinburgh 1928).

her womb, give us birth, nourish us at her breast, and lastly, unless she keep us under her care and guidance until, putting off mortal flesh, we become like the angels [*Matt.* 22:30]. Our weakness does not allow us to be dismissed from her school until we have been pupils all our lives. Furthermore, away from her bosom one cannot hope for any forgiveness of sins or any salvation ...'[175]

There are for Calvin two marks of the church, the Word of God purely preached and heard, and the sacraments administered according to Christ's Institution. These signs of the true church are not only evidence of its existence, but duties and aims of the church. They are in effect the primary mission of the church. In Calvin's understanding the church cannot exist without being involved in local mission.

Within a settled church, pastors and teachers are essential 'to keep doctrine whole and pure',[176] while apostles and prophets have no place, for as Calvin explains: 'The nature of the apostles' function is clear from this command: "Go preach the gospel to every creature" [*Mark* 16:15]. No set limits are allotted to them, but the whole earth is assigned to them to bring into obedience to Christ, in order that by spreading the gospel wherever they can among the nations, they may raise up his kingdom everywhere.[177]

Calvin goes on with his definition in this way: '"Evangelists" I take to be those who, although lower in rank than apostles, were next to them in office and functioned in their place.'[178] Calvin believed there were evangelists in his own day, as the following words show: 'I do not deny that the Lord has sometimes at a later period raised up apostles, or at least evangelists in their place, *as has happened in our own day!*[179] (Our italics.)

The church, then (with its various offices), had a vital place in the Reformer's missionary thought.

Calvin also stressed the responsibility which the individual member of the church had for mission. He did this by emphasising the Christian's concern for his neighbour. This neighbour included the heathen man or woman: 'Christ has shown in the parable of the Samaritan that the term "neighbour" includes even the most remote person' [*Luke* 10:36].[180] 'We

---

[175] *Institutes*, IV:I:4.
[176] *Institutes*, IV:III:4.
[177] *Ibid.*, IV:III:4.
[178] *Ibid.*, IV:III:4.
[179] *Ibid.*, IV:III:4.
[180] *Ibid.*, II:VIII:55.

ought to embrace the whole human race without exception in a single feeling of love.'[181] The Christian has a responsibility to pray for 'all men who dwell on earth'.[182] 'When we think and pray only about our own needs and do not remember those of our neighbours, we cut ourselves loose from the body of Christ Jesus our Lord, and how can we then be joined to God?'[183] In a sermon on I Timothy he says: 'We must not only pray for believers which are our brethren already, but for them that are very far off, as the poor unbelievers: although there seem to be a great distance and thick wall between both, yet must we notwithstanding have pity of their destruction, to the end that we may pray to God, that he should draw them unto him. Seeing it is so, let us mark, how awful a thing it is for every man to be taken up with his own interests and have no care and regard to his neighbours.'[184]

Calvin made it plain, then, that mission was to be the concern not only of the church as a whole, but also of each individual member.

The primary motive for mission in Calvin's thought was the glory of God. In his exposition of the Lord's Prayer he writes: 'We should wish God to have the honour he deserves.'[185] 'If holiness is associated with God's name where separated from all other names, it breathes pure glory; here we are bidden to request not only that God vindicate his sacred name of all contempt and dishonour, but also that he subdue the whole race of mankind to reverence for it.'[186] He concludes the first three petitions of the prayer with these words: 'In making these requests we are to keep God's glory alone before our eyes.'[187]

A further motive for mission was that of compassion for one's neighbour. These motives are found side by side in the following quotation from a sermon on Deuteronomy 33:18-19: 'We must as much as in us lieth, endeavour to draw all men on the earth to God, that all men may fear him and worship him with one accord. And indeed if we have any kindness in us, if we see that men go to destruction till God has them under his obedience: ought we not be moved with pity to draw the poor souls out of hell,

---

[181] *Ibid.*, II:VIII:55.

[182] *Ibid.*, III:XX:38.

[183] Quoted in S. M. Zwemer, 'Calvinism and the Missionary Enterprise', *Theology Today* (1950) 206-216.

[184] Sermon on 1 Tim. 2:1, 2.

[185] *Institutes*, III:XX:41.

[186] *Ibid.*, III:XX:41.

[187] *Ibid.*, III:XX:43.

and to bring them into the way of salvation? Again on the other side, if we know that God is our Father, should we be not desirous to have him known to be such of all men? And if we cannot find in our hearts that all creatures should do him homage, is it not a sign that we have no great regard for his honour?'

Any account of Calvin's practice in mission would be incomplete if reference to the practical problems of his time were omitted. But space does not allow. Let it suffice to say, that despite great practical problems Calvin still evidenced an obvious zeal for mission. Before 1555 only a few men had been sent from Geneva to other countries 'usually by Calvin himself.'[188] In April 1555, the first formal mission was sent to Piedmont. Then later in the year a mission was dispatched to France. 'In 1556 three more missionaries went out, one to Bourges and two to French colonies that were to be organised on an island off Rio de Janeiro (Brazil). Calvin, who was attending the Frankfort fair in Germany when the 1556 missions were sent, was told of them in a letter from Nicolas des Gallars, the pastor functioning as a substitute Moderator while Calvin was absent.'[189] The latter attempt to found a settlement in Brazil and make the colony a base for mission work among the Topinombou Indians came to a sad end when three of the Calvinists were martyred in 1558.[190] 'By 1557 the sending of emissaries to France had become a regular part of the Geneva Company's business. In that year eleven churches received pastors; in 1558, twenty-two; in 1559, thirty-two; and in 1560, 1561 and 1562, twelve churches a year. (These figures, taken from the official Registers of the Company, do not reveal that 1561 was actually the peak year, when, as we learn from records supplementing the Registers, more than one hundred men were sent out.)'[191] This record does not take into account the direct influence of Calvin's sermons and correspondence upon men who read them. It cannot be doubted that many of these, because of his influence, were keen for mission, certainly the later Calvinists were.[192]

---

[188] R. M. Kingdom: *Geneva and the Coming of the Wars of Religion in France 1555-1563* (1956) p. 2.

[189] *Ibid.*, p. 2.

[190] Cf. W. Schlatter, 'Kalvin und die Mission', *Evangelisches Missions-Magazin,* 53 (1909) 333ff.

[191] Kingdom (p. 2).

[192] Cf. Van den Berg, 'Calvin's Missionary Message; some remarks about the relation between Calvinism and Missions', *The Evangelical Quarterly* (July 1950), pp. 174-187.

In giving the above account of Calvin's missionary thought and practice, we would not like to overstate *man's* activity. The Reformer, however, saw no contradiction in the view 'that the kingdom of Christ is neither to be advanced nor maintained by the industry of men, but this is the work of God alone; for believers are taught to rest solely on his blessing'.[193]

The above is not just a positive statement of Calvin's missionary thought and practice. It is also a challenge to let our present understanding of mission be enriched by the contribution of a theologian of the past so that the entire world 'should be the theatre of his glory by the spread of his gospel'.[194]

---

[193] Quoted in Warneck, *Outline of a History of Protestant Missions 8* (ed. by George Robson, Edinburgh, 1901), p. 20.

[194] Quoted in Zwemer, *op. cit.*

The Theology of William Carey (1993)

BRUCE J. NICHOLLS

Bruce J. Nicholls was a career missionary in India working in theological education and in pastoral ministry with the Church of North India, than executive secretary of the World Evangelical Fellowship (now World Evangelical Alliance) Theological Commission 1968-1988 and Editor of the Evangelical Review of Theology for 18 years and is now Editor of the Asia Bible Commentary series and seen as an outstanding elder statesman in missiology and theological education all over the world. He authored and edited dozens of books in his long career.

World Evangelical Fellowship. Theological Commission. (2000, 1993). Vol. 17: Evangelical review of theology: Volume 17. "A digest of articles and book reviews selected from publications worldwide for an international readership, interpreting the Christian faith for contemporary living." (electronic ed.). Logos Library System; Evangelical Review of Theology (369). Carlisle, Cumbria, UK: Paternoster Periodicals.

Little has been written on Carey's theology. It was more implicit in his correspondence and work than explicit. Except for the Enquiry which Carey published before he left England, we have little to guide us. In this article I seek to probe five areas of Carey's theological concerns. More research is needed if we are to understand better Carey's motivation, his priorities and his message.

Editor of the ERT

William Carey's involvement in evangelism, church planting, language learning, translation work and institutional building left him no time for theological reflection. His gifts lay in linguistics and administration and not in theological formulations. No record of his sermons remains. The *Enquiry*, his letters, articles in the *Friends of India* and *Samarchar Darpan* and the numerous biographies are the only source materials for understanding and evaluating his theology. It is clear that his general theological outlook took shape during his youthful years in England prior to sailing to India in June 1793. He was caught up in the impact of the first Evangelical Awakening of the 18th Century which impacted the lives of the working class people in rural England as well as in the towns and cities. John Wesley was at the heart of this movement. Its theological origins were in the Protestant Reformation but spiritually it was in the succession of the mystical and ascetic traditions of the medieval and early Church, the Puritan revival of the 17th Century and the pietism of the Moravian movement in Germany. John Wesley's theology led him in the direction of Arminianism while Whitefield and Jonathan Edwards in the American colonies were more influenced by the Puritan Calvinism. His own particular group of dissenters, the Particular Baptists were Calvinistic while the General Baptists were more moderate. Carey was caught in this tension, as is clearly evident in the *Enquiry*.

Biblical Foundations

The Bible was the common manifesto of the Evangelical Movement and it became the controlling factor in Carey's life. His conversion experience which began under the influence of his fellow apprentice journeyman shoemaker John Warr in his 17th year, was the turning point of his life. He left the Church of England and was baptized as a believer four years later (7th October 1783). During this period Carey's theology was shaped by his close association with the leaders of the Northamptonshire Baptist churches and in particular by John Ryland, Andrew Fuller, Robert Hall Snr. and John Sutcliff. Carey became 'an ardent student of the scriptures'. From a New Testament commentary on the shelf of his employer Clarke Nichols, Carey was introduced to the Greek text. Thereafter Latin, Greek and later Hebrew, became the centre of his studies and the foundation for his later translation work. He studied the Bible with implicit trust in its truthfulness, reliability and authority all of which characterized the Evangelical Movement. For Carey the Bible was the word of God to be loved and obeyed. His passion was to be a preacher of the Word.

Carey's hermeneutical principles were literalistic and uncomplicated. He took literally the commands of Jesus and expected God to fulfil his promises. The Bible was his sole means of knowing the truth of God and the way of salvation. An example of his proof text method was his use of the Great Commission of Matthew 28:18-20 in his pioneering booklet *An Enquiry into the Obligations of Christians to use means for the Conversion of the Heathens*. David Bosch notes that Carey 'based his entire case on the argument that the Great Commission (Matthew 28:18-20) was as valid in his day (1792) as it had been in the days of the Apostle'.[195] On this basis

---

[195] David J. Bosch 'The How and Why of a True Biblical Foundation for Missions', Zending op weg Naor de Toekopmst (Kampen U.J.H. Kok. 1978), p. 34.

Carey stressed the obligation of Christians to proclaim the gospel worldwide and to use every means possible for the conversion of those who heard it.

Carey followed the expository model of the Baptist preachers of Northamptonshire. This can be seen in his so-called 'Deathless Sermon' preached to seventeen pastors of the Northamptonshire Association of Baptist churches on the 31st May 1792. With graphic illustrations on enlarging the tent Carey expounded Isaiah 54:v2, dividing the text into his two memorable principles, 'Expect great things from God. Attempt great things for God.'[196] This sermon proved to be a milestone in Carey's appeal to Andrew Fuller and others to form the Baptist Missionary Society, an event which took place four months later. The sermon reflects Carey's confidence in the sovereignty of God and his love for the world and his own certainty of the need to use every possible means to proclaim the gospel worldwide.

Throughout Carey's forty years of missionary service in India he was motivated by this consuming passion to translate the Bible into as many languages of the common people as possible so that all might hear and believe the gospel. Like other evangelicals of his day Carey believed that unless the heathen hear the gospel they are eternally lost; a conviction that continues to motivate evangelical missionaries today.

Christology for Mission

William Carey's theology was clearly Christocentric. Jesus Christ was the centre of his spiritual pilgrimage and the only hope for the salvation of the world. Having imbibed the piety of Moravian missionaries and having been inspired by the prayer life of David Brainerd (missionary to the American Indians), Carey was disciplined in maintaining his daily early morning devotional life of Bible reading and prayer. He often talked aloud with his Lord as he walked in his garden. Carey sought to bring every thought captive to Christ and he refused to speculate beyond the revelations of scripture. It cannot be over-emphasized that the cross was the centre of his preaching whether in the church or in the bazaar. He believed Christ's death was a substitutionary atonement for sin. In preaching the cross, Carey called upon his hearers to repent of their sins and put their trust in Christ for salvation alone. He had little confidence in himself and

---

[196] A. Christopher Smith has argued that the words 'from God' and 'for God' were not part of the original sermon. See A. Christopher Smith, 'The Spirit and Letter of Carey's Catalytic Watchword' (*Baptist Quarterly* 33, January 1990, 266-37).

through the stress and sorrows of his missionary career Carey turned again and again to his Lord for solace and strength. This is beautifully illustrated in the epitaph he prepared for himself, taken from the first couplet of Isaac Watt's hymn:

A guilty weak and helpless worm,
On thy kind arms I fall.
Be thou my strength and righteousness
My Jesus – and my all.

This moving testimony reveals Carey's humble piety, his Christ-centred hope and his trust in the sovereign grace of God. His sense of personal unworthiness before the righteousness of God sheds light on his Calvinistic faith. There is no doubt that his moderate Calvinism had sustained him through the crises in his life. It is also reflected in his love of nature as the handiwork of the Creator. He does not appear to have given very much emphasis to the work of the Holy Spirit as in the later Missionary Movement. Carey was a man of the Book and of his Lord, Jesus Christ.

In these early years, Carey the pastor felt deeply the conflict among his contemporaries concerning the sovereignty of God and human obligation to proclaim the gospel. The alleged comment of John Ryland Sr. at a ministerial fraternal of the Baptist Association about 1786 hurt him deeply. In response to his questioning as to whether the Lord's command was still binding, Ryland is supposed to have replied 'Young man, sit down. When God pleases to convert the heathen, he'll do it without consulting you or me. Besides, there must be another Pentecostal gift of tongues!'[197]

The Gathered Church

William Carey's theology was not only Christ-centred; it was Church-centred. Having left the Anglican Church of his fathers, Carey became an enthusiastic Dissenter and a committed member of the Particular Baptist church in which he had been baptized. Following Carey's baptism at the age of 22, John Sutcliff, the pastor at Olney, recognized his gifts and encouraged him to seek recognition as a lay preacher. This led to his being called as pastor to the village church of Moulton in 1787 and two years later to the Harvey Lane Baptist Church at Leicester. His six years in pastoral ministry, much of which was spent in controversy owing to the low

---

[197] There is no proof that these were Ryland's exact words. His son, John Ryland Jnr. denied the authenticity of the anecdote. See Iain H. Murray, 'William Carey: Climbing the Rainbow', *The Banner of Truth*, October 1992, p. 21, n. 1.

level of spirituality in his churches, laid the foundation of his Church-centred understanding of mission. Here too he was influenced by his friends John Ryland, Andrew Fuller and John Sutcliff. It was to be expected that the missionary structure Carey pioneered was a denominational one.

Carey's Doctrine of the Church followed the 'primitive' New Testament model which stressed preaching, spontaneous spirituality in worship, emphasis on fellowship, the ordinances of believers' baptism and on the Lord's Supper and on independency in church organization.[198] Carey carried this model to India. It is significant that with the arrival of the new missionaries in Serampore early in the year 1800, Carey and his colleagues immediately constituted themselves as the local Baptist Church and elected Carey as pastor. The first convert, Krishna Pal, upon his baptism in December 1800, was admitted without delay to the membership of this church and invited to participate in the service of the Lord's Supper. Thus the concept of the gathered church with its emphasis on the fellowship of believers became the guiding principle of Carey's evangelistic and church planting ministries.

Carey and his colleagues carried this principle into the structuring of the Serampore Mission. As a community they covenanted together to live as an extended family, sharing in a common table, common purse and in rotating leadership. Carey had been inspired to follow this joint family lifestyle by the example of the Moravian missionaries, except in the concept of a permanent house father. In October 1805 they drew up a 'Form of Agreement' in which in eleven points they outlined their Mission strategy. This included the resolution that the church must be indigenous from the beginning. The 8th principle stated: 'it is only by means of native preachers that we can hope for the universal spread of the Gospel throughout this immense continent. We think it is our duty as soon as possible, to advise the native brethren who may be formed into separate churches, to choose their pastors and deacons from their own countrymen.'[199]

It was often stated that Carey failed as an evangelist and in establishing new churches. John Mack of Serampore College, in a funeral sermon on

---

[198] Christopher Smith contrasts the 'primitive' model with the 'professional' institutional model of the later church. He argues that the Serampore trio operated simultaneously in the spiritual world of personal piety and the commercial world of technologically-impressive capitalism. See his article 'A Tale of Many Models', *International Bulletin of Missionary Research 1992*.

[199] Cited *Christian History* (Vol. XI. No. 4) p. 34.

Carey (reprinted in the *Bengal Hurkaru*, Calcutta 14th August 1834) remarked that he had never heard of a single Indian converted directly by Carey's preaching and that in the last twelve years of his life Carey only once, to his knowledge, addressed the gospel to 'the heathen'.[200] This harsh judgement hardly does justice to the priority Carey gave to preaching and to establishing new churches in the earlier years of his ministry. It is understandable that in his later years Carey was preoccupied with his translation work, his teaching at Fort William College and the founding and developing of Serampore College and he was overwhelmed by personal controversy. It is clear from his letters and biographers that in his early years in Serampore Carey preached regularly in the bazaar and entered into serious dialogue with Hindus and others. The statistics of the Serampore Mission suggest that by 1812 there were eleven Bengali churches and twenty native evangelists and by 1813 five hundred had been baptized. This would have included Anglo-Indians and Europeans as well as Hindus. These figures represent the work of the Mission as a whole, not just of Carey. Considering the suspicion and resentment of the European community, the fanaticism of the Brahmins, and the low moral standards of the people, the slow growth of the church is understandable. The Hindu reform movement beginning with Rammohan Roy after 1815 proved an effective half-way house for would-be converts from the upper classes. They accepted Christian ethical teaching but chose to remain within the Hindu caste community. In a letter to his son Jabez dated 26th January 1824, Carey shared his distress that the people seem 'as insensible as ever' to Christianity.[201] Even if Carey saw little direct fruit for his preaching he was instrumental in the conversion of many through his multi-faceted ministries.

The Serampore trio, Carey, Marshman and Ward, were much more committed to the principle of establishing indigenous churches than were the Calcutta and General Baptist missionaries. This created some friction between them. The Serampore trio recognized that native pastors needed to be properly trained and to become self supporting, and that the churches must be self governing. Their first step in this policy was to establish as many schools as possible giving a general education in the Bengali language and seeking to make the schools self-supporting. Joshua Marshman drew up guidelines in *Hints relative to Native Schools, together with an*

---

[200] E. Daniel Potts, *British Baptist Missionaries in India 1793-1837* Cambridge CUP 1967) p. 35, n. 1.
[201] Potts, *ibid.*, p. 36.

outline of an Institution for their Extension and Management.²⁰² The success of their educational system led the Serampore missionaries to recognize the need for a higher institution to train teachers for the schools and to prepare native preachers as evangelists and pastors for the work of the churches. In the prospectus for the proposed College at Serampore they emphasized both Sanskrit, Eastern literature and European science and knowledge as being essential to the training of national church leaders. It is also significant that in addition to training Christians as teachers and evangelists they opened the College to youth from all parts of India 'without distinction in caste or creed'. Eleven Brahmin students enrolled in the first session.

The Serampore missionaries saw that though the church was called out of the world to be a new fellowship, it must be engaged in witness in the world; thus Serampore symbolized all that Carey and his colleagues stood for – respect for Indian language, literature and culture, the values of Western science and knowledge and a commitment to the message of the Bible and to Christian ethical lifestyle. The original vision for Serampore College continues to be maintained to the present day, both as a University College with faculties in Arts, Science and Commerce and as a Theological faculty for training men and women for the service of the Church.

William Carey's Doctrine of the Church was not only that of the local church but of the ecumenical family of Churches. In Calcutta Carey had a good working relationship with the evangelical Church of England chaplains. He met regularly with Henry Martyn for fellowship in the restructured pagoda at Serampore. Carey was a catalyst for world evangelization. In 1806 he proposed to Andrew Fuller, the Secretary of the Baptist Missionary Society, that they should summon 'a meeting of all denominations of Christians at the Cape of Good Hope somewhere about 1910 to be followed by another such conference every ten years'. Andrew Fuller turned the project down, replying, 'I consider this as one of Br'r Carey's pleasing dreams'.²⁰³ It was not until the World Missionary Conference of Edinburgh in 1910 that Carey's vision was realized. In a real sense it may be said that Carey's vision for world evangelization also anticipated the slogan of the contempory Lausanne Movement for World Evangelism, 'calling the Whole Church to take the Whole Gospel to the Whole World'.

---

²⁰² John D. W. Watts, 'Baptists and the Transformation of Culture: A Case Study from the Career of William Carey' *Review and Expositor* 89, (1992) No. 1, p. 16.

²⁰³ Ruth Rouse 'William Carey's "Pleasing Dream"' *International Review of Missions* (1949) p. 181.

Faith and Culture

For William Carey the Christian faith and Indian culture were not irreconcilable. He strove to affirm Bengali culture where it did not conflict with the gospel so that converts could retain their cultural self-identity and give leadership in evangelism and to the emerging church. He resisted attempts to replace Indian culture by the so-called Christian culture of the west. Carey was motivated by his respect for the highest values in Indian culture as well as by his conviction that evangelism was primarily the task of the national Christians.

This culture-affirming attitude was expressed in a number of ways. For example, Carey did not ask his first convert Krishna Pal to change his name even though he carried the name of a Hindu god. The prevailing spirit then and until recently was that converts at their baptism should take an anglicized biblical name or the western name of their missionary benefactor. Similarly in regard to dress, Carey and his colleagues encouraged new believers to retain their traditional dress and even the sacred thread of the higher castes.[204]

When the Brahmin convert Krishna Prasad disregarded and trampled on his sacred thread before his baptism, Ward kept it and later sent it to England for safe keeping. Then Ward gave Krishna Prasad money to buy another *paita* and for some years Krishna Prasad wore his thread on his preaching tours.

However, the most significant factor in Carey's approach to Indian culture was his insistence that education be in the vernacular language.[205] While other missionaries and social workers were emphasizing the use of the English language and western education, on the assumption that the Enlightenment culture of the west was superior to native language and

---

[204] It is perhaps significant that despite his commitment to affirming national culture, Carey himself continued to wear the dress of his own English culture and of his status as a college professor. For Carey there was no single Christian culture; each was valid in its own context.

[205] In his translation work Carey not only translated the Bible into many Indian languages but, with Marshman, one third of the Hindu epic *Ramayana*, into Bengali (5 volumes) and with Ward into English (3 volumes). He also published *Itihasamala* in Bengali, an anthology of prose stories of Bengali life. It can be argued that he wanted to show the superiority of the teaching of the Bible to other scriptures, and at the same time win respect in official circles. This was no doubt true, but it does not fully explain the enormous effort put into this work in spite of the criticism of other missionaries and the Society in England.

culture, Carey insisted on Bengali as the medium of education from primary school through to university education in Serampore College. As we have seen, Carey recognized the importance of both Eastern and Western knowledge and these were taught side by side at Serampore College.

While endorsing Bengali cultural values Carey and his colleagues rejected those cultural practices that conflicted with biblical ethics and social justice. Carey opposed idolatrous practices such as the Jagannath festival in which worshippers lost their lives, but he did not attack idolatry as such in public.

Carey was a vigorous opponent of the evils of the caste system. Upon profession of faith, Krishna Pal was invited by Thomas and Carey to share a meal with the missionaries and so break caste. Only then was he baptized and admitted to the Church. At his first communion Krishna Prasad the Brahmin convert received the common communion cup from the hands and lips of Krishna Pal, the Sudra. This was no doubt an intentional breaking of caste. Carey's life-long campaign against the evils of infanticide, the burning of widows (*sati*) reflected his commitment to biblical ethics and to compassionate justice. Carey was committed to the social transformation of culture.

This raises an important question as to how far Carey's action for social change was the consequence of his theological convictions or of his instinctive response to injustices that he experienced in his early years. Carey was no systematic theologian and the answer is probably both/and rather than either/or. Carey's acceptance of and love for the Bible and his sense of obligation to obey its teaching shaped his faith and action. Frederick Downs argues that in the New Testament conflict between James and Paul on the issue of Gentile converts accepting Palestinian Jewish culture, Carey was clearly on the side of Paul, who recognized that there was no single Christian culture but that the Christian faith must be incarnate in every culture.[206] Yet there can be no doubt that Carey's own cultural background prepared him in a unique way to feel deeply about the injustices of Indian society. Throughout his life in England he lived in constant poverty, and as a dissenter was disadvantaged in education, employment and social acceptance. The spirit of the second half of the 18th Century in England was one of radicalism and revolt, reformers clamouring for freedom of the press and dissenters expressing their resentment of the Test and Cooperation Acts. The idealism of the French and American revolutions encouraged

---

[206] Frederick S. Downs 'Reflections on the Culture/Society Issue in Contemporary Mission', *American Baptist Quarterly* (December 1989) pp. 239-246.

republican inclinations to overthrow the monarchy. Carey the young radical was caught up in this ferment. On one occasion Andrew Fuller his mentor chided him for not drinking to the King's health.[207]

Carey had also imbibed the social conscience of the pre-Victorian Evangelical Movement. Throughout his life he identified with the evangelical revolt against the slave trade. For example, he stopped eating sugar from the West Indies. In India, Carey constantly prayed for the emancipation of the West Indian slaves. With tears of joy he thanked God when the news came in September 1833 of their intended release.[208] Carey's cultural background made it inevitable that he would be opposed to the many social injustices he faced during his missionary career.

Integral Mission

Another significant and abiding factor in Carey's theology was his commitment to what we may call integral mission – social justice and the renewal of society integrated with compassionate service, universal education, fearless evangelism and church planting. Carey and his colleagues, Joshua and Hannah Marshman and William Ward, without whom he would never have succeeded, were pioneers and catalysts for change 150 years ahead of their time. Carey's respect for the best of Indian language and literature, his compassion for the suffering and the oppressed, his ceaseless campaign for social justice won him the respect of both the British imperialistic bureaucrats and the social activists among Hindu Reformers such as Raja Rammohan Roy. He is called Mahatma Carey – the Great Spirit – by Hindu leaders in Bengal today. However, his policies were not accepted by all. His own Baptist missionary colleagues in Calcutta who separated themselves from him, were critical of his indigenous policies, his autocratic methods and his independent spirit. As a catalyst for change, he inevitably attracted criticism. It is Carey's translation work and his holistic approach to mission that have inspired the leaders of churches and of many Christian agencies in India today to call for the bicentenary celebrations of Carey's arrival in India on 11th November 1793. Irrespective of denominational allegiance, the churches want to recognize his unique contribution to the founding and development of Christian witness in North India. Christopher Smith notes that Carey was a self-educated tradesman who rose to become a linguist and orientalist, a penniless cottager who founded a grand scholarly institution, and a shoemaker who married an aristocratic lady. He

---

[207] S. Pearce Carey, *William Carey* (London, Carey Press, 1934), p. 6.
[208] Carey, *ibid.*, p. 436.

was accessible to both the humble poor, to the Anglo Saxon middle class and to the ruling aristocracy. Smith adds: 'He was a catalyst extraordinary who operated during an unrepeatable and critical *kairos* in world history.'[209] He belongs to the whole Church and to India.

As we have already suggested, Carey's theology was shaped by his biblical faith, his social background and early struggles, the radical spirit of his age and by the impact of the Evangelical pre-Victorian Movement for social reform. *The Enquiry* represents the summation of his thinking prior to going to India. During his forty year missionary career he built on this foundation and made no radical departure from it. His thought naturally matured and his commitment to holistic and integral mission strengthened, despite the fact that he himself became less involved in direct evangelistic work. it has been left to others to build on these foundations.

Carey's working relationship with William Ward from 1800 until Ward's sudden death in 1823 and with Joshua and Hannah Marshman until his own death in 1834 is unique in the history of missions. Although different in temperament they were of one heart and mind in their mision. Without Ward and the Marshmans, Carey would never have achieved his holistic and integral Mission.

Part of the Serampore Mission's unique contribution to missions was their ability to develop structures and institutions to carry through the functional programmes they initiated. For example, William Ward pioneered the printing press as a vehicle to publish Carey's biblical translations and as a means of self-support for the Serampore Mission. Carey and Marshman opened numerous schools to give education to the poor. Again, Carey and Marshman established Serampore College to provide training for Indian pastors and teachers for the schools. Carey started a Savings Bank to enable the poor to provide for the education of their children and to assist the unemployed. He was instrumental in the founding of the Agro-Horticulture Society in order to raise the level of agricultural production to provide a better diet for the poor. He entered into an ongoing dialogue with the political leaders to carry through the needed social reforms. He appealed directly to the British authorities in India and to the Parliament in London. In the periodicals which he and Marshman founded, *Samachar Darpan* and *Friend of India*, they brought to the attention of their political rulers cases of infanticide, *sati*, the ill treatment of lepers and instances of slavery. They believed that word and deed were inseparable. Thus by every

---

[209] A. Christopher Smith, 'The Legacy of William Carey', *International Bulletin of Missionary Research* (16/1, 1992) p. 7.

means Carey and his colleagues sought to arouse the consciences of both the educated national leaders and their people and the political authorities on issues of social injustice. The two most notable examples of Carey's successful influence on the political structures were the action of the Governor General Lord Wellesley in 1802 to make the practice of infanticide illegal, and the action of Governor General Lord Bentinck in abolishing *sati* in December 1829. The latter action was the culmination of Carey's protest against this social evil from the beginning of his ministry in Serampore thirty years before. At the same time it is probable that Carey's efforts inspired Rammohan Roy in his campaign against *sati*. It appears that these two leaders rarely met.

The work of William Carey cannot be judged only by the immediate successes and failures of the Serampore Mission, for as his friend Christopher Anderson declared in a memorial sermon in Edinburgh in 1834, Carey's labours, however great, were 'chiefly preparatory or prospective.'[210] arey expected great things from God and he attempted great things for God. He was a man of vision and a man of action. Some of Carey's achievements have stood the test of time, notably Serampore College; others have not. His translation of the Bible into the languages of India was less than satisfactory and has been replaced by others, especially those working under the guidance of the Bible Society. Yet his Bengali grammar and his 87,000 word *Dictionary of the Bengali Language* (1824) helped to raise Bengali from an unsettled dialect to the level of a national language. Carey's role in the Bengali Renaissance is acknowledged by all. In the words of John Watts, 'Carey embraced Bengali and Asian culture in the name of Christ and accomplished much more for the Kingdom and for humanity than he could ever know. And generations rise up to call him blessed.'[211]

Despite the limitations of Carey's work as an evangelist, his principles for indigenous self-supporting churches are standard practices today. The heart of Carey's theology is summed up in the words he whispered to Alexander Duff on his death bed: 'Mr Duff, you have been speaking about Dr Carey, Dr Carey: when I am gone say nothing about Dr Carey. Speak only about Dr Carey's Saviour.'[212]

---

[210] Smith *ibid.*, p. 7.
[211] Watts *op. cit.*, p. 19.
[212] Pearce Carey, *op. cit.*, p. 428.

John Calvin and his Missionary Enterprise (1998)

ERROLL HULSE

Erroll Hulse was trained as an architect in South Africa, but has pastored several churches in Great Britain. He is the editor of Reformation Today and on the board of Evangelical Press. He also was one of the founders of Banner of Truth Trust in the 1950s.

Originally published in Reformation Today (1998). Reprinted with permission by Reformation Today and the author.

An Outline of Calvin's Life

John Calvin was born in 1509 in the town of Noyon in Picardy, northwest of Paris. He studied law and was so gifted that he was able to take the place of his lecturers when they were absent. In due course he earned his doctorate in law.

During the latter studies in about 1531 he was suddenly converted from Rome to Christ. He left Paris in 1533, being in danger because of his Christian faith. He lived in various places and began to devote his time to producing a systematic theology which was to become famous under the name *The Institutes of the Christian Religion*. He continued to work on and enlarge this work throughout his life. The first edition, published in 1536, was modest in size but over the years Calvin extended this work which soon became a classic and has continued as such ever since.[213]

In 1536 Calvin travelled from Italy to Strasbourg. On the way he stopped at the city of Geneva where he intended to stay just one night. However there he met the fiery Reformer Farel.

At this point we need to look at the background as it will not only explain why Farel was so keen to engage Calvin's help but also show how these cities became Protestant. Geneva had seven regions (parishes) and about 300 priests and nuns. Farel had sought to reform the city but had

---

[213] *Calvin's Institutes*. The two volumes, edited by John T McNeil and translated by Ford Lewis Battles, form part of the *Library of Christian Classics*. 1,500 pages, Westminster Press, USA.

been expelled. He then persuaded a friend by the name of Froment to begin teaching French in Geneva. This French language school attracted many prominent women students. Froment chose the New Testament as his textbook which was used by the Holy Spirit to convict the women who then influenced their husbands. In due course the evangelical party in the city increased in number. The way in which these cities were won was by challenging the Roman Catholic priests to a public debate which the city leaders were invited to attend. There were 200 City Council members in Geneva. The priests were mostly ignorant and unable to defend the Roman Catholic position. The Reformers would demonstrate the Roman Catholic teaching to be without biblical foundation and this convinced the City Council to reject Roman Catholic practice and control.

It was just when Farel was involved in this desperate struggle to persuade the leaders of Geneva to reject Romanism that Calvin arrived, then only 27 years old. Farel immediately saw in Calvin the teacher needed to consolidate the work. But Calvin had no desire to stay in Geneva. He was tired and longed for rest. 'May God curse your rest!!' shouted Farel. These words made Calvin tremble. Later he wrote in the introduction to his *Commentary on the Book of Psalms*, 'I was terrified by Farel's words and made conscious of being a coward.' So Calvin was persuaded to stay and he began to preach in Geneva. Not long after this the Roman Catholic priests of the nearby city of Lausanne were challenged to a public debate by the Reformers. Of 337 priests only 174 arrived and only 4 had any ability to defend their doctrine. Farel and Viret, a foremost Swiss Reformer of those times, were the spokesmen for the Bible. They took Calvin with them as an observer as he had no experience of these debates. The debate went on for several days. One priest in defence of transubstantiation started to quote from the Early Church Fathers. Farel and Viret were unable to handle this and looked to Calvin for help. Standing up, the latter proceeded to quote from memory passages from the Early Church Fathers, giving the exact source in each case. It was an amazing display of learning and had an electrifying effect on the assembly. The opposition was completely confounded. One priest was converted immediately. As a result of this astonishing performance not only did Lausanne turn Protestant but 200 priests renounced the Roman Catholic Church.

The work in Geneva however was not easy. Calvin wished to bring everything under the authority of Scripture. The City Council would not agree and this led to such a division that they expelled Calvin who then went to live in Strasbourg. There he was influenced by two outstanding Reformers, Bucer and Capito. They recognized Calvin's gifts and invited him to pastor a church with a congregation numbering 500 which he did from 1538 to 1541.

It was in 1541 that a Roman Catholic cardinal by the name of Sadoleto wrote to the Council of Geneva inviting them to return to the Roman Catholic Church. Sadoleto badly miscalculated because the people hated Romanism even though they had not agreed to all Calvin's reforms. They did not know how to reply to Sadoleto's letter. The humble course was followed which was to invite Calvin to return to Geneva. At first he refused but when he did return it was through a long and patient work that Geneva became the foremost centre for Protestantism, a city where many persecuted Christians from all over Europe were able to find refuge as well as a ministry that inspired them with missionary zeal.

Calvin's method was to expound the Scriptures systematically. He would preach almost every day in the morning and afternoon, expounding the Old Testament during the week and the New Testament on Sundays. He preached without notes directly from the Hebrew or the Greek. His expositions were written down by scribes. This is how his valuable commentaries came into being. He also kept up a huge correspondence. Up to 1553 much of his time was spent working at reformation in Geneva. Thereafter up until the time of his death in 1564 aged 54 he concentrated on the evangelisation of France.

Missionaries sent into France

It is widely believed that the Reformers of the sixteenth century were not involved in missionary activity. That is simply not the case.[214] John Calvin was involved in the work of sending missionaries to Brazil. Doors into Brazil did not open at that time and those involved in the attempt lost their lives. However the mission field is not only lands far off. Indeed France constituted a mission field.[215]

Unlike present day France, which is almost entirely secular in outlook, the France of the 16th century was religious but dominated by the priesthood of the Roman Catholic Church. Persecution by the priests against

---

[214] For a detailed description of the Brazilian saga see *The Heritage of John Calvin* edited by John Bratt, pages 40-73, Eerdmans, 1973.

[215] John Calvin's enterprise in the evangelisation of France is described by Jean-Marc Berthoud in a carefully researched treatise of 53 pages, *Westminster Conference Papers for 1992* obtainable from John Harris, 8 Back Knowl Road, Mirfield, WF14 9SA, UK _4.00 including postage. It is from this treatise that I have extracted the material about France.

evangelicals was fierce. It could cost your life to actively propagate the evangelical faith. However within the Roman Church a very considerable Bible movement had taken place through the secret reading of books by Luther as well as through the teaching of a well-known Catholic, Lefèvre d'Etaples. A great spiritual harvest was there to be reaped.

From 1555 to 1562 we know for sure that 88 preachers were sent from Geneva into France. Of these, nine laid down their lives as martyrs. There may have been more than 88. Historical research is hampered by the fact that everything in that period was done in a secretive way for security reasons. Also we must account for many short term missions into France. Those who were ordained and sent out as church planters were exceptionally gifted men. Some of them were from aristocratic families and most were from a well-educated upper middle class background in France. Very few were from artisan origin and none from a peasant background. With the exception of Pierre Viret who was Swiss, (he became the pastor of the largest church of 8,000 communicants at Nîmes), these church planting missionaries originated from almost every province of France. This fact helps explain how it was that almost all regions of France were permeated with the gospel.

Of these missionaries those who were not already accredited pastors were obliged to conform to rigorous standards set up by Calvin. The moral life of the candidate, his theological integrity and his preaching ability were subject to careful examination. With regard to moral discipline a system was established by which the pastors were responsible to each other. There was an exacting code listing offences that were not to be tolerated in a minister. Offences in money, dishonesty or sexual misconduct meant instant dismissal.

All Calvin's students had to be fully proficient in Latin, Hebrew and Greek, in order to be thoroughly proficient in line by line exegesis of the Scriptures.

They were required to be trained in Church History and Systematic Theology. Character training was paramount. These pastors had to face the reality of martyrdom. Only when Calvin judged a man to possess the necessary fibre and stamina would he be sent into France to preach and plant churches. Each church began by a group gathering in a home, and then out of that a fully disciplined church would be constituted. Such was termed 'a dressed church'.

In 1555 there was only one 'dressed church'. Seven years later, in 1562, there were 2150 such churches! This represents growth of extraordinary proportions. Eventually there were over two million Protestant church members out of a French population of twenty million. This multiplication came in spite of fierce persecution. For instance in 1572, 70,000 Protestants lost their lives. The church order used was Presbyterian. There were 29 national synods from about 1562 to 1685 when persecution forced most of the believers to leave France.

The real character of John Calvin is revealed in his letter-writing which was very extensive and pastoral in character. Besides personal letters he also wrote to the French churches as a whole. For instance in November 1559 he wrote: 'Persecutions are the real battles of Christians, to test the constancy and firmness of their faith; we should hold in high esteem the blood of the martyrs shed for a testimony to the truth.'

Conclusion

From the example provided above we need above all to recapture the biblical idea that a missionary is a male preacher/pastor who engages in church planting. There are many ancillary services and many ancillary agencies but without the application in practice of preaching and pastoring in the work of church planting the prospect of Christianity in any unevangelised land will be bleak.

John Calvin on Evangelism and Missions (1998)

RAY VAN NESTE

Dr. Ray Van Neste is assistant professor of Christians Studies and Director of the R. C. Ryan Center of Biblical Studies of Union University, Jackson, TN.

Originally published in The Founders Journal, issue 33 (summer 1998). Reprinted by permission of the author (www.uu.edu/personal/rvannest) and of the Founders Ministries, Cape Coral, FL (www.founders.org).

Introduction

From his own lifetime onward John Calvin has been a controversial person. One controversy stems from the accusations leveled against him by many that he was completely unevangelistic and unconcerned about missions. A. M. Hunter, in his book on Calvin's teaching, said, "Certainly he [Calvin] displayed no trace of missionary enthusiasm."[216] Some have even said that Calvin's teaching on predestination necessarily destroyed evangelistic fervor; "we are all familiar with the scornful rationalization that facilely asserts that his horrible doctrine of divine election makes nonsense of all missionary and evangelistic activity."[217] Others, however, have said: "One of the natural results of Calvin's perspective of predestination was an intensified zeal for evangelism."[218] Though some have used Calvin's teachings to excuse their apathy towards evangelism, a close examination of Calvin's historical context, his writings, and his actions would prove John Calvin to be a man truly committed to the spread of the gospel.

Historical Context

In order to understand John Calvin, or any other historical figure, one must understand the time in which the person lived and worked. Calvin

---

[216] A. Mitchell Hunter, *The Teaching of Calvin, a Modern Interpretation* (Glasgow: Maclehose, Jackson, and Company, 1920), 154.

[217] Philip E. Hughes, "John Calvin: Director of Missions," in *The Heritage of John Calvin*, ed., J. H. Bratt (Grand Rapids: Wm. B. Eerdmans, 1973), 42.

[218] Frank A. James, III, "It was both 'a horrible decree' and 'very sweet fruit'", *Christian History* 5, no. 4 (Fall 1986): 26.

emerged as a Reformation leader in 1536 with the publication of *The Institutes of the Christian Religion* and remained in leadership until his death in 1564. Thus, Calvin was a generation after Luther, and the Reformation, well entrenched in Germany, was spreading all over Europe. However, there was little organization among the churches that had split with Rome. Historian Owen Chadwick noted that

> The problem now was not the overthrow of the papacy, but the construction of new modes of power ... In breaking down papal authority, the Reformation seemed to have left the authority of the Christian ministry vague and uncertain.[219]

Protestant groups, who had been accustomed to strong central authority in Rome, were now only loosely organized and, though they claimed scripture for their authority, they disagreed on what the scriptures meant with regard to certain doctrines. By the time that Calvin gained prominence in 1536, Protestant churches were in great need of organization and structure in their doctrine and practice.

In addition to the disorganization within, there was persecution from without. The scattered condition of Protestantism was only worsened by the intense efforts of the Roman Church to eradicate the Protestant movement. Protestant churches were struggling not only for their identity but also for their very survival. Calvin himself had to leave France for personal safety, and he wrote the first edition of the *Institutes* in response to the ill treatment of French Protestants. Identification with Protestantism brought immediate punishment, including torture and even death.

Obviously, Calvin's era was a time of intense difficulty for Protestant churches. The demands of the day led him to spend a considerable amount of his energy developing a church organization, writing theology, and training ministers. With such pressing needs one *might* understand if Calvin neglected evangelism or missions. After all, the church itself and its message must first be established. Moreover, preaching Reformation doctrine in areas other than the Protestant cities would mean almost certain death. However, even these pressing needs and problems, which would immobilize many churches today, did not stop the evangelistic efforts of Calvin and his followers.

---

[219] Owen Chadwick, *The Reformation* (Pelican Books, 1964; reprint, New York: Penguin Group, Penguin Books, 1990), vol. 3, *The Penguin History of the Church*, ed., Owen Chadwick, 83.

Calvin's Writings

Calvin's writings on predestination have most often been targeted as unevangelistic and destructive to missionary zeal. Calvin addressed predestination primarily in related parts of his *Institutes* and in his treatise, *Concerning the Eternal Predestination of God*, which J. K. S. Reid called "the longest and most sustained exposition which Calvin wrote on the subject."[220] Dealing with predestination in the *Institutes*, Calvin does not directly address evangelism specifically, but neither does he describe it as unnecessary. He does, in fact, write several times about the gospel being preached to the masses, resulting in the salvation of the elect and the hardening of the non-elect (III.23.10; II.5.10). In other words, Calvin did not limit the preaching of the gospel to those considered to be elect. He explains his views more fully in his treatise on predestination:

> Since we do not know who belongs to the number of the predestined and who does not, it befits us so to feel as to wish that all be saved. So it will come about that, whoever we come across, we shall study to make him a sharer of peace ... even severe rebuke will be administered like medicine, lest they should perish or cause others to perish. But it will be for God to make it effective in those whom He foreknew and predestined.[221]

Calvin clearly encouraged Christians to be involved in evangelism! "It befits us" to desire all people to be saved. The result of this proper desire should make us try to lead everyone "we come across" to faith in Christ, for that is the only way they could share in peace. This is not to be a halfhearted effort. Christians are to use "even severe rebuke" if necessary to prevent others from ignoring the gospel and perishing. Christians must make the effort to evangelize everyone knowing that only God can save.

Calvin's doctrine of predestination did not make the preaching of the gospel unnecessary; instead, it made preaching necessary because it was by the preaching of the gospel that God had chosen to save the predestined.

Aside from his writings on predestination, Calvin also strongly supported the idea of missions with passages widely scattered throughout his commentaries.[222] Commenting on Micah 2:1-4, Calvin states, "The Kingdom of Christ was only begun in the world when God commanded the

---

[220] John Calvin, *Concerning the Eternal Predestination of God*, trans. J. K. S. Reid (London: James Clarke and Co., Limited, 1961), 9.

[221] Ibid., 138.

[222] R. Pierce Beaver, "The Genevan Mission to Brazil," in *The Heritage of John Calvin*, ed., J. H. Bratt (Grand Rapids: Wm. B. Eerdmans, 1973), 56.

gospel to be every where proclaimed and ... at this day its course is not as yet complete."²²³ In other words the Great Commission was not fulfilled by the apostles and, consequently, this mission is still the responsibility of Christians.

Calvin expressed similar views as he commented on 1 Tim. 2:4, saying "there is no people and no rank in the world that is excluded from salvation; because God wishes that the gospel should be proclaimed to all without exception."²²⁴ He is not, of course, saying that everyone in the world would be saved, but that certain people from all parts of the world would be saved. The whole idea of the passage is that God desires "foreign nations" to hear the gospel and to be included in salvation. It is the Christian's duty "to be solicitous and to do our endeavor for the salvation of all whom God includes in his calling."²²⁵

No one should be denied the opportunity of hearing the gospel proclaimed. Continuing to verse five of the same passage, Calvin writes that those people insult God "who, by their opinion, shut out any person from the hope of salvation."²²⁶ The gospel is to be preached indiscriminately to all people, and the decision about who will believe is to be left to God.

Indeed, Calvin never portrays God as a cruel tyrant grudgingly allowing some to be saved. In a comment on Ezek. 18:23, he states:

> God certainly desires nothing more than for those who are perishing and rushing toward death to return to the way of safety. This is why the gospel is today proclaimed throughout the world, for God wished to testify to all the ages that he is greatly inclined to pity.²²⁷

God desires for men to be saved and by His election has assured that some will be. It is the fact that God will definitely call some that encourages believers to "bestow more toil and exertion for the instruction of rebels," realizing that "our duty is, to be employed in sowing and watering, and while we do this we must look for the increase from God."²²⁸ Clearly, Calvin recognized the need for Christians to exert effort in evangelism in

---

[223] Ibid., 57.

[224] John Calvin, *Calvin's Commentaries, Ephesians – Jude* (Wilmington, DE: Associated Publishers and Authors, n.d.), 2172.

[225] Ibid.

[226] Ibid., 2173.

[227] John Calvin, *Calvin: Commentaries* (Philadelphia: Westminster Press, 1963), vol. 23, *The Library of Christian Classics*, eds. Baillie, McNeill, and Van Dusen, 402.

[228] Calvin, *Ephesians – Jude*, 2247.

order to be used of God to call out His elect. He saw evangelism as a duty and employment involving "toil and exertion." Such is far from an indifferent attitude toward evangelism.

Calvin's Activity

Perhaps the best evidence of Calvin's concern for missions is the mission activity of the Genevan church under his leadership. Under Calvin's leadership, Geneva became "the hub of a vast missionary enterprise"[229] and "a dynamic center or nucleus from which the vital missionary energy it generated radiated out into the world beyond."[230] Protestant refugees from all over Europe fled to Geneva; they came not merely for safety but also to learn from Calvin the doctrines of the Reformation so they could return home to spread the true gospel. Philip Hughes notes that Geneva became a "school of missions" which had as one of its purposes

> "to send out witnesses who would spread the teaching of the Reformation far and wide .... It [Geneva] was a dynamic centre of missionary concern and activity, an axis from which the light of the Good News radiated forth through the testimony of those who, after thorough preparation in this school, were sent forth in the service of Jesus Christ."[231]

Thus was Calvin's missionary concern reflected in the church he served and the students he taught.

The pastors of Geneva, including Calvin himself, met regularly and kept sporadic notes of their actions in a register, which became the greatest source of information on the missionary activity in Geneva. In April 1555 the *Register of the Company of Pastors* for the first time listed men who were sent out from Geneva to "evangelize Foreign Parts."[232] The entry that mentioned these men stated that they had been sent out prior to April 1555, and they were already ministering in the Piedmont valleys.[233] More ministers may have been sent out before this time without being recorded in the

---

[229] Raymond K. Anderson, "Calvin and Missions," *Christian History*, 5 no. 4 (Fall 1986): 23.
[230] Hughes, "John Calvin: D. O. M.," 45.
[231] Philip Hughes, ed. and trans., *The Register of the Company of Pastors of Geneva in the Time of Calvin* (Grand Rapids: Wm. B. Eerdmans, 1966), 25.
[232] Alister McGrath, *A Life of John Calvin, a Study in the Shaping of Western Culture* (Oxford; Basil Blackwell Ltd., 1990), 182. Cf. Hughes, *Register*, 308.
[233] Hughes, *Register*, 308.

Register because the notes were not complete and it was often dangerous to record the names of missionaries.

By 1557 it was a normal part of business for the Genevan pastors to send missionaries into France. Robert M. Kingdon called it a "concentrated missionary effort."[234] By 1562, religious wars had broken out in France, and it was no longer safe to record the names of missionaries. However, between 1555 and 1562 the *Register* records 88 men by name who were sent out from Geneva to different places as "bearers of the gospel."[235]

In reality many more than 88 were sent. In one year, 1561, though the *Register* mentions only twelve missionaries, other sources indicate that at least 142 missionaries were sent![236] Hundreds of men were sent out, reaching Italy, Germany, Scotland, England, and practically covering France.[237] From all over Europe requests came to Geneva for ministers of the gospel and the Genevan Company of Pastors filled as many as possible. At times even their own churches were deprived of pastors in order to meet the needs of struggling groups abroad.[238] Thus, Geneva, under Calvin's direction, served as the heart of the Reformation in Europe, pumping out the lifeblood of trained ministers into all areas.

In addition to the extensive work in Europe, one group of Genevan missionaries was sent to Brazil. The *Register* simply states that on Tuesday, August 25, 1556, M. Pierre Richier and M. Guillaume were sent as ministers to Brazil. "These two were subsequently commended to the care of the Lord and sent off with a letter from this church."[239] The ministers were sent in response to a request from Admiral Coligny, a Huguenot leader. They were to serve as chaplains for a group of Protestants who were going to Brazil to establish a colony, and they would have opportunity to instruct

---

[234] Robert M. Kingdon, "Calvinist Religious Aggression," in *The French Wars of Religion, How Important Were Religious Factors?*, ed. J. H. M. Salmon (Lexington, MA: D. C. Heath and Company, 1967), 6.

[235] Hughes, "John Calvin: D. O. M," 46; cf. also McGrath, 184. McGrath mentions some of the areas to which these men went: Poitiers, Paris, Lyons, Bergerac, Dieppe (which he calls an important jumping-off point for England and Scotland, Issoudun, and Orleans).

[236] Ibid.

[237] Anderson, 23.

[238] Hughes, *Register*, 27.

[239] Ibid., 317.

the natives in the gospel.[240] One man who went on the trip wrote that, upon receiving the request,

> the church of Geneva at once gave thanks to God for the extension of the reign of Jesus Christ in a country so distant and likewise so foreign and among a nation entirely without knowledge of the true God.[241]

Sadly, the mission was not successful because the leader of the group betrayed the Protestants. Some were killed, and others were sent back to Europe. Though the mission failed, it remains "a striking testimony to the far reaching missionary vision of Calvin and his Genevan colleagues."[242]

Conclusion

Though evangelism was not discussed as much in the sixteenth century as it would be later, Calvin proved himself to be genuinely concerned for the spread of the true gospel. In light of the situation of the world around him, his mission activity, and that of his colleagues, is truly admirable. His writings also show that he believed the gospel should be preached to all. The missionary endeavors of the Genevan church especially prove Calvin's commitment to missions. Speaking of these efforts, Philip Hughes states,

> Here is irrefutable proof of the falsity of the too common conclusion that Calvinism is incompatible with evangelism and spells death to all missionary enterprise.[243]

Clearly, Calvin must have believed his teachings were compatible with mission work since he was so involved in such work himself. Whether or not one agrees with all of Calvin's views or actions, one must admit the great reformer's teachings (including predestination) do indeed support evangelism and mission work.

Selected Bibliography

Anderson, Raymond K. "Calvin and Missions." ChristianHistory, 5, no. 4 (Fall 1986): 23.

Beaver, R. Pierce. "The Genevan Mission to Brazil." In The Heritage of John Calvin, ed. J. H. Bratt, 55-73. Grand Rapids: William B. Eerdmans Publishing Company, 1973.

---

[240] Hughes, "John Calvin: D. O. M.," 47.
[241] Beaver, 61.
[242] Anderson, 23.
[243] Hughes, *Register*, 25.

Calvin, John. Calvin's Commentaries. Ephesians – Jude. Wilmington, DE: Associated Publishers and Authors, n.d.

_____. Calvin's Commentaries. Vol. 7, The Gospels. Grand Rapids: Associated Publishers and Authors, Inc., n.d.

_____. Calvin: Commentaries. Edited by Joseph Haroutunian. Vol. 23, The Library of Christian Classics, eds. Baillie, McNeill, Van Dusen. Philadelphia: Westminster Press, 1963.

_____. Calvin: Institutes of the Christian Religion. Edited by John T. McNeill. Translated by Ford Lewis Battles. Vols. 20-21, The Library of Christian Classics, eds. Baillie, McNeill, Van Dusen. Philadelphia: Westminster Press, 1960.

_____. Calvin's New Testament Commentaries. The Epistles Paul the Apostle to the Galatians, Ephesians, Philippians, and Colossians. Edited by David W. Torrance and Thomas F. Torrance. Translated by T. H. L. Parker. Grand Rapids: William B. Eerdmans Publishing Company, 1965.

_____. Concerning the Eternal Predestination of God. Translated by J. K. S. Reid. London: James Clarke and Co. Limited, 1961.

Chadwick, Owen. The Reformation. Vol. 3, The Penguin History of the Church, ed. Owen Chadwick. Pelican Books, 1964; reprint, New York: Penguin Group, Penguin Books, 1990.

George, Timothy. Theology of the Reformers. Nashville: Broadman Press, 1988.

Hughes, Philip E. "John Calvin: Director of Missions." In The Heritage of John Calvin, ed. J. H. Bratt, 40-54. Grand Rapids: William B. Eerdmans, 1973.

_____. ed. and trans. The Register of the Company of Pastors of Geneva in the Time of Calvin. Grand Rapids: William B. Eerdmans Publishing Company, 1966.

Hunter, A. Mitchell. The Teaching of Calvin, A Modern Interpretation. Glasgow: Maclehose, Jackson, and Company, 1920.

James, Frank A., III. "It was both 'a horrible decree' and 'very sweet fruit.'" Christian History, 5, no. 4 (Fall 1986): 24-26.

Kingdon, Robert M. "Calvinist Religious Aggression." In The French Wars of Religion, How Important Were Religious Factors?, ed. J. H. M. Salmon, 6-11. Problems in European Civilization, eds. Ralph W. Greenlaw and Dwight E. Lee. Lexington, MA: D. C. Heath and Company, 1967.

Kuiper, R. B. God Centered Evangelism. Grand Rapids: Baker Book House, 1961; reprint, Carlisle, PA: Banner of Truth Trust, 1978.

McGrath, Alister E. A Life of John Calvin, a Study in the Shaping of Western Culture. Oxford: Basil Blackwell Ltd., 1990.

McNeill, John T. The History and Character of Calvinism. Oxford: Oxford University Press, 1954.

Calvin the Evangelist (2001)

FRANK A. JAMES, III

Frank Allison James III is President of Reformed Theological Seminary in Orlando, Florida. He also serves as Professor of Historical and Systematic Theology and Professor of Church History. He was awarded the D.Phil. in History from Oxford University in 1993 and a Ph.D. in Theology from Westminster Theological Seminary/Pennsylvania in 2000.

Originally published in Reformed Quarterly, Vol 19 (2001), No. 2/3 (http://www.rts.edu/ quarterly/fall01/james.html). Reprinted by permission of publisher and author.

There are many popular misconceptions about John Calvin. Who is the true Calvin behind the image?

Will Durant, the famous author of the eleven-volume series on the History of Western Civilization, said of Calvin: "We shall always find it hard to love the man, John Calvin, who darkened the human soul with the most absurd and blasphemous conception of God in all the long and honored history of nonsense."

Even the defrocked TV evangelist, Jimmy Swaggart, has something to say about Calvin. "Calvin," said Swaggart, "has caused untold millions of souls to be damned."

Such judgements, besides being uncharitable, fail to get at the real John Calvin – a man with a strong evangelical heart.

One of the most pervasive criticisms of Calvin is that he had no interest in missions. The well-known Protestant missiologist, Gustav Warneck, portrayed the Reformers, including Calvin, as missiologically challenged merely because they believed in predestination. "We miss in the Reformers, not only missionary action, but even the idea of missions ... because fundamental theological views hindered them from giving their activity and even their thoughts a missionary direction."

But history tells another story.

The city of Geneva, long associated with Calvin, was also an important refugee center in the Reformer's day. Throughout sixteenth century Europe, persecuted Protestants fled their homelands, many of whom found their way to Geneva. In the 1550s, the population of Geneva literally doubled.

One of those refugees who came to Geneva was the Englishman John Bale, who wrote: "Geneva seems to me to be the wonderful miracle of the whole world. For so many from all countries come here, as it were, to a sanctuary. Is it not wonderful that Spaniards, Italians, Scots, Englishmen, Frenchmen, Germans, disagreeing in manners, speech, and apparel, should live so lovingly and friendly, and dwell together like a ... Christian congregation?"

Since Geneva was French-speaking, the vast majority of refugees came from France. As they sat under Calvin's teaching in the Cathedral of St. Pierre, the French refugees' hearts stirred for their homeland. Many of them felt compelled to return to France with the Protestant gospel.

Calvin, however, did not want to send uneducated missionaries back to the dangers of Catholic France. He believed that a good missionary had to be a good theologian first. And so he inspired and educated them. He trained them theologically, tested their preaching ability, and carefully scrutinized their moral character. Calvin and the Genevan Consistory sent properly trained missionaries back to France to share the Gospel.

Calvin did not just educate them and send men back to France. These missionaries did not just become photographic memories on Calvin's refrigerator door. On the contrary; Calvin remained intimately involved in all that they were doing.

The Genevan archives hold hundreds of letters containing Calvin's pastoral and practical advice on establishing underground churches. He did not just send missionaries; he invested himself in long-term relationships with them.

Concrete information exists from the year 1555 onwards. The data indicate that by 1555, there were five underground Protestant churches in France. By 1559, the number of these Protestant churches jumped to more than one hundred. And scholars estimate that by 1562 there were more than 2,150 churches established in France with approximately three-million Protestant souls in attendance.

This can only be described as an explosion of missionary activity; detonated in large part by the Genevan Consistory and other Swiss Protestant cities. Far from being disinterested in missions, history shows that Calvin was enraptured by it.

To be a missionary in France was so dangerous that the Genevan Consistory decided not to keep any record of such missionary activity in order to protect their lives. And so the Genevan Consistory deliberately obscured the names and the numbers of missionaries sent out from Geneva.

Scholar peter Wilcox has combed the Genevan archives and dusted off some of Calvin's five hundred-year old correspondence. Much to his surprise, Wilcox discovered a treasure trove of material indicating that the last ten years of Calvin's life in Geneva (1555-1564) were preoccupied with missions' Among the dusty tomes were letters written by the Genevan missionaries themselves revealing just how successful they had been. One French church in Bergerac boasted to Calvin:

"There is, by the grace of God, such a movement in our district, that the devil is already for the most part driven out, so that we are able to provide ministers for ourselves. From day to day, we are growing, and God has caused His Word to bear such fruit that at sermons on Sundays, there are about four- to five-thousand people."

Another letter from Montpelier rejoiced, "Our church, thanks to the Lord, has so grown and so continues to grow every day that we are obliged to preach three sermons on Sundays to a total of five- to six-thousand people."

And it gets better. A pastor in Toulouse wrote to the Genevan Consistory: "Our church has grown to the astonishing number of about eight- to nine-thousand souls."

Calvin didn't just plant small fledgling churches; he planted megachurches that in turn planted more churches. It is difficult to fathom the extraordinary success of these Genevan sponsored missionaries. Even in our modern era, such statistics are unheard of.

The French government became so concerned about all these churches being planted that they sent a letter of protest to the Genevan city council. The Genevan city council responded by saying, "What missionaries?"

Genevan missionaries planted churches in other European destinations. Records indicate missionaries also were sent to Italy; the Netherlands, Hungary; Poland, and the free Imperial city-states in the Rhineland. The late Philip Edgcumbe Hughes, one of the few modern scholars aware of this extraordinary achievement, concluded that Calvin's Geneva was a "school of missions ... [and] a dynamic centre of missionary concern and activity."

There is still more to the story of Genevan missions. It is one thing to send missionaries to Europe, but what about transcontinental missions?

Once again, Calvin earns high masks. As a matter of historical fact, Calvin also sent missionaries across the Atlantic Ocean to South America. It is a little known missionary episode that reads like an adventure story.

Because of increasing persecution, the leading Protestant in France, Admiral Coligny, embraced a grand vision for establishing a French Protestant colony in the New World where Protestants would be free to worship. Coligny sent out an expedition that eventually landed in what is now Brazil.

Along with his plans to establish a colony in Brazil, Coligny collaborated with Calvin to provide missionaries to the new settlement.

We actually know the names of the two missionaries that Geneva sent to Brazil – Pierre Richier and William Chartier. These two Genevan trained missionaries were to serve as chaplains to the settlers and bring the gospel to Brazil's natives.

The French expedition landed in Rio de Janeiro on March 10, 1557, and suddenly things took a turn for the worse. Nicholas Durand de Villegagnon, the leader of the expedition, turned traitor to the Protestant cause. He decided to create his own South American fiefdom. When the French Protestant settlers disapproved, he actually killed a number of them. The Protestant colonists and the Genevan missionaries fled into the Brazilian jungle where they found refuge, believe it or not, with a tribe of cannibals.

Over time, the Protestant colonists and missionaries eventually made their way back to France where one of them (Jean de Lery) wrote a book describing his Brazilian adventures. He described how the colonists and missionaries made every effort to share the gospel with the cannibals. Although their efforts ultimately proved unsuccessful, they nevertheless exhibited an abiding missionary interest – even in the midst of a terrible trial.

What motivated Calvin's extraordinary missions interests? The answer, in part, can be found in Calvin's sermons.

Calvin's sermons typically offer a concluding prayer. These prayers often repeated his most deeply held convictions. After preaching a sermon on 1 Timothy 2:3, Calvin offered this prayer:

"Seeing that God has given us such a treasure and so inestimable a thing as His Word, we must employ ourselves as much as we can, that it may be kept safe and sound and not perish. And let every man be sure to lock it up securely in his own heart. But it is not enough to have an eye to his own salvation, but the knowledge of God must shine generally throughout the whole world."

Similar sentiments are found in many of his concluding pastoral prayers. For Calvin, it was axiomatic that the salvation of our souls necessarily carries with it an inevitable desire to share the gospel with others.

Calvin was missions-minded because he understood the transformational character of the gospel. He understood that when God saves a person, it makes a profound difference in that person's life and in the lives of others.

If Calvin is taken as a model, Reformed theology ought to produce not only the best theologians. but also the best pastors and missionaries. These convictions reveal the true Calvin behind the image.

John Calvin: Teacher and Practitioner of Evangelism (2001)

JOEL R. BEEKE

Rev. Dr. Joel R. Beeke is founder and president of Puritan Reformed Theological Seminary, Grand Rapids, MI, and its Professor of Systematic Theology and Homiletics. He is also pastor of the Heritage Netherlands Reformed congregation in Grand Rapids.

Originally published 2001 in Credo Quarterly and in Reformation & Revival, and edited 2003 by the author for this volume.

Many scholars would take issue with the title of this chapter. Some would say that Roman Catholicism kept the evangelistic torch of Christianity lit via the powerful forces of the papacy, the monasteries, and the monarch while Calvin and the Reformers tried to extinguish it.[244] But others would assert that John Calvin (1509-1564), the father of Reformed and Presbyterian doctrine and theology, was largely responsible for relighting the torch of biblical evangelism during the Reformation.[245]

Some also credit Calvin with being a theological father of the Reformed missionary movement.[246] Views of Calvin's attitude toward evangelism and missions have ranged from hearty to moderate support on the positive side,[247] and from indifference to active opposition on the negative side.[248]

---

[244] William Richey Hogg, "The Rise of Protestant Missionary Concern, 1517-1914," in *Theology of Christian Mission,* ed. G. Anderson (New York: McGraw-Hill, 1961), pp. 96-97.

[245] David B. Calhoun, "John Calvin: Missionary Hero or Missionary Failure?," *Presbuterion* 5,1 (Spr 1979):16-33 – to which I am greatly indebted in the first part of this article; W. Stanford Reid, "Calvin's Geneva: A Missionary Centre," *Reformed Theological Review* 42,3 (1983):65-74.

[246] Samuel M. Zwemer, "Calvinism and the Missionary Enterprise," *Theology Today* 7,2 (July 1950):206-216; J. Douglas MacMillan, "Calvin, Geneva, and Christian Mission," *Reformed Theological Journal* 5 (Nov 1989):5-17.

[247] Johannes van den Berg, "Calvin's Missionary Message," *The Evangelical Quarterly* 22 (1950):174-87; Walter Holsten, "Reformation und Mission," *Archiv für Reformationsgeschichte* 44,1 (1953):1-32; Charles E. Edwards, "Calvin and Missions," *The Evangelical Quarterly* 39 (1967):47-51; Charles Chaney, "The Mis-

A negative view of Calvin's evangelism is a result of:

- A failure to study Calvin's writings prior to drawing their conclusions,
- A failure to understand Calvin's view of evangelism within his own historical context,
- Preconceived doctrinal notions about Calvin and his theology to their study. Some critics naively assert that Calvin's doctrine of election virtually negates evangelism.

To assess Calvin's view of evangelism correctly, we must understand what Calvin himself had to say on the subject. Second, we must look at the entire scope of Calvin's evangelism, both in his teaching and his practice. We can find scores of references to evangelism in Calvin's *Institutes*, commentaries, sermons, and letters. Then we can look at Calvin's evangelistic work (1) in his own flock, (2) in his home city of Geneva, (3) in greater Europe, and (4) in mission opportunities overseas. As we shall see, Calvin was more of an evangelist than is commonly recognized.

Calvin: Teacher of Evangelism

How was Calvin's teaching evangelistic? In what way did his instruction oblige believers to seek the conversion of all people, those within the church as well as those in the world outside it?

Along with other Reformers, Calvin taught evangelism in a general way by earnestly proclaiming the gospel and by reforming the church according to biblical requirements. More specifically, Calvin taught evangelism by focusing on the universality of Christ's kingdom and the responsibility of Christians to help extend that kingdom.

The universality of Christ's kingdom is an oft-repeated theme in Calvin's teaching.[249] Calvin says all three persons of the Trinity are involved in the spreading of the kingdom. The Father will show "not only in one corner, what true religion is ... but he will send forth his voice to the ex-

---

sionary Dynamic in the Theology of John Calvin," *Reformed Review* 17,3 (Mar 1964): 24-38.

[248] Gustav Warneck, *Outline of a History of Protestant Missions* (London: Oliphant Anderson & Ferrier, 1906), pp. 19-20.

[249] John Calvin, *Commentaries of Calvin* (Grand Rapids: Eerdmans, 1950ff.), on Psalm 2:8, 110:2, Matt. 6:10, 12:31, John 13:31. (Hereafter the format, *Commentary* on Psalm 2:8, will be used.)

treme limits of the earth."[250] Jesus came "to extend his grace over all the world."[251] And the Holy Spirit descended to "reach all the ends and extremities of the world."[252] In short, innumerable offspring "who shall be spread over the whole earth" will be born to Christ.[253] And the triumph of Christ's kingdom will become manifest everywhere among the nations.[254]

How will the triune God extend His kingdom throughout the world? Calvin's answer involves both God's sovereignty and our responsibility. He says the work of evangelism is God's work, not ours, but God will use us as His instruments. Citing the parable of the sower, Calvin explains that Christ sows the seed of life everywhere (Matt. 13:24-30), gathering His church not by human means but by heavenly power.[255] The gospel "does not fall from the clouds like rain," however, but is "brought by the hands of men to where God has sent it."[256] Jesus teaches us that God "uses our work and summons us to be his instruments in cultivating his field."[257] The power to save rests with God, but He reveals His salvation through the preaching of the gospel.[258] God's evangelism causes our evangelism.[259] We are His co-workers, and He allows us to participate in "the honor of constituting his own Son governor over the whole world."[260]

Calvin taught that the ordinary method of "collecting a church" is by the outward voice of men; "for though God might bring each person to himself by a secret influence, yet he employs the agency of men, that he may awaken in them an anxiety about the salvation of each other."[261] He goes so far as to say, "Nothing retards so much the progress of Christ's kingdom

---

[250] *Commentary* on Micah 4:3.

[251] John Calvin, *Sermons of M. John Calvin on the Epistles of S. Paule to Timothy and Titus,* trans. L. T. (Edinburgh: Banner of Truth Trust reprint, 1983), sermon on 1 Timothy 2:5-6, pp. 161-72.

[252] *Commentary* on Acts 2:1-4.

[253] *Commentary* on Psalm 110:3.

[254] T. F. Torrance, *Kingdom and Church* (London: Oliver and Boyd, 1956), p. 161.

[255] *Commentary* on Matthew 24:30.

[256] *Commentary* on Romans 10:15.

[257] *Commentary* on Matthew 13:24-30.

[258] John Calvin, *Institutes of the Christian Religion,* ed. John T. McNeill and trans. Ford Lewis Battles (Philadelphia: Westminster Press, 1960), Book 4, chapter 1, section 5. (Hereafter the format, *Institutes* 4.1.5, will be used.)

[259] *Commentary* on Romans 10:14-17.

[260] *Commentary* on Psalm 2:8.

[261] *Commentary* on Isaiah 2:3.

as the paucity of ministers."[262] Still, no human effort has the final word. It is the Lord, says Calvin, who "causes the voice of the gospel to resound not only in one place, but far and wide through the whole world."[263] The gospel is not preached at random to all nations but by the decree of God.[264]

According to Calvin, this joining together of divine sovereignty and human responsibility in evangelism offers the following lessons:

1. As Reformed evangelists, we must pray daily for the extension of Christ's kingdom. As Calvin says, "We must daily desire that God gather churches unto himself from all parts of the earth."[265] Since it pleases God to use our prayers to accomplish His purposes, we must pray for the conversion of the heathen.[266] Calvin writes, "It ought to be the great object of our daily wishes, that God would collect churches for himself from all the countries of the earth, that he would enlarge their numbers, enrich them with gifts, and establish a legitimate order among them."[267] By daily prayer for God's kingdom to come, we "profess ourselves servants and children of God deeply committed to his reputation."[268]

2. We must not become discouraged at a lack of visible success in evangelistic effort, but pray on. "Our Lord exercises the faith of his children, in that he doth not out of hand perform the things which he had promised them. And this thing ought specially to be applied to the reign of our Lord Jesus Christ," Calvin writes. "If God pass over a day or a year [without giving fruit], it is not for us to give over, but we must in the meanwhile pray and not doubt but that he heareth our voice."[269] We must keep praying, believing that "Christ shall manifestly exercise the power given to him for our salvation and for that of the whole world."[270]

---

[262] Jules Bonnet, ed., *Letters of Calvin*, trans. David Constable and Marcus Robert Gilchrist, 4 vols. (New York, reprint), 4:263.

[263] *Commentary* on Isaiah 49:2.

[264] *Commentary* on Isaiah 45:22.

[265] *Institutes* 3.20.42.

[266] *Sermons of Master John Calvin upon the Fifthe Book of Moses called Deuteronomie,* trans. Arthur Golding (Edinburgh: Banner of Truth Trust reprint, 1987), sermon on Deuteronomy 33:18-19. (Hereafter *Sermon on Deuteronomy* 33:18-19.)

[267] *Institutes* 3.20.42.

[268] *Institutes* 3.20.43.

[269] Sermon on Deuteronomy 33:7-8.

[270] *Commentary* on Micah 7:10-14.

3. We must work diligently for the extension of Christ's kingdom, knowing that our work will not be in vain. Our salvation obligates us to work for the salvation of others. Calvin says, "We are called by the Lord on this condition, that everyone should afterwards strive to lead others to the truth, to restore the wandering to the right way, to extend a helping hand to the fallen, to win over those that are without."[271] Moreover, it is not enough for every man to be busy with other ways of serving God. "Our zeal must extend yet further to the drawing of other men." We must do everything we are capable of to draw all men on earth to God.[272]

There are many reasons why we must evangelize. Calvin offers the following:

- God commands us to do so. "We should remember that the gospel is preached not only by the command of Christ but at his urging and leading."[273]

- God leads us by example. Like our gracious God who wooed us, we must have our "arms extended, as he has, toward those outside" of us.[274]

- We want to glorify God. True Christians yearn to extend God's truth everywhere that "God may be glorified."[275]

- We want to please God. As Calvin writes, "It is a sacrifice well-pleasing to God to advance the spread of the gospel."[276] To five students who were sentenced to death for preaching in France, Calvin wrote, "Seeing that [God] employs your life in so worthy a cause as is the witness of the gospel, doubt not that it must be precious to Him."[277]

- We have a duty to God. "It is very just that we should labor ... to further the progress of the gospel," says Calvin;[278] "it is our duty to

---

[271] *Commentary* on Hebrews 10:24.

[272] *Sermon on Deuteronomy* 33:18-19.

[273] *Commentary* on Matthew 13:24-20.

[274] John Calvin, *Sermons on the Epistle to the Ephesians,* trans. Arthur Golding (Edinburgh: Banner of Truth Trust, 1973), sermon on Ephesians 4:15-16.

[275] Bonnet, *Letters of Calvin*, 4:169.

[276] Bonnet, *Letters of Calvin*, 2:453.

[277] Bonnet, *Letters of Calvin*, 2:407.

[278] Bonnet, *Letters of Calvin*, 2:453.

proclaim the goodness of God to every nation."[279]

- We have a duty to our fellow sinners. Our compassion for sinners should be intensified by our knowledge that "God cannot be sincerely called upon by others than those to whom, through the preaching of the gospel, his kindness and gentle dealings have become known."[280] Consequently, every encounter with other human beings should motivate us to bring them to the knowledge of God.[281]

- We are grateful to God. Those who are indebted to God's mercy are bound to become, like the psalmist, "the loud herald of the grace of God" to all men.[282] If salvation is possible for me, a great sinner, then it is possible for others. I owe it to God to strive for the salvation of others; if I do not, I am a contradiction. As Calvin says, "Nothing could be more inconsistent concerning the nature of faith than that deadness which would lead a man to disregard his brethren, and to keep the light of knowledge ... in his own breast."[283] We must, out of gratitude, bring the gospel to others in distress, or appear ungrateful to God for our own salvation.[284]

Calvin never assumed that the missionary task was completed by the apostles. Instead, he taught that every Christian must testify by word and deed of God's grace to everyone he or she meets.[285] Calvin's affirmation of the priesthood of all believers involves the church's participation in Christ's prophetic, priestly, and kingly ministry. It commissions believers to confess Christ's name to others (prophetical task), to pray for their salvation (priestly task), and to disciple them (kingly task). It is the basis for powerful evangelistic activity on the part of the entire living church "to the world's end."[286]

Calvin: Practitioner of Evangelism

Calvin believed we must make full use of the opportunities God gives to evangelize. "When an opportunity for edification presents itself, we should

---

[279] *Commentary* on Isaiah 12:5.
[280] *Institutes* 3.20.11.
[281] *Sermon on Deuteronomy* 33:18-19.
[282] *Commentary* on Psalm 51:16.
[283] *Commentary* on Isaiah 2:3.
[284] *Sermon on Deuteronomy* 24:10-13.
[285] *Institutes* 4.20.4.
[286] *Sermon on Deuteronomy* 18:9-15.

realize that a door has been opened for us by the hand of God in order that we may introduce Christ into that place and we should not refuse to accept the generous invitation that God thus gives us," he writes.[287]

On the other hand, when opportunities are restricted and doors of evangelism are closed to our witness, we should not persist in trying to do what cannot be done. Rather, we should pray and seek for other opportunities. "The door is shut when there is no hope of success. [Then] we have to go a different way rather than wear ourselves out in vain efforts to get through it," Calvin writes.[288]

Difficulties in witnessing are not an excuse to stop trying, however. To those suffering severe restrictions and persecutions in France, Calvin wrote: "Let every one strive to attract and win over to Jesus Christ those whom he can."[289] "Each man must perform his duty without yielding to any impediment. At the end our effort and our labors shall not fail; they shall receive the success which does not yet appear."[290]

Let's examine Calvin's practice of evangelism in his own congregation, in his home city of Geneva, in Europe (particularly France), and in missionary efforts overseas (particularly Brazil).

Evangelism in the Congregation

Too often we think of evangelism today only as the Spirit's regenerating work and the sinner's consequent receiving of Christ by faith. In this, we reject Calvin's emphasis on conversion as a continuous process involving the whole person.

For Calvin, evangelism involved a continual, authoritative call to the believer to exercise faith and repentance in the crucified and risen Christ. This summons is a whole-life commitment. Evangelism means presenting Christ so that people, by the power of the Spirit, may come to God in Christ. But it also means presenting Christ so that the believer may serve Christ as Lord in the fellowship of His church and in the world. Evangelism demands building up believers in the most holy faith according to the five key tenets of the Reformation: Scripture alone, grace alone, faith alone, Christ alone, the glory of God alone.

---

[287] *Commentary* on 2 Corinthians 2:12.
[288] Ibid.
[289] Bonnet, *Letters of Calvin*, 3:134.
[290] *Commentary* on Genesis 17:23.

Calvin was an outstanding practitioner of this kind of evangelism within his own congregation. For Calvin, evangelism began with preaching. As William Bouwsma writes, "He preached regularly and often: on the Old Testament on weekdays at six in the morning (seven in winter), every other week; on the New Testament on Sunday mornings; and on the Psalms on Sunday afternoons. During his lifetime he preached, on this schedule, some 4,000 sermons after his return to Geneva: more than 170 sermons a year." Preaching was so important to Calvin that when he was reviewing the accomplishments of his lifetime on his deathbed, he mentioned his sermons ahead of his writings.[291]

Calvin's intent in preaching was to evangelize as well as edify. On average, he would preach on four or five verses in the Old Testament and two or three verses in the New Testament. He would consider a small portion of the text at a time, first explaining the text, then applying it to the lives of his congregation. Calvin's sermons were never short on application; rather, the application was often longer than the exposition in his sermons. Preachers must be like fathers, he wrote, "dividing bread into small pieces to feed their children."

He was also succinct. As Calvin's successor, Theodore Beza, said of the Reformer's preaching, "Every word weighed a pound."

Calvin frequently instructed his congregation on how to listen to a sermon. He told them what to look for in preaching, in what spirit they should listen, and how they should listen. His goal was to help people participate in the sermon as much as they could so that it would feed their souls. Coming to a sermon, Calvin said, should include "willingness to obey God completely and with no reserve."[292] "We have not come to the preaching merely to hear what we do not know," Calvin added, "but to be incited to do our duty."[293]

Calvin also reached out to unsaved people through his preaching, impressing them with the necessity of faith in Christ and what that meant. Calvin made it clear that he did not believe everyone in his flock was saved. Though charitable toward church members who maintained a com-

---

[291] William Bouwsma, *John Calvin: A Sixteenth-Century Portrait* (New York: Oxford, 1988), p. 29.

[292] Leroy Nixon, *John Calvin, Expository Preacher* (Grand Rapids: Eerdmans, 1950), p. 65.

[293] John Calvin, *Opera quae supersunt omnia,* ed. Guilielmus Baum, Eduardus Cunitz, and Eduardus Reuss, in *Corpus Reformatorum* (Brunsvigae: C. A. Schwetschke et filium, 1895), 79:783.

mendable, outward lifestyle, he also referred more than thirty times in his commentaries and nine times in his *Institutes* (only counting references within 3.21 to 3.24) to the small numbers of those who receive the preached Word with saving faith. "If the same sermon is preached, say, to a hundred people, twenty receive it with the ready obedience of faith, while the rest hold it valueless, or laugh, or hiss, or loathe it," Calvin says.[294] He writes, "For though all, without exception, to whom God's Word is preached, are taught, yet scarce one in ten so much as tastes it; yea, scarce one in a hundred profits to the extent of being enabled, thereby, to proceed in a right course to the end."[295]

For Calvin, the most important tasks of evangelism were building up the children of God in the most holy faith, and convicting unbelievers of the heinousness of sin and directing them to Christ Jesus as the only Redeemer.

Evangelism in Geneva

Calvin did not confine preaching to his own congregation. He also used it as a tool to spread the Reformation throughout the city of Geneva. On Sundays, the Genevan Ordinances required sermons in each of the three churches at daybreak and 9 a.m. At noon, children went to catechism classes. At 3 p.m., sermons were preached again in each church.

Weekday sermons were scheduled at various times in the three churches on Mondays, Wednesdays, and Fridays. By the time Calvin died, a sermon was preached in every church each day of the week.

Even that wasn't enough. Calvin wanted to reform Genevans in all spheres of life. In his ecclesiastical ordinances he required three additional functions besides preaching that each church should offer:

1. Teaching. Doctors of theology should explain the Word of God, first in informal lectures, then in the more formal setting of the Geneva Academy, established in 1559. By the time Calvin's successor, Theodore Beza, retired, the Geneva Academy had trained 1,600 men for the ministry.

2. Discipline. Elders appointed within each congregation were, with the assistance of the pastors, to maintain Christian discipline, watching over the conduct of church members and their leaders.

---

[294] *Institutes* 3.24.12.
[295] *Commentary* on Psalm 119:101.

3. Charity. Deacons in each church were to receive contributions and distribute them to the poor.

Initially, Calvin's reforms met stiff local opposition. People particularly objected to the church's use of excommunication to enforce church discipline. After months of bitter controversy, the local citizens and religious refugees who supported Calvin won control of the city. For the last nine years of his life, Calvin's control over Geneva was nearly complete.

Calvin wanted to do more than reform Geneva, however; he wanted the city to become a kind of model for Christ's reign throughout the world. Indeed, the reputation and influence of the Genevan community spread to neighboring France, then to Scotland, England, the Netherlands, parts of western Germany, and sections of Poland, Czechoslovakia, and Hungary. The Genevan church became a model for the entire Reformed movement.

The Geneva Academy also assumed a critically important role as it quickly became more than a place to learn theology. In "John Calvin: Director of Missions," Philip Hughes writes:

Calvin's Geneva was something very much more than a haven and a school. It was not a theological ivory tower that lived to itself and for itself, oblivious to its responsibility in the gospel to the needs of others. Human vessels were equipped and refitted in this haven ... that they might launch out into the surrounding ocean of the world's need, bravely facing every storm and peril that awaited them in order to bring the light of Christ's gospel to those who were in the ignorance and darkness from which they themselves had originally come. They were taught in this school in order that they in turn might teach others the truth that had set them free.[296]

Influenced by the Academy, John Knox took the evangelical doctrine back to his native Scotland. Englishmen were equipped to lead the cause in England; Italians had what they needed to teach in Italy; and Frenchmen (who formed the great bulk of refugees) spread Calvinism to France. Inspired by Calvin's truly ecumenical vision, Geneva became a nucleus from which evangelism spread throughout the world. According to the Register of the Company of Pastors, eighty-eight men were sent out between 1555 and 1562 from Geneva to different places in the world. These figures are woefully incomplete. In 1561, which appears to have been the peak year for missionary activity, the dispatch of only twelve men is recorded,

---

[296] Philip Hughes, *The Heritage of John Calvin,* ed. John H. Bratt (Grand Rapids: Eerdmans, 1973), p. 44.

whereas other sources indicate that nearly twelve times that number – no less than 142 – went forth on respective missions.[297]

That is an amazing accomplishment for an effort that began with a small church struggling within a tiny city-republic. Yet Calvin himself recognized the strategic value of the effort. He wrote to Bullinger, "When I consider how very important this corner [of Geneva] is for the propagation of the kingdom of Christ, I have good reason to be anxious that it should be carefully watched over."[298]

In a sermon on 1 Timothy 3:14, Calvin preached, "May we attend to what God has enjoined upon us, that he would be pleased to show his grace, not only to one city or a little handful of people, but that he would reign over all the world; that everyone may serve and worship him in truth."

Evangelistic Efforts in France

To understand how Calvin promoted the Reformation throughout Europe, we need to look at what he did in France.

France was only partially open to Reformed evangelism. Religious and political hostilities, which also threatened Geneva, were a constant danger in France. Nonetheless, Calvin and his colleagues made the most of the small opening they had. The minutes of the Company of Pastors in Geneva deal with the supervision of the missionary efforts in France more than in any other country.[299]

Here's how it worked. Reformed believers from France took refuge in Geneva. While there, many began to study theology. They then felt compelled to return to their own people as Reformed evangelists and pastors. After passing a rigorous theological examination, each was given an assignment by the Genevan Company of Pastors, usually in response to a formal request from a French church needing a pastor. In most cases, the receiving church was fighting for its life under persecution.

The French refugees who returned as pastors were eventually killed, but their zeal encouraged the hopes of their parishioners. Their mission, which, according to the pastors, sought "to advance the knowledge of the gospel in

---

[297] Ibid., pp. 45-46.
[298] Bonnet, *Letters of Calvin*, 2:227.
[299] Robert M. Kingdon, *Geneva and the Consolidation of the French Protestant Movement* (Madison: University of Wisconsin Press, 1967), p. 31.

France, as our Lord commands," was successful. Reformed evangelistic preaching produced a remarkable revival. In 1555, there was only one fully organized Reformed church in France. Seven years later, there were close to two thousand.

The French Reformed pastors were on fire for God and, despite massive persecution, God used their work to convert thousands. This is one of the most remarkable examples of effective home missions work in the history of Protestantism, and one of the most astonishing revivals in church history.

Some of the French Reformed congregations became very large. For example, Pierre Viret pastored a church of 8,000 communicants in Nimes. More than 10 percent of the French population in the 1560s – as many as three million – belonged to these churches.

During the St. Bartholomew's Day massacre of 1572, 70,000 Protestants were killed. Nevertheless, the church continued. Persecution eventually drove out many of the French Protestants, known as the Huguenots. They left France for many different nations, enriching the Church wherever they went.

Not all of the refugee pastors were sent to French churches. Some went to Northern Italy, others to Antwerp, London, and other cities in Europe. Some even went beyond Europe to far-off Brazil. Regardless of where they went, their preaching was strong and powerful, and God blessed their efforts.

Evangelism in Brazil

Calvin knew there were nations and people who had not yet heard the gospel and he keenly felt the burden. Though there is no record that he ever came into contact with the newly discovered world of Asian and African paganism, Calvin was involved with the Indians of South America through the Genevan mission to Brazil.

With the help of a Huguenot sympathizer, Gaspard de Coligny, and the support of Henry II, Nicolas Durand (also called Villegagnon) led an expedition to Brazil in 1555 to establish a colony there. The colonists included former prisoners, some of whom were Huguenots. When trouble erupted in the new colony near Rio de Janeiro, Villegagnon turned to the Huguenots in France, asking for better settlers. He appealed to Coligny as well as to Calvin and the church in Geneva. That letter was not preserved and there is only a brief summary in the account of the Company of Pastors of what happened.

Nonetheless, we have some insight into those events because of what Jean de Lery, a shoemaker and student of theology in Geneva who was soon to join the Brazilian colony, recorded in his personal journal. He wrote, "The letter asked that the church of Geneva send Villegagnon immediately ministers of the Word of God and with them numerous other persons 'well instructed in the Christian religion' in order better to reform him and his people and 'to bring the savages to the knowledge of their salvation.'"[300] Responsibility for evangelism to the heathen was thus laid squarely at the feet of the church of Geneva.

The church's reaction, according to Jean de Lery, was this: "Upon receiving these letters and hearing this news, the church of Geneva at once gave thanks to God for the extension of the reign of Jesus Christ in a country so distant and likewise so foreign and among a nation entirely without knowledge of the true God."[301]

The Company of Pastors chose two ministers to send to Brazil. The Register succinctly notes: "On Tuesday 25 August [1556], in consequence of the receipt of a letter requesting this church to send ministers to the new islands [Brazil], which the French had conquered, M. Pierre Richer and M. Guillaume Charretier were elected. These two were subsequently commended to the care of the Lord and sent off with a letter from this church."[302] Eleven laymen were also recruited for the colony, including Jean de Lery.

Although Calvin was not in Geneva at this time, he was kept informed of what was happening and offered his advice in letters that were sent on to Villegagnon.

The work with Indians in Brazil did not go well. Pastor Richier wrote to Calvin in April 1557 that the savages were incredibly barbaric. "The result is we are frustrated in our hope of revealing Christ to them," he said.[303] Richier did not want to abandon the mission, however. He told Calvin that the missionaries would advance the work in stages and wait patiently for

---

[300] R. Pierce Beaver, "The Genevan Mission to Brazil," in *The Heritage of John Calvin,* ed. John H. Bratt, p. 61.

[301] Ibid.

[302] Philip E. Hughes, ed. and trans., *The Register of the Company of Pastors of Geneva in the Time of Calvin* (Grand Rapids: Eerdmans, 1966), p. 317.

[303] Beaver, "The Genevan Mission to Brazil," p. 62.

the six young boys who were placed with the Indians (the Tupinambas) to learn their language. "Since the Most High has given us this task, we expect this Edom to become a future possession for Christ," he added confidently. Meanwhile, he trusted that the witness of pious and industrious members of the Reformed Church in the colony would influence the Indians.

Richier was a striking witness of Calvin's missionary emphasis in four ways: (1) obedience to God in doing what is possible in a difficult situation, (2) trust in God to create opportunities for further witness, (3) insistence on the importance of the lives and actions of Christians as a means of witness, and (4) confidence that God will advance His kingdom.

The rest of the story is tragic. Villegagnon became disenchanted with Calvin and the Reformers. On February 9, 1558, just outside of Rio de Janeiro, he strangled three Calvinists and threw them into the sea. Believers fled for their lives. Later, the Portuguese attacked and destroyed the remainder of the settlement.

Thus ended the mission to the Indians. There is no record of any Indian converts. But was that the true end of the story? When an account of the martyrs of Rio de Janeiro was published six years later, it began with these words: "A barbarous land, utterly astonished at seeing the martyrs of our Lord Jesus Christ die, will some day produce the fruits that such precious blood has been at all times wont to produce."[304] Or, as Tertullian once wrote, "The blood of the martyrs is the seed of the church." Today, the Reformed faith is growing in Brazil among conservative Presbyterians through Reformed preaching, the Puritan Project, and various ministries that reprint Reformed and Puritan titles in Portuguese.

It is clear that Calvin was interested in spreading the gospel overseas, but that interest was limited by the following realities of the sixteenth century:

1. Time constraints. The Reformation was still so new in Calvin's time that he needed to concentrate on building up the truth in the churches. A mission church that is not built on foundational truth is not equipped to carry its message to foreign lands.

2. Work at home. Those who critique Calvin, saying his evangelistic efforts failed to extend to the foreign mission field, are quite unfair. After all, did not Christ command his disciples to begin spreading the gospel in Jerusalem and Judea (home missions) and then move on to Samaria and the

---

[304] G. Baez-Camargo, "The Earlist Protestant Missionary Venture in Latin America," *Church History* 21, 2 (June 1952):144.

uttermost parts of the earth (foreign missions)? Obviously, the established church should be involved in both home and foreign missions, but we err when we judge one more important than the other. A genuine spirit of evangelism sees need everywhere. It does not fall prey to the worldly spirit that "The farther from home, the better."

3. Government restrictions. Overseas mission work for the Reformers was virtually impossible because most of the governments in Europe were controlled by Roman Catholic princes, kings, and emperors. Persecution of Protestants was widespread. As Calvin wrote, "Today, when God wishes his gospel to be preached in the whole world, so that the world may be restored from death to life, he seems to ask for the impossible. We see how greatly we are resisted everywhere and with how many and what potent machinations Satan works against us, so that all roads are blocked by the princes themselves."[305]

Nearly every door to the heathen world was closed for Calvin and his fellow Reformers. The world of Islam to the south and east was guarded by Turkish armies, while the navies of Spain and Portugal prevented access to the recently discovered new world. In 1493, Pope Alexander VI gave the Spanish and Portuguese rulers exclusive rights to these areas, which were reaffirmed by popes and treaties that followed.

Going out into the world for Calvin and other Reformers didn't necessarily mean leaving Europe. The mission field of unbelief was right within the realm of Christendom. For the Genevan church, France and Europe were open. Strengthened by Calvin's evangelistic theology, believers zealously responded to the mission call.

Calvin did what he could to support evangelism on the foreign front. Despite its tragic failure, the pioneer Protestant project off the coast of Brazil from 1550-1560 evoked Calvin's wholehearted sympathy, interest, and continued correspondence.[306]

Calvin's Missionary Spirit and Election

Though Calvin's specific writings on missiology are limited, his *Institutes*, commentaries, sermons, letters, and life glow with a missionary spirit. It is abundantly clear that John Calvin had a heart for evangelism to extend the kingdom of our Lord Jesus Christ to the ends of the earth. It was Calvin's wish that "the kingdom of Christ should flourish everywhere."

---

[305] *Commentary* on Genesis 17:23.
[306] Beaver, "The Genevan Mission to Brazil," pp. 55-73.

Establishing the heavenly reign of God upon earth was so important, Calvin said, that it "ought not only to occupy the chief place among our cares, but even absorb all our thoughts."[307]

All of this should dispel the myth that Calvin and his followers promoted inactivity and disinterest in evangelism. Rather, the truths of sovereign grace taught by Calvin such as election are precisely the doctrines that encourage

missionary activity. Where biblical, Reformed truth is loved, appreciated, and rightly taught, evangelism and mission activity abounds.

Election encourages evangelistic activity, for God sovereignly links election with the means of grace (Acts 13:44-49). Election evokes mission activity characterized by a humble dependence on God for blessing. The doctrine of free grace is not a barrier to God-centered, God-glorifying evangelism; it is a barrier against a humanistic concept of evangelistic task and methods.[308]

Calvin never allowed election to limit the free offer of the gospel. He taught that since no one knows who are elect, preachers must operate on the principle that God wills all to be saved.[309] Election undergirds rather than limits evangelism. Election belongs to the special category of God's secret purposes, not to the evangelistic activity of the church. Consequently, the gospel must be preached to every sinner; the sinner's believing response to the free offer of salvation in Christ reveals whether or not he is elect. For though the gospel call comes to all who hear the Word, that call is only made effectual by the Holy Spirit in the elect.[310] God opens doors for the church that the gospel may go into all the world, and His elect will hear it and respond in faith.[311]

Election thus is the impetus and guarantor of the success of Reformed evangelism. As Isaiah 55:11 says, "My word ... that goeth forth out of my mouth ... shall not return unto me void, but it shall accomplish that which I please, and it shall prosper in the thing whereto I sent it."

---

[307] Bonnet, *Letters of Calvin*, 2:134-35.
[308] Van den Berg, "Calvin's Missionary Message," p. 179.
[309] *Institutes* 3.24.16-17.
[310] Ibid.
[311] *Institutes* 3.21.7.

Is it any wonder, then, that Calvin called election the church's heart, hope, and comfort? Totally depraved creatures such as you and I may hope in an electing God.

A Word of Encouragement

Calvin has been criticized for his supposed failure to support evangelistic efforts. We have seen that this is simply not so, and the lessons ought to give us encouragement.

For one, it tells us we ought to stay on task and worry less about what others say of us. If Calvin could not shield himself from critics even when he worked twenty hours a day, preaching, teaching, and writing, what does that say about our work for God's kingdom? If Calvin was not evangelistic, who is? Are we willing to confess with William Carey as we labor for the souls of sinners, "I had rather wear out than rust out"?

Perhaps some of us are tired. We fear we are wearing out without seeing fruit from our evangelistic efforts. We are burdened with work. Spiritual labor has produced spiritual weariness, which in turn has produced spiritual discouragement. Our eye has not dimmed, but our physical and spiritual energy has been seriously depleted by the constant giving of ourselves for the good of others.

That may be particularly true for those of us who are pastors. On Saturday evenings we are anxious because we do not feel adequately prepared for worship; our responsibilities have been too heavy. We have been overwhelmed with church administration, personal counseling, and correspondence. By Sunday evening we are completely drained. Unable to sustain our responsibilities, we labor under a continual sense of inadequacy. We lack family time; we lack private time with God. Like Moses, our hands grow heavy in intercession. Like Paul, we cry out, "Who is sufficient for these things?" (2 Cor. 2:16). The routines of daily ministry become overwhelming; we experience what Spurgeon called "the minister's fainting fits," and we wonder if we are being used by God after all. Our vision of ministry is sadly diminished.

In such times, we should follow Calvin's example. Some lessons from him include:

- Look more to Christ. Rest more in His perseverance, for your perseverance rests in His. Seek grace to imitate His patience under affliction. Your trials may alarm you, but they will not destroy you. Your crosses are God's way to royal crowning (Rev. 7:14).

- Take the long view. Seek to live in light of eternity. The Chinese bamboo tree appears to do absolutely nothing for four years. Then, during its fifth year, it suddenly shoots up ninety feet in sixty days. Would you say that this tree grew in six weeks or in five years? If you follow the Lord in obedience, you will generally see your efforts rewarded eventually. Remember, however, that God never asked you to produce growth; He only asks you to continue working.

- Realize that times of discouragement are often followed by times of revival. While we predict the church's ruin, God is preparing for her renewal. The church will survive through all time and come to glory while the ungodly will come to ruin. So gird up the loins of your mind and stand fast, for the Lord is greater than both Apollyon and the times. Look to God, not man, for the church belongs to God.

- Rely on God. Though friends may fail you, God will not. The Father is worthy. Christ is worthy. The Holy Spirit is worthy. Seeing that you have a great high priest, Jesus, the Son of God, who rules from the heavens, draw near to Him in faith, and wait upon Him, and He will renew your strength. We are not all Calvins. Actually, none of us can be Calvins. But we can keep working by God's grace, looking to Jesus for daily strength. If Calvin, one man, did so much good for the cause of evangelism, shouldn't we ask God to also use our efforts, making them fruitful by His blessing?

Heed the advice of the Puritan, John Flavel, who wrote, "Bury not the church before she be dead." Pray more and look at circumstances less. Continue with double earnestness to serve the Lord when no visible result is before you. Endure hardship as good soldiers of Christ. Be willing to be counted fools for Christ's sake. Be sure that you are in God, for you may then be sure that God is in you.

In M'Cheyne's words, "Let your life speak even louder than your sermons. Let your life be the life of your ministry." Be exemplary on and off the pulpit, and leave the fruits of your ministry to our sovereign God who makes no mistakes and who never forsakes the work of His hands.

Finally, take heart from Calvin's approach to "the open door." Do we not err in spending our energies trying to pry open doors that God has closed? Shouldn't we rather pray more for new doors to open for our ministries? Shouldn't we ask for God's guidance in recognizing which doors are open and for His strength to walk through them? May God give us grace not to lead Him but rather to follow Him in all our evangelistic efforts. Isn't the very heartbeat of Reformed evangelism to follow God rather than try to lead Him?

May the Lord Jesus be able to say of us what he said to the church in Philadelphia in Revelation 3:8, "I know thy works: behold, I have set before thee an open door, and no man can shut it: for thou hast a little strength, and hast kept my word, and hast not denied my name."

That is what Calvin's Reformed evangelism is all about, and that is what our evangelism must be all about. May God help us to be true to His Name, to be obedient to His Word, to look for the doors He will open before us, and to pray with Calvin: "May we daily solicit thee in our prayers, and never doubt, but that under the government of thy Christ, thou canst again gather together the whole world ... when Christ shall exercise the power given to him for our salvation and for that of the whole world."[312]

---

[312] Cited in J. Graham Miller, *Calvin's Wisdom* (Edinburgh: Banner of Truth Trust, 1992), p. 221.

John Calvin and Missions: A Historical Study (2002)

SCOTT J. SIMMONS

Scott J. Simmons is graduated from James Madison University in 1991 with a degree in Geology, worked as a geologist and became involved in the mission program of a local church. He then went to Reformed Theological Seminary in Orlando, and graduated in 1997. For the next four years, Scott became a high school teacher at Chapelgate Christian Academy, where he taught Bible, consumer math, and New Testament Greek. Scott also worked in the Chapelgate mission department until he was called as an Assistant Pastor in 2001. He eventually became the Pastor of Missions and Spiritual Formation there.

Published in the web under http://www.aplacefortruth.org/calvin.missions1.htm, "A Place for Truth Studies – Reformed and Post-Reformation Creeds and Councils", in 2002 and edited for this volume by the author in 2003.

Introduction

There is a long-standing tradition that claims that Calvin and the early Protestant movement took no interest in missions. Gustav Warneck wrote early in this century, "We miss in the Reformers not only missionary action, but even the idea of missions ... [in part] because fundamental theological views hindered them from giving their activity, and even their thoughts, a missionary direction."[313] Warneck went on to state that Calvin claimed that the Church had no duty to send out missionaries.[314] This misunderstanding has continued even into the present day. Ralph D. Winter, for instance, writes that the Reformers "did not even talk of mission outreach."[315] He claims that the Protestant missionary movement can be divided into three eras: the first beginning in 1792 with William Carey, the

---

[313] Gustav Warneck, History of Protestant Missions, trans. G. Robinson (Edinburgh: Oliphant Anderson & Ferrier, 1906), 9, cited in Fred H. Klooster, "Missions – The Heidelberg Catechism and Calvin," Calvin Theological Journal 7 (Nov. 1972): 182.

[314] Ibid., 19.

[315] Ralph D. Winter, "The Kingdom Strikes Back," in Perspectives on the World Christian Movement (Pasadena: William Carey Library, 1992), B–18.

second beginning 1865 with Hudson Taylor, and the third beginning in 1934 with Cameron Townsend and Donald McGavran. Winter describes missionary efforts prior to 1792 by saying, "our Protestant tradition plugged along for over 250 years minding its own business and its own blessing (like Israel of old)."[316]

While these charges may be brought against many churches in the Protestant tradition, and even against some Calvinistic churches, it is simply untrue that John Calvin took no interest in missions. In fact, Calvin sent hundreds of missionaries to France, the rest of Europe, and even to the New World. The following discussion, therefore, will not only demonstrate that John Calvin had a coherent theology of missions, but will provide a summary of how his theology took action in his missionary endeavors throughout the world.

Calvin's Theology of Missions

Calvin never wrote a systematic treatment of his theology of missions. However, his Institutes, commentaries, and letters contain many references to his theology of missions and his missionary spirit. An accurate description of his theology of missions can be reconstructed from these statements made by Calvin in his writings. The following will provide a summary of his theology of missions as well as answers to common objections to his theology as they relate to missions.

A Positive Statement

The basis for Christian missions, according to Calvin, is the present reign of Jesus Christ. In his commentaries on the Psalms and prophets, it is clear that Calvin considered the kingdom of David to be a shadow of the greater Kingdom to come. For instance, commenting on Isaiah 2:4, Calvin writes, "the difference between the kingdom of David, which was but a shadow, and this other Kingdom," is that "by the coming of Christ, [God] began to reign ... in the person of his only-begotten Son."[317] Commenting on Psalm 22:28, Calvin writes, "This passage, I have no doubt, agrees with many other prophecies which represent the throne of God as erected, on

---

[316] Ralph D. Winter, "Four Men, Three Eras, Two Transitions," in Perspectives on the World Christian Movement, B–34.

[317] John Calvin, Calvin's Commentaries, vol. 7, Isaiah 1-32 (Grand Rapids: Baker, 1979), 98-99.

which Christ may sit to superintend and govern the world."[318] This present reign of God through Christ is presupposed throughout his writings when he speaks of the basis for world missions.

One important dynamic that takes effect in this new Kingdom is the break down of the distinction between Jew and Gentile. Calvin frequently makes use of Ephesians 2:14 to insist that the partition-wall between Jew and Gentile has been broken down and the gospel has been promulgated, so that "we [both Jew and Gentile] have been gathered together into the body of the Church, and Christ's power is put forth to uphold and defend us."[319] Since Christ's rule extends over not only Jews, but over the whole world, Gentiles are called along with Jews into His Kingdom.[320] It is the inclusion of Gentiles into the commonwealth of Israel that allows the gospel of the Jewish Messiah to be proclaimed to Gentiles throughout the world.

Christ's task while ruling over the earth from heaven is to subdue the earth to Himself. This happens in two ways. First, the reprobate who refuse to submit to Christ's rule will "assail" the kingdom of Christ "from time to time until the end of the world," at which time they will be laid prostrate at His feet.[321] Second, the elect are "brought to yield a willing obedience to Him," being subdued and humbled by Him. After the last day these will be made "partakers with Him in glory."[322] By these two methods the kingdom will be extended throughout the world. At no time can the progress of this kingdom be hindered. Commenting on Isaiah 2:2, Calvin writes that there will be "uninterrupted progress" in the spread of His kingdom "until he appears a second time for our salvation."[323] The kingdom of Christ, the "invincible Kingdom," will be "vastly extended" because God makes "his scepter stretch far and wide."[324] Throughout the Church age, according to Calvin, Christ's kingdom is being extended throughout the world.

---

[318] John Calvin, Calvin's Commentaries, vol. 4, Johsua–Psalms 1-35, 385.

[319] Commentary on Ps. 110:2, in Calvin's Commentaries, vol. 6, Psalms 93-150, 301; see also his commentaries on Isaiah 45:22, Matthew 24:19, and Acts 8:1.

[320] See Calvin's commentary on Isaiah 2:4, in Calvin's Commentaries, vol. 7, Isaiah 1-32, 98-102.

[321] See Calvin's commentary on Psalm 110:1 in Calvin's Commentaries, vol. 6, Psalms 93-150, 299.

[322] Ibid., 300.

[323] John Calvin, Calvin's Commentaries, vol. 7, Isaiah 1-32, 92.

[324] Commentary on Psalm 110:2 in Calvin's Commentaries, vol. 6, Psalms 93-150, 300.

The means by which Christ's kingdom is spread on earth is through the preaching of the gospel to the nations. Calvin writes, "There is no other way of raising up the church of God than by the light of the word, in which God himself, by his own voice, points out the way of salvation. Until the truth shines, men cannot be united together, so as to form a true church."[325] Calvin insisted that Christians bear the responsibility to spread the gospel. He writes, "for it is our duty to proclaim the goodness of God to every nation ... the work is such as ought not to be concealed in a corner, but to be everywhere proclaimed."[326] While God could have used other means, He chose to "employ the agency of men" through the preaching of the gospel.[327]

Calvin's theology of missions is thus God-centered and Christ-centered, focusing on the glory of God in Christ as well as the duty of man. All of life was to be lived for the glory of God. While the Catholic Church used meritorious works and asceticism as tools of motivation for missions, Protestants would not use this type of motivation.[328] For Calvin, the motivating factor for world missions was the glory of God. When the gospel is proclaimed and accepted among the nations, God is worshipped and glorified. This is the chief end of man. Charles Chaney writes of him, "The fact that the glory of God was the prime motive in early Protestant missions and that it has played such a vital part in later missionary thought and activity can be traced directly to Calvin's theology."[329]

Charges against Calvin's Theology of Missions

There have been many who say that Calvin's theology was a hindrance to missions throughout the sixteenth and seventeenth centuries. Two charges are usually given against Calvin's theology of mission. These are his understanding of the Great Commission and his doctrine of predestina-

---

[325] Commentary on Micah 4:1-2, cited in Charles Chaney, "The Missionary Dynamic in the Theology of John Calvin," Reformed Review 17 (Mar. 1964): 28.

[326] Commentary on Isaiah 12:5, in Calvin's Commentaries, vol. 7, Isaiah 1-32, 403.

[327] Commentary on Isaiah 2:3, in Charles Chaney, "The Missionary Dynamic in the Theology of John Calvin," 28.

[328] J. van den Berg, "Calvin's Missionary Message: Some Remarks About the Relation Between Calvinism and Missions." Evangelical Quarterly 22 (Jul. 1950): 177.

[329] Charles Chaney, "The Missionary Dynamic in the Theology of John Calvin," Reformed Review 17 (Mar. 1964): 36-37. See also Samuel Zwemer, "Calvinism and the Missionary Enterprise," Theology Today 7 (Jul. 1950): 211.

tion. However, both these charges reflect a poor understanding of Calvin's theology.

The Great Commission

Some have objected to Calvin's understanding of missions by claiming that Calvin believed that the Great Commission (Matt. 28:18-20) was binding only on the first century apostles, making missions unnecessary for future generations.[330] It is true that Calvin interpreted the Great Commission as referring to the apostolic ministry.[331] However, his reasoning for interpreting the Great Commission in this way was not to de-emphasize the necessity of missions in the present time. He was fighting a different battle – namely, the battle against the Catholic doctrine of apostolic succession. Calvin intended to show that the Apostolate was a temporary munus extraordinarium that ceased after the twelve apostles. The Great Commission was brought into this discussion to argue against Catholicism, not missionary activity.[332]

Calvin never expressed the idea that the apostles fulfilled the missionary command such that missionary activity is no longer necessary. He only saw the beginning of the spread of the gospel to all nations being fulfilled by the apostles.[333] Calvin wrote of the apostolic ministry, "Christ, we know, penetrated with amazing speed, from the east to west, like the lightning's flash, in order to bring into the Church the Gentiles from all parts of the world."[334] Yet Calvin also wrote of the necessity of missionary activity in the present time. For instance, commenting on Matthew 24:19, he wrote, "the Lord commands the ministers of the gospel to go a distance, in order to spread the doctrine of salvation in every part of the world."[335] Calvin made similar statements in his comments on Isaiah 12:5; 45:23; Matt. 24:14; and 2 Cor. 2:12. While there were some after Calvin who taught

---

[330] This is implied by Ruth A. Tucker in Jerusalem to Irian Jaya: A Biographical History of Christian Missions (Grand Rapids: Zondervan, 1983), 67.

[331] John Calvin, Institutes of the Christian Religion, 4.8.4; 4.8.8.

[332] J. van den Berg, "Calvin's Missionary Message," 178.

[333] Ibid., 179.

[334] Commentary on Psalm 22:27, in Calvin's Commentaries, vol. 4, Joshua–Psalms 1-35, 386.

[335] John Calvin, Calvin's Commentaries, vol. 17, Harmony of Matthew, Mark, and Luke, 384.

that the missionary mandate had been fulfilled,[336] this view cannot be attributed to Calvin himself.

Predestination

It has been objected that if Calvin's doctrine of predestination is true, then there is no reason to be involved in missions, for all the elect will surely be saved and all the reprobate will surely be eternally damned. Ruth Tucker, for instance, writes in her history of Christian missions that the doctrine of predestination taught by Calvinists "made missions extraneous if God had already chosen those he would save."[337] However, according to Calvin, this objection forgets the doctrine of the preached word. Calvin insisted that God uses the preaching of the gospel by men to bring people to faith. Calvin writes,

although he is able to accomplish the secret work of his holy Spirit without any means or assistance, he has nevertheless ordained outward preaching, to use it as it were as a means. But to make such a means effective and fruitful he inscribes in our hearts with his own finger those very words which he speaks in our ears by the mouth of a human being.[338]

Not only has God ordained the preaching of the gospel as a means of salvation, it is the only means of salvation. Calvin writes, "God cannot be called upon by any except those who have learned of his mercy from the gospel."[339]

Furthermore, Calvin insisted that the number of the elect is unknown. Therefore, the gospel ought to be freely proclaimed to everyone. Quoting Augustine, Calvin writes, "For as we know not who belongs to the number of the predestined or who does not belong, we ought to be so minded as to wish that all men be saved."[340] In this way, the preaching of the gospel to the nations is not hindered, but encouraged. The will of man is captive to

---

[336] For instance, Beza taught that the apostles had taken the gospel even to America. See J. van den Berg, "Calvin's Missionary Message," 179.

[337] Ruth A. Tucker, From Jerusalem to Irian Jaya, 67.

[338] John Calvin, The Bondage and Liberation of the Will: A Defence of the Orthodox Doctrine of Human Choice against Pighius, ed. A.N.S. Lane, trans. G. I. Davies (Grand Rapids: Baker, 1996), 215.

[339] See John Calvin, Institutes of the Christian Religion, 3.20.12. See also 3:20.1; 3.20.11.

[340] John Calvin, Institutes of the Christian Religion, 3.23.14. See also, The Bondage and Liberation of the Will, 160.

Satan's will (2 Tim. 2:25-26), such that it is impossible for anyone to will his own salvation. However, the preacher knows that there are elect who will be saved at the preaching of the gospel through the inward work of the Holy Spirit.[341] Therefore, the preacher can proclaim the gospel with confidence that those elected to eternal life will heed the call.

Calvin's Missionary Endeavors

Charles Edwards was certainly correct when he stated that "The Reformation was a missionary movement on a grand, international scale."[342] As the Reformation spread throughout Europe, missionary activity was taking place. The sacramentalism of Catholicism gave way to a truer Christianity based on sola scriptura, sola fide, and sola gratia. In fact, even the Catholic understanding of the gospel likely did not reach many in the uneducated classes. The Scriptures were written and the mass was conducted in Latin. Many of those who were unable to understand Latin likely never had any gospel preached to them in an understandable manner. As the reformation spread throughout Europe, the Bible was translated into common tongues and church services were understandable to the masses. In all likelihood, unreached peoples in Europe were reached with the gospel through the reformation. The Reformers continually had to fight for their very survival, fighting to establish their own identity over their Roman Catholic adversaries.[343] Yet even with this opposition, Calvin was able to make an extraordinary effort to evangelize France, the rest of Europe, and even the New World.

France

Calvin had an intense passion for the conversion of France to the Reformed faith. In 1553, Calvin began sending missionaries to France. Most of these missionaries had come to Geneva as refugees from France while fleeing persecution. Yet after being trained by Calvin in theology, moral character, and preaching, he sent them back to plant churches in France. These efforts by Calvin had tremendous success. In 1555, there were five Reformed churches in France. In 1559, there were almost 100. In 1562, the

---

[341] John Calvin, The Bondage and Liberation of the Will, 163-65.

[342] Charles E. Edwards, "Calvin and Missions," The Evangelical Quarterly 8 (1936): 47.

[343] Gordon D. Laman, "The Origin of Protestant Missions," Reformed Review 43 (Aut. 1989): 53.

number had reached 2,150.³⁴⁴ The total membership of these churches in 1562 is estimated at three million (out of a total population in France of about 20 million).³⁴⁵

When requests for new ministers were received in Geneva from France, Calvin did his best to send pastors to fill those pulpits. The Register of the Company of Pastors mentions 88 men who were sent from Geneva between 1555 and 1562.³⁴⁶ However, this was not a complete list. Some names were changed and even omitted to protect them from possible religious persecution. Also, before 1555 and after 1562, it was deemed unwise to keep records for fear of persecution. Yet it has been determined from other sources that no less than 142 missionaries were sent from Geneva (a city of 20,000) in 1561 alone.³⁴⁷ The picture that remains is that an astounding number of missionaries were sent out from Geneva under Calvin's influence. Fred Klooster even writes, "the mission activity that emanated from Geneva under Calvin's inspiration was itself of monumental proportions. It was perhaps the greatest home missions project that history has yet seen since the time of the apostles."³⁴⁸

So successful was this church planting effort that it drew the attention of the king of France. In 1561 Charles IX, the new king of France, sent a letter to the Council of Geneva. The letter claimed that preachers sent from Geneva were causing "seditions and dissensions which had been disturbing his reign."³⁴⁹ The king then asked that the pastors be recalled from France in order to maintain peace in the land. Calvin replied to the king saying that "we have never attempted to send persons into your kingdom as your majesty has been told ...; so that it will be found that no one, with our knowledge and permission, has ever gone from here to preach except a single individual who was asked of us for the city of London." He admits that some people had come to them, but they had simply instructed them "to

---

[344] Ibid., 59.

[345] Robert M. Kingdon, *Geneva and the Coming of the Wars of Religion in France* (Genève: Libraire E. Droz, 1956), 79.

[346] Preface to Robert M. Kingdon, *Geneva and the Coming of the Wars of Religion in France*.

[347] Philip E. Hughes, "John Calvin: Director of Missions," *Columbia Theological Seminary Bulletin* 59 (Dec. 1966): 20.

[348] Fred H. Klooster, "Missions – The Heidelberg Catechism and Calvin," *Calvin Theological Journal* 7 (Nov. 1972): 192.

[349] Robert M. Kingdon, *Geneva and the Coming of the Wars of Religion in France*, 34.

exercise their gifts wherever they should go for the advancement of the gospel."[350]

The result of Calvin's extraordinary efforts to evangelize France was that a Protestant church was formed by peaceful means. Williston Walker writes that "A great national Church, for the first time in Reformation history, was created independent of a hostile State; and the work was one for which Calvin had given the model, the inspiration, and the training."[351] Blood was spilt in France over the Protestant cause. However, after the massacre at Vassy and the peace of Amboise in 1563, Calvin wrote, "I would always counsel that arms be laid aside, and that we all perish rather than enter again on the confusions that have been witnessed."[352]

His desire to bring reformation to France through peaceful means is also evident in his correspondence with kings Francis I and Henry II. In 1536, three years after his conversion, Calvin addressed his first edition of the Institutes of the Christian Religion to king Francis I. In this address, he sought the conversion of the king to the Protestant faith.[353] In 1557, Calvin wrote to king Henry II explaining the faith of the French Reformed churches. In this letter he gave the king of France a brief statement of faith in order to encourage the king "to have compassion on those who seek but to serve God in simplicity, while they loyally acquit themselves of their duty towards you."[354]

The Rest of Europe

Geneva: Refugee Center and Missionary Center

Since about 1542, Calvin's Geneva became a refugee center. Protestants from all over Europe, including the Netherlands, England, Scotland, and Italy, came to Geneva for refuge from religious persecution. By 1555, the population of Geneva doubled. Calvin himself was pleased to take in these refugees, though at times it was extremely difficult to accommodate them. Calvin wrote in a letter to Farel dated 1551, "I am, meanwhile, much preoccupied with the foreigners who daily pass through this place in great

---

[350] John Calvin, Selected Works, Vol. 7, Letters, Part 4, 168.
[351] Williston Walker, John Calvin: The Organizer of Reformed Protestantism 1509-1564 (New York: Knickerbocker Press, 1906), 385.
[352] Ibid., 387.
[353] Gordon D. Laman, "The Origin of Protestant Missions," 58.
[354] John Calvin, Selected Works, Vol. 6, Letters, Part 3, 372.

numbers, or who have come here to live ... Should you pay us a visit next autumn, you will find our city considerably increased – a pleasing spectacle to me, if they do not overwhelm me with their visits."[355]

Yet Calvin's Geneva can be considered not only a refugee center, but a missionary center for the propagating of the gospel and the establishment of Reformed churches throughout Europe. People who came from all over Europe were trained as missionaries and sent back out as ministers of the gospel. Laman writes that

Through the coming and going of these refugees, and through the evangelical writings from the printing presses of Geneva and elsewhere in Latin, French, English, and Dutch, the Reformed faith was exported widely, even to Poland and Hungary. By correspondence, Calvin encouraged, guided, and dialogued with this diaspora of evangelical Christians witnessing under persecution.[356]

It is impossible, given the scope of this paper, to explore in detail the results of Calvin's endeavors throughout Europe. The following, therefore, will simply bring to light some of the highlights of Calvin's involvement, focusing only on the Netherlands, England, Scotland, Poland, and Hungary.

The Netherlands

In 1544, Calvin sent the first Reformed missionary to the Netherlands. Pierre Brully worked to establish a Reformed church there, but was martyred after only three months.[357] Lutherans and Anabaptists had seen some converts in the 1520's and 30's, but the Calvinists carried the day, possibly because of the Calvinistic form of church government and discipline.[358] Guy de Bray, who had met with Calvin in Frankfort in 1556, wrote the so-called Belgic Confession in 1559. This confession was printed in 1561 in Geneva.[359] This confession has become the foundation for the Reformed Church of Holland.

---

[355] Corpus Reformatum, XLII, col. 134, cited in G.R. Potter and M. Greengrass, John Calvin, Documents of Modern History (New York: St. Martins Press, 1983), 123.

[356] Ibid., 59.

[357] Gordon D. Laman, "The Origin of Protestant Missions," 59.

[358] W. Fred Graham, ed., Later Calvinism: International Perspectives, Sixteenth Century Essays and Studies, vol. 22 (Kirksville, MO: Sixteenth Century Journal Publisher, 1994), 386.

[359] Ibid. See also Williston Walker, John Calvin, 388.

The Netherlands produced missionaries of their own, largely through the writings of Hadrianus Saravia (1531-1613). He undertook the task of developing a reformed perspective on missiology, though he was influenced in many ways by the Anglican system of church government. In 1590, he wrote a treatise entitled, On the Various Levels of Ministers of the Gospel as They have been Instituted by the Lord, which argued against the view that the Great Commission ended with the apostolic age. Saravia's writings influenced later Dutch missionaries in India such as Justus Heurnius (1587-1651). Missionaries were sent to India from the Netherlands nearly two hundred years before Carey wrote his Enquiry in 1792.[360] Saravia's work also influenced the early Puritans in America such as John Eliot, who ministered to the American Indians in New England during the seventeenth century.[361]

England

Calvin had gained some influence in England during the reign of Edward VI, as evidenced by his letters to Cramner.[362] Acceptance of Calvin's theology increased throughout Edward's reign. However, it was through Calvin's ministry to the Marian exiles in Geneva that Calvinism took hold in England.[363] Large numbers of exiles were admitted in Geneva during the reign of Mary. At least 50 exiles were received on one day in 1557. John Knox, a devout disciple of Calvin, who was later to return to Scotland in 1559, pastored these refugees. During the reign of Elizabeth, these Marian exiles returned to England with their Calvinistic doctrine. The eventual result was the formation of the Puritan party and the drafting of the Westminster Confession of Faith in 1646.[364]

During the reign of Edward VI, London also became a refugee center. In 1550, John à Lasco (or Jan Laski), a Polish nobleman and friend of Calvin, was installed pastor over a "foreigners' church" of French and German exiles in London. A Lasco's church was modeled after Calvin's ordinances for Geneva, though with some modifications. Calvin kept in regular contact with a Lasco and the London church, which existed until disbanded by Mary I. Potter and Greengrass write that after the church was disbanded, a

---

[360] Carey's writing was probably heavily influenced by the writings of Justus Heurnius. See Ibid., 63.
[361] Gordon D. Laman, "The Origin of Protestant Missions," 62-3.
[362] Williston Walker, John Calvin, 389.
[363] Ibid., 389-90.
[364] Ibid., 390-91.

Lasco and other members "were to prove important catalysts for Swiss reform elsewhere in Europe."[365] Many of these exiles made it to Frankfurt and formed a congregation there in 1554. A Lasco went to Norway and Emden before arriving in Frankfurt to once again pastor the "foreigners' church" there.[366]

In 1544, a Lasco was in Emden, where he was superintendent of churches in East Friesland. A Lasco met with Simon Menno with the purpose of converting Menno and his followers to the Reformed faith. One writer states,

The discussion was held on Jan. 28-31, 1544, when the articles pertaining to the Incarnation, baptism, original sin, justification, and the call of ministers were discussed. Although the two men did not agree concerning all articles, Menno and his followers were dismissed by a Lasco in a friendly manner. Menno had promised to present a written confession regarding the Incarnation, and he now wrote ... A brief and clear confession and scriptural declaration concerning the Incarnation.[367]

Although a Lasco later published this confession "without Menno's knowledge or consent," this exchange demonstrates a Lasco's desire to convert even the Radical reformers to the Protestant cause without resorting to violence.[368]

Scotland

Calvin aided in bringing the reformation to Scotland through the ministry of John Knox. Knox had fled England after Mary ascended to the throne and arrived in Geneva in 1554. He returned to Scotland in 1555 in a failed attempt to bring reform, and shortly returned to Geneva.[369] In 1556, he began to pastor the English fugitive congregation in Geneva. Knox was sent back to Scotland in 1559 and successfully established Protestantism in

---

[365] G.R. Potter and M. Greengrass, John Calvin, 134-35.
[366] Ibid., 138. See also Williston Walker, John Calvin, 393.
[367] Canadian Mennonite Encyclopedia On Line: http://www.mhsc.ca/encyclopedia/contents/M4636ME.html.
[368] Ibid. At the same time, it should be noted that a Lasco believed Menno's theology was misleading many from the true faith and sought to hinder its progress. In 1554, after some of the Mennonites had come to the aid of some of those in a Lasco's group, a second discussion between the a Lasco and Menno groups ended inhospitably.
[369] Williston Walker, John Calvin, 392-93.

that country. In 1560, the Scottish parliament denounced papal authority and drafted the First Confession of Faith, which was thoroughly Calvinistic in orientation. The Kirk of Scotland was then fashioned after the Calvinistic model found in the Institutes and in the practice of the French Reformed churches.[370]

While Calvin was generally in approval of John Knox and his ministry, there were some tensions. In 1558, while Knox was still in Geneva, he published a pamphlet without Calvin's knowledge entitled The First Blast of the Trumpet against the Monstrous Regiment of Women. This pamphlet was written in response to Mary's reign and argued that women rulers were against God's law. Calvin banned the sale of the book in Geneva. When Elizabeth I became queen later in 1558, Calvin dedicated his commentary on Isaiah to her in an attempt to repair the damaged relationship between Geneva and England. However, the damage was done and in 1566 Beza stated that Elizabeth's hostility toward Calvinism was as a result of this incident. After Knox returned to Scotland, Calvin continued to be concerned about Knox's abrasive and uncompromising nature. Nevertheless, there appears to have been a good relationship between the two reformers. Yet Calvin's concern about Knox demonstrates his own missionary mindset. Calvin wanted to bring reform to England and Scotland in full submission to the proper authorities.[371]

Poland

Calvin had much success early on in the evangelization of Poland. By 1545, Calvinism was spreading widely among the nobility of Poland. King Sigismund Augustus of Poland himself was a tolerant, "enlightened" Catholic who even took a Protestant wife.[372] Calvin dedicated his commentary on Hebrews to him in 1549. He wrote, "Your kingdom is extensive and renowned, and abounds in many excellencies; but its happiness will then only be solid when it adopts Christ as its chief ruler and governor."[373] Calvin again wrote him on Christmas Eve 1555 and stated that "in Poland true religion has already begun to dawn on the darkness of the Popery ... I whom the King of kings has appointed a preacher of the gospel, and a minister of his church, call upon your majesty in his name, to make this work

---

[370] G.R. Potter and M. Greengrass, John Calvin, 157.
[371] Ibid., 156-57.
[372] Williston Walker, John Calvin, 394.
[373] Charles E. Edwards, "Calvin and Missions," 50.

above all others your special care."³⁷⁴ In effect, Calvin preached the gospel to the king of Poland and asked him to encourage the work of the Reformation there.

While Calvin and Sigismund Augustus remained on good terms, the king never agreed to undertake a national Reformation. Nevertheless, John à Lasco (Jan Laski) returned to Poland in 1557, where he spent the last three to four years of his life "in an evangelical campaign to create a proper evangelical Church in Poland.³⁷⁵ Lasco was the leading reformer in Poland. He was originally a priest and friend of Erasmus before undertaking the task of furthering the Reformation in several countries, including England and Germany. After his return, he busied himself "preaching, holding synods, stimulating the translation of the Bible into Polish, and seeking to bring the varieties of Protestantism into one ecclesiastical structure."³⁷⁶

In many ways, Lasco was a model Prostestant leader. Kenneth Scott Latourette writes that he "was an irenic soul who exerted himself in behalf of accord among the Protestants."³⁷⁷ Calvin viewed him with similar regard. He wrote to John Utenhoven, also laboring in Poland, "I am fully convinced he will labour faithfully and strenuously in extending the kingdom of Christ."³⁷⁸ While Calvin's and Lasco's efforts had initial success, it did not last long past Calvin's death. Conflicts with Lutherans, Anti-Trinitarians, and Jesuits caused Calvinism to decline and it never achieved a lasting foothold in Poland.³⁷⁹

Hungary

The stage for reformation in Hungary was set at least in part by three factors. First, the ministry and martyrdom of John Hus (1373-1415), whose teachings were widely spread in Hungary in the 15th century,³⁸⁰ incited sympathy for the protestant cause. Second, 1541, the entire New Testament

---

[374] John Calvin, Selected Works, Vol. 6, Letters, Part 3, 246.
[375] John Calvin, Selected Works, Vol. 6, Letters, Part 3, 323-24 n. See also G.R. Potter and M. Greengrass, John Calvin, 140-41.
[376] Kenneth Scott Latourette, A History of Christianity, vol. 2, Reformation to Present (Peabody, MA: Prince Press, 1975), 793-94.
[377] Ibid., 891.
[378] John Calvin, Selected Works, Vol. 6, Letters, Part 3. Ibid., 325.
[379] Williston Walker, John Calvin, 394.
[380] James Aitken Wylie, Protestantism in Hungary and Transylvania, vol. 3, bk. 20. On line: www.whatsaiththescripture.com/Voice/History.Protestant.v3.b20.html.

was translated into the Hungarian language. Third, in 1536, King Soliman the Magnificent threatened Hungary. In 1526, King Louis went to meet him at Mohácz with only 27,000 men – a mere fraction of the Turkish army. The result was a massacre, and king Louis fled the country, leaving a power vacuum in Hungary. James Wylie continues the story:

Two candidates now contested the scepter of Hungary – John Zapolya, the unpatriotic grandee who saw his king march to death, but sat still in his castle, and the Archduke Ferdinand of Austria. Both caused themselves to be crowned, and hence arose a civil war, which, complicated with occasional appearances of Soliman upon the scene, occupied the two rivals for years, and left them no leisure to carry out the persecuting edicts. In the midst of these troubles Protestantism made rapid progress. Peter Perenyi, a powerful noble, embraced the Gospel, with his two sons. Many other magnates followed his example, and-settled Protestant ministers upon their domains, built churches, planted schools, and sent their sons to study at Wittenberg. The greater number of the towns of Hungary embraced the Reformation.[381]

Whatever the reasons, By the 1550's, Calvinism was becoming established in Hungary. In 1557 and 1558 a synod was held which resulted in the Hungarian Confession, exhibiting a distinct Calvinistic theology. In 1567, at the Synod of Debrecen, the Hungarian Reformed Church adopted the Heidelberg Catechism and the Second Helvetic Confession.[382] Calvinism has survived in Hungary despite much persecution, though during the seventeenth century the Counter Reformation reclaimed many converts to the Catholic faith. However, at the turn of this century, two-thirds of the evangelical churches of Hungary were Calvinistic in origin.[383] Of the nearly 2.6 million people associated with Christian denominations in Hungary today (population 10.5 million), approximately 2 million are affiliated with the Reformed Church.[384]

Overseas Missions in Brazil

Protestants were greatly hindered in any attempt to bring the gospel overseas. Prior to 1588 (when the Spanish Armada was defeated) the Span-

---

[381] James Aitken Wylie, Protestantism in Hungary and Transylvania, vol. 3, bk. 20.

[382] Encyclopedia Britannica, s.v. "Reformed Church in Hungary." Online: www.britannica.com.

[383] Ibid., 395.

[384] Patrick Johnstone, Operation World (Grand Rapids: Zondervan, 1993), 268.

ish and the Portuguese controlled the sea-lanes.[385] The Pope had divided the New World between them. The French defied the Pope in this matter and sent out ships to the New World themselves.[386] Since these countries were Catholic, they did not permit Protestant missionaries to sail overseas with the gospel. As Gordon Laman has noted, a kind of "religious imperialism" had joined with the "commercial and political imperialism" of the Spain and Portugal.[387] Therefore, it was astonishing that Calvin was able to send missionaries to Brazil.

Nicolas Durand, who received the title sieur de Villegagnon from his father, was a fellow student with John Calvin in Paris. However, Villegagnon joined the military and became Knight of Malta. He was later appointed Vice-admiral of Britanny. After a quarrel with a governor, he decided to start a colonial expedition in Brazil. Villegagnon sought the aid of the Coligny the Grand Admiral of France, who was a supporter and protector of the Reformed Church. Villegagnon told him that he desired to start a colony that would offer protection for Protestants being persecuted in France. This convinced Coligny and Coligny in turn convinced Henry II to grant ships towards the expedition.[388]

On November 10, 1555, Villegagnon set sail and after four months, they landed in Rio de Janeiro. After his arrival in Brazil, he sent word back to Coligny asking for reinforcements and for ministers to evangelize the Tupinamba Indians. Coligny was all too happy to oblige his request. He wrote Calvin about the matter, and according to Baez-Camargo, Calvin "saw a wonderful door opening here for the extension of the Geneva Church, and so he took steps at once to organize a missionary force."[389] Two pastors and eleven laymen volunteered for the mission. They left Geneva in September 1556 and landed in Fort Coligny (in Rio de Janeiro) in March 1557.[390]

The Genevan missionaries were received with gladness. Pierre Richier and Guillaume Chartier, the two pastors, began to organize the church in Fort Coligny. On March 21, 1557, they held their first communion service.

---

[385] Charles E. Edwards, "Calvin and Missions," 47.
[386] R. Pierce Beaver, "The Genevan Mission to Brazil," The Reformed Journal 17 (1967): 15.
[387] Gordon Laman, "The Origin of Protestant Missions," 53.
[388] R. Pierce Beaver, "The Genevan Mission to Brazil," 14.
[389] G. Baez-Camargo, "The Earliest Protestant Missionary Venture in Latin America," Church History 21 (Jun. 1952): 135.
[390] Ibid., 136.

Villegagnon appeared to be a model Protestant leader. However, things soon began to change. Villegagnon began to interfere with the pastors in matters of church discipline and even on "matters of faith." He began to demand that baptism and the Lord's Supper be administered in a similar fashion to Catholic teachings. To rectify this situation, both sides agreed to send Chartier back to Geneva to discuss the matter and Villegagnon said he would abide by what Calvin said on the matter. However, as soon as Chartier left, Villegagnon began to call Calvin a heretic. He also began to punish the Genevan missionaries by over working them in the construction of the fort and not giving them adequate food. At this point, Richier confronted Villegagnon face to face and told him that the Geneva missionaries would return to Geneva on the next ship.[391]

In January 1558, the missionaries set sail to return home. Yet the ship began to leak, so five of the Geneva men decided to return to the mission. Villegagnon initially welcomed them back, but then grew suspicious. He demanded a statement of faith from the Genevan Calvinists. When he received the statement, he had three out of the five men strangled and thrown into the ocean (the other two were spared because Villegagnon was in need of a tailor and a cutler). Villegagnon later returned to France for reinforcements, and in 1560, the Portuguese attacked and destroyed the fort, and the French colony was ended.[392]

From all practical standpoints, the mission to Brazil was a failure. Yet during the short time the Genevan missionaries were in Brazil, attempts were made to evangelize the Indians. Richier was discouraged by the nature of the Indian cannibals. He saw them as "crassly stupid" and "incapable of distinguishing good from evil." He was also discouraged by the greatness of the language barrier. Nevertheless, he wrote Calvin, "Since where the Most High has given us this task, we expect this Edom to become a future possession for Christ."[393] In a more optimistic moment, Richier recognized the opportunity he had in evangelizing these Indians and wrote to Calvin that they are "like a tabula rasa easy to paint on."[394] So Richier never gave up his desire for the conversion of these Indians.

One of the laymen, a theological student named Jean de Léry, was less pessimistic. He spent time in their villages and took notes on their religious

---

[391] Ibid., 138.
[392] R. Pierce Beaver, "The Genevan Mission to Brazil," 20.
[393] Ibid., 17.
[394] G. Baez-Camargo, "The Earliest Protestant Missionary Venture in Latin America," 140.

beliefs and customs. He even found some good traits among them. At one time he wrote that "if we had been able to remain in that country for a longer time, we would have drawn and won over some of them to Christ."[395] Léry gave an example of a time when he was crossing the jungle with three Indian friends. Compelled by the beauty of his surroundings, Léry began to sing Psalm 104, "Bless the Lord, O my Soul." The Indians asked him to explain the song. Léry did not know the Indian dialect very well, but proceeded to explain the song and the gospel in the span of a half an hour. The Indians were pleased with what they heard and presented him with an aguti (a kind of rabbit-sized rodent) as a gift.[396]

Therefore, while there was never a single Indian convert from the Brazil mission, the reason was more for lack of time than for lack of effort. Calvin took the only opportunity he had to start a mission in the New World. Though the mission failed, this effort demonstrates Calvin's desire to see Christ's kingdom extended to every nation on earth. Calvin never had another opportunity to send out more missionaries. It would be the New England Puritans of the seventeenth century who would carry on the work begun by Calvin.

Conclusion

John Calvin never presented a systematic theology of missions in his writings. However, it has been shown not only that a coherent theology of missions can be reconstructed from his writings, but that Calvin considered Geneva to be a "missionary center" for the evangelization of France, the rest of Europe, and even the New World. Perhaps the reason why no systematic theology of missions can be found in his writings is because missions was central to his ministry in Geneva. Missions was not a "section" of his systematic theology, it was central to what he was trying to accomplish in his ministry. Does Calvin fit a twentieth century definition of what a missionary should be like? Probably not, but neither did William Carey or Hudson Taylor. The fact remains that Calvin's theology and missionary efforts constitute a major step forward in protestant missiology.

After discussing Calvin's missionary endeavors and highlighting the efforts of the Puritans in New England and the Dutch missionaries in the Orient (not to mention the Moravian missions), it should be evident that a

---

[395] R. Pierce Beaver, "The Genevan Mission to Brazil," 17-18.
[396] G. Baez-Camargo, "The Earliest Protestant Missionary Venture in Latin America," 141-42.

fourth era of missionary activity should be added to Winter's scheme, beginning in 1544 when John Calvin sent his first missionaries to the Netherlands. While this era may seem small when compared to the movement begun by William Carey (a Calvinist), it still deserves its proper recognition in any history of Protestant missions.

Bibliography

Works Cited

Beaver, R. Pierce. "The Genevan Mission to Brazil." The Reformed Journal 17 (Jul.-Aug., 1967): 14-20.

Baez-Camargo, G. "The Earliest Protestant Missionary Venture in Latin America." Church History 21 (Jun. 1952): 135-145.

Calvin, John. The Bondage and Liberation of the Will: A Defence of the Orthodox Doctrine of Human Choice against Pighius. Ed. A.N.S. Lane. Trans. G. I. Davies. Grand Rapids: Baker Books, 1996.

_____. Calvin's Commentaries. Vol. 4. Joshua – Psalms 1-35. Grand Rapids: Baker, 1979.

_____. Calvin's Commentaries. Vol. 6. Psalms 93-150. Grand Rapids: Baker, 1979.

_____. Calvin's Commentaries. Vol. 7. Isaiah 1-32. Grand Rapids: Baker, 1979.

_____. Calvin's Commentaries. Vol. 8. Isaiah 33-66. Grand Rapids: Baker, 1979.

_____. Calvin's Commentaries. Vol. 17. Harmony of Matthew, Mark, and Luke. Grand Rapids: Baker, 1979.

_____. The Institutes of the Christian Religion. Philadelphia: Westminster Press, 1960.

_____. Selected Works of John Calvin: Tracts and Letters. Vols. 4-7. Letters, Parts 1-4. Eds. Henry Beveridge and Jules Bonnet. Grand Rapids: Baker, 1983.

Chaney, Charles. "The Missionary Dynamic in the Theology of John Calvin." Reformed Review 17 (Mar. 1964): 24-38.

Edwards, Charles E. "Calvin and Missions." The Evangelical Quarterly 8 (1936): 47-51.

Graham, W. Fred, ed. Later Calvinism: International Perspectives. Sixteenth Century Essays and Studies. Vol. 22. Kirksville, MO: Sixteenth Century Journal Publisher, 1994.

Hughes, Philip Edgcumbe. "John Calvin: Director of Missions." Columbia Theological Seminary Bulletin 59 (Dec. 1966): 17-25.

Johnstone, Patrick. Operation World. Grand Rapids: Zondervan, 1993.

Kingdon, Robert M. Geneva and the Coming of the Wars of Religion in France. Genève: Libraire E. Droz, 1956.

Klooster, Fred H. "Missions – The Heidelberg Catechism and Calvin." Calvin Theological Journal 7 (Nov. 1972): 181-208.

Laman, Gordon D. "The Origin of Protestant Missions." Reformed Review 43 (Aut. 1989): 52-67.

Latourette, Kenneth Scott. A History of Christianity. Vol. 2. Reformation to Present. Peabody, MA: Prince Press, 1975.

Potter, G. R. and M. Greengrass. John Calvin: Documents of Modern History. New York: St. Martins Press, 1983.

The Register of the Company of Pastors of Geneva in the Time of Calvin. Ed. Philip Edgcumbe Hughes. Grand Rapids: Wm. B. Eerdmans, 1966.

Tucker, Ruth. From Jerusalem to Irian Jaya: A Biographical History of Christian Missions. Grand Rapids: Zondervan, 1983.

Van den Berg, J. "Calvin's Missionary Message: Some Remarks About the Relation Between Calvinism and Missions." Evangelical Quarterly 22 (Jul. 1950): 174-187.

Walker, Williston. John Calvin: The Organizer of Reformed Protestantism 1509-1564. New York: Knickerbocker Press, 1906.

Winter, Ralph D. and Steven C. Hawthorne, eds. Perspectives on the World Christian Movement. Rev. Ed. Pasadena, CA: William Carey Library, 1992.

Zwemer, Samuel M. "Calvinism and the Missionary Enterprise." Theology Today 7 (Jul. 1950): 206-16.

Extended Bibliography

Avis, The Church in the Theology of the Reformers. Atlanta: John Knox Press, 1981.

Benz, Ernst. "The Pietist and Puritan Sources of Early Protestant World Missions." Church History 20 (Jun. 1951): 28-55.

Bonar, Horatius. Words to Winners of Souls. Originally Published 1866. Phillipsburg, NJ: Presbyterian and Reformed, 1995.

Calvin, John. Tracts and Treatises. Vol. 1. On the Reformation of the Church. Trans. Henry Beveridge. Grand Rapids: Wm. B. Eerdmans, 1958.

_____. Tracts and Treatises. Vol. 2. On the Doctrine and Worship of the Church. Trans. Henry Beveridge. Grand Rapids: Wm. B. Eerdmans, 1958.

_____. Tracts and Treatises. Vol. 3. In Defense of the Reformed Faith. Trans. Henry Beveridge. Grand Rapids: Wm. B. Eerdmans, 1958.

Carey, William. An Inquiry into the Obligations of Christians to Use Means for the Conversion of the Heathens. Ed. John L. Pretlove. Dallas, TX: Criswell Publications, 1988.

Cogley, Richard W. "Idealism vs. Materialism in the Study of Puritan Missions to the Indians." Method and Theory in the Study of Religion 3.2 (1991): 165-182.

Colbert, Charles. "They are our Brothers: Raphael and the American Indian." Sixteenth Century Journal 16.2 (1985): 181-90.

Conn, Harvie M. "The Missionary Task of Theology: A Love/Hate Relationship?" Westminster Theological Journal 45 (Spr. 1983): 1-21.

De Greef, W. The Writings of John Calvin: An Introductory Guide. Grand Rapids: Baker Book House, 1993.

Gibbons, Richard. "Aspects of the Preaching of John Calvin." Glasgow University: Unpublished Paper, 1996.

Glaser, Mitch. "The Reformed Movement and Jewish Evangelism." Presbyterion 11.2 (Fall 1985): 101-117.

Gordon, Amy Glassner. "The First Protestant Missionary Effort: Why Did it Fail?" International Bulletin of Missionary Research 8 (Jan. 1984): 12-18.

Kasdorf, Hans. "The Reformation and Mission: A Bibliographical Survey of Secondary Literature." Occasional Bulletin of Missionary Research 4 (Oct. 1980): 169-175.

Noel, Charles C. "Missionary Preachers in Spain: Teaching Social Virtue in the 18th Century." American Historical Review 90 (Oct. 1985): 866-92.

Packer, J. I. Evangelism and the Sovereignty of God. Downers Grove, IL: InterVarsity Press, 1961.

––––––––. Introductory Essay to John Owen's Death of Death in the Death of Christ. Pensacola, FL: Chapel Library.

Peyer, Bernd. "Samson Occom: Mohegan Missionary and Writer of the 18th Century." American Indian Quarterly 6 (1982): 208-17.

Piper, John. Let the Nations be Glad! The Supremacy of God in Missions. Grand Rapids: Baker Book House, 1993.

Pulloppillil, Thomas. "Missionaries in Arunachal Pradesh During the 18th Century." Indian Church History Review 16 (1982): 5-9.

Reid, W. Stanford. "Calvin's Geneva: A Missionary Centre." Reformed Theological Review 42 (Sept.-Dec. 1983): 65-74.

Reisinger, Ernest C. What Should We think of Evangelism and Calvinism? Maitland, FL: Orlando Grace Church.

Richardson, Don. Eternity in their Hearts. Rev. Ed. Ventura, CA: Regal Books, 1984.

Schattschneider, David. A. Pioneers in Mission: Zinzendorf and the Moravians." International Bulletin of Missionary Research (Apr. 1984): 63-67.

Simmons, William S. "Conversion from Indian to Purtian." New England Quarterly 52.2 (Jun. 1979): 197-218.

Van den Berg, J. "Calvin and Missions." In John Calvin: Contemporary Prophet. Ed. Hoogstra, J. Philadelphia: Presbyterian. & Reformed, 1959. Pp. 167-83.

Van Rooy, Jacobus, A. "Christ and the Religions: The Issues at Stake." Missionalia 13.1 (Apr. 1985): 3-13.

Warneck, Gustav. History of Protestant Missions. Trans. G. Robinson. Edinburgh: Oliphant Anderson & Ferrier, 1906.

Warren, Max. "Revivals in Religion." Churchman 91 (Jan. 1977): 6-18.

Woudstra, Marten H., Henry Zwaanstra, and Henry Stob, eds. "Mission and Reformed Creeds." Calvin Theological Journal 7 (Nov. 1972): 133-220.

Youngs, J. William T. "The Indian Saints of Early New England," Early American Literature 16.3 (Wint. 1981-82): 241-56.

www.ingramcontent.com/pod-product-compliance
Lightning Source LLC
Chambersburg PA
CBHW060953230426
43665CB00015B/2179